MY LIFE WITH MARTIN LUTHER KING, JR.

"People are always asking me, 'When is another Martin Luther King, Jr., going to come along?' I answer, 'Never.' There will never be another Martin Luther King, Jr. Martin would be very disappointed if he thought people were waiting for someone like him. He tried to open doors so that many people could be leaders. Because of him we now have African-American educational leaders, political leaders, business leaders, and so on. That is his heritage, and his challenge to those who will become leaders in the future. I have written this book in order to inspire young people to take up my husband's challenge."

— *Coretta Scott King*

MY LIFE WITH

Martin Luther King, Jr.

· REVISED EDITION ·

CORETTA SCOTT KING

*Introduction by Bernice, Dexter,
Martin, and Yolanda King*

PUFFIN BOOKS

PUFFIN BOOKS
Published by the Penguin Group
Penguin Books USA Inc., 375 Hudson Street, New York, New York 10014, U.S.A.
Penguin Books Ltd, 27 Wrights Lane, London W8 5TZ, England
Penguin Books Australia Ltd, Ringwood, Victoria, Australia
Penguin Books Canada Ltd, 10 Alcorn Avenue, Toronto, Ontario, Canada M4V 3B2
Penguin Books (N.Z.) Ltd, 182–190 Wairau Road, Auckland 10, New Zealand

Penguin Books Ltd, Registered Offices: Harmondsworth, Middlesex, England

First published in the United States of America by Henry Holt and Company, 1969
Revised edition published by Henry Holt and Company, 1993
Published in Puffin Books, 1994

3 5 7 9 10 8 6 4

Grateful acknowledgment is made for the following:
"Mother to Son" from *Selected Poems* by Langston Hughes.
Copyright © 1926 by Alfred A. Knopf, Inc., and renewed in 1954
by Langston Hughes.
Reprinted by permission of the publisher.

Excerpts from a tribute to Martin Luther King, Jr., by Harry Belafonte
and Stanley Levison from the *Encyclopedia Year Book*, 1969 edition.
Copyright © 1969 by Grolier Incorporated. Reprinted by permission.

LIBRARY OF CONGRESS CATALOGING-IN-PUBLICATION DATA
King, Coretta Scott.
My life with Martin Luther King, Jr./Coretta Scott King;
introduction by Bernice, Dexter, Martin, and Yolanda King.—Rev. ed.
p. cm.
Previously published: Rev. ed. New York: H. Holt, 1993
Includes index.
ISBN 0-14-036805-1
1. King, Martin Luther, Jr., 1929–1968—Juvenile literature.
2. King, Coretta Scott, 1927– —Juvenile literature. 3. Afro-
Americans—Biography—Juvenile literature. 4. Civil rights
workers—United States—Biography—Juvenile literature.
5. Baptist—United States—Clergy—Biography—Juvenile literature.
I. Title.
[E185.97.K5K5   1994   323'.092—dc20   93-36237   CIP   AC

Printed in the United States of America

This book is dedicated
to the memory of my late husband
whose noble life of unselfish devotion to love,
justice, and truth I was privileged to share,
and from that sharing
derived immeasurable fulfillment;
and to our four children,
Yolanda, Martin III, Dexter,
and Bernice, who may live to see
the realization of The Dream.

Contents

Introduction

We are proud to be the sons and daughters of Dr. Martin Luther King, Jr., and equally proud to be the offspring of such a woman as Coretta Scott King.

She has always been the unsung strength of our family in even the darkest of times. As our father said in his book *Stride Toward Freedom*, "Calm and unruffled, Coretta moved quietly about the business of keeping the household going. When I needed to talk things out, she was ready to listen, or to offer suggestions when I asked for them. Her fortitude was my strength. Afraid for me at times, she never allowed her fears to worry me or impede my work in the protest. And she seemed to have no fear for herself."

Like our father, she has encouraged each of us to find our own calling—Yolanda as an actress/lecturer; Martin as Fulton County Commissioner in Atlanta, Georgia; Dexter as a businessman; and Bernice as a minister and lawyer.

Our parents have taught us, in finding ourselves, to hold fast to the traditions of family. It is the basis upon which we continue their legacy and begin to establish our own.

With a foundation of love—for God, family, and the citizens of the world—we have all the ammunition we need to find our place in the sun.

We encourage the youth of today and every day to find strength through the example of their ancestors and find family within the world community. We believe they will find that their predecessors have traveled many of the same roads and have been faced with finding the proper path to follow at the forks in those roads. There are lessons to be learned by their example so that the mistakes of the past will not become the mistakes of the future.

Despite the generational differences between our mother and our contemporaries, we believe that the example she has set in her life through her work as an activist for human rights and non-violence can be a lesson for all people in all times.

We love you, Mother, and hope that our lives will begin to touch as many people as your life has.

Yolanda, Martin, Dexter, and Bernice

Preface

It is difficult to revise a book that contains so much memory. People who have passed away, and those whose names may not be familiar to young readers, are very alive and important to me. I feel as if I could speak with them and as if they were still with us. Keeping some people in the book and cutting others has not been easy. My family, including my parents, my grown children, my sister Edythe, Naomi King, Christine Farris, and Isaac, are a constant support. But Daddy and Mamma King, A.D., and, of course, Martin seem present as well. In the interest of a new generation of readers I have had to make some cuts. But, whether mentioned by name or not, I want to stress the importance of everyone who shared in our lives and participated in the Civil Rights Movement.

Martin always talked about the "ground crew," the people in the background whom nobody cared about except those directly involved in the Movement. We could not have done without the "crew"—from the secretaries and custodians to the unsung leaders—even though they got little recognition from the public. I remember them; they are family too. We have to remember them for what they meant, and for the fact that the Civil Rights Movement was a people's Movement—that was what made it great. I hope that readers discovering these events for the first time will go on to learn more about everyone who participated in the Movement. Many of them were young people.

Martin understood that college, high school, and even elementary school students could help to lead what he called "the worldwide struggle for freedom." A whole generation was rising up and taking things into its own hands. Those students worked with the Movement, and the Movement itself was led by people who were just a little bit older than the students. Martin himself was only twenty-six years old when he was called to be the spokesperson for the Montgomery Movement. The young people worked with older people and they were assisted by them, but they were also allowed to do their own thing. We adults need to sponsor students once again and to allow them to organize themselves as they see fit.

Unfortunately, most young people do not understand nonviolence. Today they are really turned off by the word "nonviolence." However, there are also a growing number of young people who realize that nonviolence is an alternative to the violence in their lives and the violence they are victimized by on a daily basis. They understand that deprivation is as much a part of the violence in their lives as the physical violence and street violence that they experience.

At the Martin Luther King, Jr., Center for Nonviolent Change we have been working with young people since the seventies and we teach nonviolence as a way of life. Some arrive at the center very angry and disbelieving, but they come around because they see that nonviolence works. At first it begins to work inside them. We teach that nonviolence first changes the individual. Young people begin to see how their whole attitude can change. They can see and feel a sense of community as they get to know people who are in the seminar and workshop with them. They get that sense of bonding, and it is a very good feeling. So then they open up and start to talk about violence in their lives. They realize that this process is a way to change that.

Nonviolence is not just about one person, one family, or one community, it is a holistic philosophy. All life is interrelated; we are all tied together. Problems that affect people in Beijing, China, also affect people in Harlem, U.S.A., and everywhere else in the world. We must be concerned about others as well as ourselves; we cannot just focus on our own problems. We must study the cultures and languages of the whole world. We need to study the history of other people who are different from ourselves, those who are outside our borders as well as those who are inside. Martin used to say we are all tied together in an escapable network of mutuality. What affects one directly affects all indirectly.

Young people today often say, "What did you get for all your sacrifice? You sold out. You were Toms." We didn't get everything we wanted, so they think we never gained anything. Though we still have severe problems in this country, we should not forget what the Movement did achieve. Many African Americans hold important positions today that were made possible by the struggles and the sacrifices of those who are now of the older generation. African Americans are policymakers running states, cities, and municipalities; we lead state legislatures, serve on corporate boards, and help to shape policy throughout the country. None of that would have been possible without the Movement. But we also need to remember that the struggle is a never-ending process. Freedom is never really won. You earn it and win it in every generation. That is what we have not taught young people, or older ones for that matter. You do not finally win a state of freedom that is protected forever. It doesn't work that way. This book records the struggle that we undertook in America. I hope it will inspire a new generation to take up their own nonviolent fight for freedom, dignity, and human rights around the world.

Coretta Scott King

MY LIFE WITH

Martin Luther King, Jr.

· REVISED EDITION ·

1

"Make it plain, son"

The summer of 1964 had been very difficult for my husband, Martin Luther King, Jr. The calls upon him were staggering and his life was filled with almost incredible pressures. He was away from our home in Atlanta much of the time, involved in the struggle for voter registration, in the Movement to integrate public facilities, in a trip to Germany, in the presidential campaign, and in many other difficult and strenuous tasks.

Because I was concerned about him, in October, soon after he returned from Germany, I encouraged my husband to go to St. Joseph's Hospital in Atlanta for a checkup, hoping that he would in that way be able to get a few days' rest. At about nine o'clock on the morning after Martin went to the hospital, the telephone rang; it rang most of the time in our house. Many of the calls were from people with whom Martin worked or who wanted to give support to the Movement or who wanted help from him. But many times the telephone brought threats, abuse, and a stream of obscenity. This time when I answered, the voice on the line said, "This is the Associated Press. I would like to speak to Dr. Martin Luther King."

I explained that Dr. King was not at home, and the reporter said, "Is this Mrs. King?" When I replied that it was, he said, "We have just received word from Norway that your husband has been given the Nobel Peace Prize for 1964."

It was too much to fully comprehend, but I tried to act calm. He asked me whether he could get in touch with Dr. King for a statement, and I told him I'd contact my husband and have him call back. When the reporter asked for my reactions, I explained that it was hard for me to tell yet what I really felt.

Of course, I had read in newspaper stories that Martin was being considered for the prize. After that we heard that he was high on the list of possible winners; but Martin and I both thought these reports were merely rumors, for we thought that the prize was given only to those occupied exclusively in international peace activities. Though Martin had often written and spoken of non-violence as the salvation of a world in peril, we did not feel others saw the broad implications of his philosophy.

"This year the prize is worth fifty-four thousand dollars," the reporter said. "What do you suppose Dr. King will do with all that money?"

"Knowing him," I answered, "I'm sure he will give it all to the Freedom Movement."

"How do you feel about that?"

"I think that is where the money should go. I believe in it wholeheartedly."

As soon as the reporter hung up, I called Martin at the hospital. When he answered in a sleepy voice, I said cheerily, "How is the Nobel Peace Prize winner for 1964 feeling this morning?"

"What's that?" Martin asked.

"Martin, the Associated Press just called to tell us that the announcement has been made, and you are the winner."

After a long silence Martin said, "I'd better check to see if this is true."

Martin told me later that he had fallen asleep after his early-morning breakfast at the hospital. When I called him with the news, he was stunned. He thought he was still dreaming.

It took me quite a while to analyze my own reactions. Of course, the phone kept ringing, and my first thought was that Martin had checked into the hospital only the day before, and this meant that he would get absolutely no rest, because there would be all kinds of people trying to get to him. It seemed as if every time he got to the point where he wanted to get away from things, something would happen.

On the other hand, I realized that this was exactly the sort of lift Martin desperately needed, and in that moment I was filled with joy. I sat quietly by the telephone and I prayed, "Thank you, Our Father. Thank you for what this means to Martin and to the children and to me. Thank you and help us to be worthy of this blessing."

A little later I had a call from the staff at the Southern Christian Leadership Conference office to tell me that Martin had set up a press conference for eleven o'clock at the hospital and had asked that I come over and join him.

Of course, I went immediately. At the hospital I found all the reporters and photographers, with flashbulbs winking, crowded into the hospital chapel. Martin had written out a statement, and he answered their questions easily and calmly, as he always did. He told them that he would give all the money he was awarded to the Cause, as I had known he would. The prize money was later divided among the Southern Christian Leadership Conference (SCLC), the Congress of Racial Equality, the Student Nonviolent Coordinating Committee, the National Association for the Advancement of Colored People, the National Council of Negro Women, and the American Foundation on Nonviolence, which had been set up to further education in nonviolence.

Finally the reporters went away, and Martin and I went up to our room where we were left alone to sort out our thoughts and our emotions.

Of course, I was pleased, but at the same time I was pondering. Why? Why was Martin's contribution considered of international importance? What was the deeper meaning of all this—some meaning that we were not yet able to understand? For this was a prize not just for civil rights, but for contributing to world peace. Though we were very happy, both Martin and I realized the tremendous responsibility that this placed on him. This was, of course, the greatest recognition that had come to him, but we both knew that to accomplish what the prize really implied, we still had a long way to go. It was a great tribute, but an even more awesome burden. I felt pride and joy, and pain too, when I thought of the added responsibilities my husband must bear; and it was my burden too. I think he put it best for both of us when he later said, in his acceptance speech, "I feel as though this prize has been given to me for something that really has *not* yet been achieved. It is a commission to go out and work even harder for the things in which we believe."

Some of Martin's minister friends generously contributed funds through their churches so that his mother, Alberta Williams King, and his father, the Reverend Martin Luther King, Sr., could go on the trip to Norway, where Martin would receive the award. Martin's father had, by that time, been pastor of Ebenezer Baptist Church on Auburn Avenue in Atlanta for thirty-three years. He was a big man, physically and spirtually. He stood strong and broad in his pulpit, afraid of no man, white or black, telling it like it is, preaching the Word to his congregation and giving them his overflowing love.

At that time, Martin was his co-pastor at Ebenezer, and the two of them were very close. Daddy King, as we all called him, was immensely proud of his son's winning the Nobel Peace Prize. At the same time, he was genuinely humble, for he too was awed by the new responsibilities that had fallen on Martin's shoulders.

I wanted to take my two oldest children; Yolanda, whom we call Yoki, was almost nine, and Martin Luther King III, Marty, was seven. They both had been through a lot with us—threats and attempted bombings and knowing that their father was in danger. And when their daddy had been in jail, or when he was called a liar, or a Communist, or an Uncle Tom, they had learned to hold their heads high and believe in him. I thought it would be good for them to see their father receive the world's highest humanitarian award, but the Nobel Committee advised us against bringing children younger than twelve years old. The children were very disappointed when I told them they could not go, though they understood the reasons.

Early in December our party of about thirty people left Atlanta for New York on two separate flights—for the protection of the children, except in unusual circumstances, Martin and I never flew together. In New York several special activities had been planned for us by United Nations Under Secretary Ralph Bunche and the President of the U.N. General Assembly. We met representatives from Norway and Sweden, from England, and from some of the African countries. We began to feel that our trip abroad had already started.

On Sunday my husband preached a sermon in St. Paul's Cathedral in London. Except for the Nobel ceremony itself, this was the high moment of the trip. The great seventeenth-century Anglican church was filled with people who had come to hear Martin.

We were tremendously moved, not only by Martin's sermon but also by the Anglican ritual, which we had never seen—the priests in their vestments, the stately ceremony of the service, and the beautiful singing by the choir of men and boys whose clear soprano voices were so pure. Martin found it a beautiful and inspiring experience.

After Martin had ascended to the pulpit, he began to preach, his clear, rich voice filling the cathedral. His style of preaching grew out of the tradition of the southern Baptist ministers, with cadences and timing which he had heard from his father and other ministers as long as he could remember. But anyone who has ever heard him knows that what made Martin's sermons memorable was not the oratorical skill with which he was so abundantly blessed, but the message which he brought and which came from his heart, straight to the heart of the listener.

He preached one of his favorite sermons that day—*Three Dimensions of a Complete Life*. It had a special meaning for me, because it was the theme of the first sermon I had ever heard him preach on a Sunday long ago in a little church at Roxbury, Massachusetts. And it was also the initial sermon he preached in the Dexter Avenue Baptist Church in Montgomery, Alabama, where he began his pastorate.

But the sermon at St. Paul's Cathedral was not simply a repetition. As always, Martin took the theme and adapted it to his audience, adding new insights, changing it in accordance with the times, and elaborating upon it extemporaneously. The text was from Revelation 21:16, "The length and the breadth and the height of it are equal." Martin described St. John's vision of "a new and holy Jerusalem descending out of heaven from God." This new heavenly city would not be an unbalanced entity with towering virtues on one side of it and degrading vices on the other. The most noble thing about the new city would be its completeness in all three of its dimensions, in its length and its breadth and its height.

The troubles of the world, my husband said, were due to incompleteness. Greece gave us noble philosophy and poetic insights, but her glorious cities were built on a foundation of slavery. Western civilization was also great, bequeathing to us glories of art and culture as well as the Industrial Revolution that was the beginning of material abundance for man, but it was based on injustice and colonialism and allowed its material means to outdistance spiritual ends.

America, he said, is a great nation, offering the world the Declaration of Independence and enormous technological advances, but it too is incomplete because of its materialism and because it has deprived twenty-two million black men and women of life, liberty, and the pursuit of happiness.

Just as the great cities, nations, and civilizations are incomplete, so have been many of our great leaders. The individual, Martin said, should strive for completeness within himself. The *first dimension* of a complete life is the development of a person's inner powers. He must work tirelessly to achieve excellence in his field of endeavor, no matter how humble. "Set yourself earnestly to discover what you are made to do and then give yourself passionately to the doing of it. This clear onward drive toward self-fulfillment is the length of a man's life."

The *second dimension* of a complete life is concern for and identification with one's fellowman. "The recognition of the oneness of humanity and the need of active brotherly concern for the welfare of others is the breadth of man's life."

There remained the *third dimension*, the height, man's upward reach. Some of us are out-and-out atheists; some are atheists in practice while giving lip service to God. Martin believed that a man must actively seek God. He said:

Where will you find Him? In a test tube? No! Where else except in Jesus Christ, the Lord of our lives? . . . Christ is the Word made flesh. He is the language of eternity translated in the words of time. . . . By committing ourselves absolutely to Christ and His way, we will participate in that marvelous act of faith that will bring us to the true knowledge of God.

Summing up, Martin said,

Love yourself, if that means healthy self-interest. . . . That is the length of life. Love your neighbor as yourself; you are commanded to do that. That is the breadth of life. But never forget that there is an even greater commandment, "Love the Lord thy God with all thy heart, and with all thy soul, and with all thy mind." This is the height of life. . . .

. . . God grant that we will catch [John's] vision and move with unrelenting passion toward that city of complete life in which the length and the breadth and the height are equal. Only by reaching this city can we achieve our true essence. Only by attaining this completeness can we be true sons of God.

As Martin was speaking, that great, sophisticated congregation sat silent and intent upon his words. He said later that he could feel the current of their overwhelming response flowing toward him, and his own emotion rose with theirs. His father sat among them, completely carried away. Members of our party teased Daddy King afterward, saying that he was muttering under his breath a favorite phrase which he would have shouted out in our own Baptist church. He was saying, "Make it plain, son, make it plain."

After the service Canon Collins of St. Paul's took us to his home for a brief reception. Then we had time to do a little sight-seeing in London—the usual things: Westminster Abbey, the Tower of London. We drove down Whitehall, with its great government buildings—the Admiralty and the Foreign Office—which stood like monuments to the great empire that had been and was no longer; past the Houses of Parliament with their long, splendid Gothic facades, and Big Ben in its tower sounding the quarter hours with the Westminster chimes. But the beauty and nobility of London were clouded for Martin by the thought, as he said, "that it was built by exploitation of Africans and Indians and other oppressed peoples."

On December 8, we took off for Oslo. Though we landed fairly early in the afternoon, the sun was setting. In that month of the shortest days, there were only about four or five hours of sunlight in Oslo. This we had to get used to, and also to the intense, crisp cold we felt as we stepped from the plane.

But if the air was chilly, our greeting was warm. Of course, officials of the Nobel Committee were there, headed by Dr. Gunnar Jahn. We expected them, but not the crowds of people who came to welcome us, and especially the hundreds of young people. Martin made a brief statement to the press expressing his thanks to the Nobel Committee and to the assembled people for the warm welcome we received. Children presented us with bouquets of flowers. Then we walked slowly along a path cleared for us through the crowd. People were smiling and waving at us. We were able to shake hands with a few of them and waved back at the rest. What impressed both Martin and me was the genuine warmth of the people. It made us feel very much at home, and we felt a release, seldom known to us, from tension.

The first evening we had no engagements. It was the birthday of Marian Logan, one of the members of our group, and we gave a surprise party for her at the hotel. It turned into a celebration of our trip, and of our hopes and expectations. Never before had so many of us been gathered together in a simple fellowship. Always there were meetings, decisions, emergencies, crises, pressures of various kinds. Martin and several of the others had been to jail many times. Some had been severely beaten. Churches and homes had been bombed. Now we were released from solemnity into joy. After dinner, Martin, Andy Young, Ralph Abernathy, Wyatt Walker, and Bernard Lee formed a quintet and sang freedom

ongs in beautiful harmony. This was something they often did to
break up the seriousness of staff conferences and retreats. Then we
all sang freedom songs and hymns together, and that night their
words rang louder than ever before. We sang "Oh Freedom," "Ain't
Gonna Let Nobody Turn Me Around," "Were You There When
They Crucified My Lord?" and "Balm in Gilead," which my husband often quoted when he needed a lift:

> Sometimes I feel discouraged
> And think my work's in vain
> But then the Holy Spirit
> Revives my soul again.
>
> There is a Balm in Gilead
> To make the wounded whole,
> There is a Balm in Gilead
> To heal the sinsick soul.

Later still, we moved out of the dining room into the lounge, and
Daddy King began to talk about his emotions. "I want to say
something to all of you now," he began, "and I want you to listen."
He raised his finger to focus our attention in the way he did when
he spoke from the pulpit in Ebenezer Church. "I want to try to tell
you how I feel. I guess most of you know this, but I just have to say
it now anyway." He stopped to draw a deep breath and let it out
slowly as he did when he was gathering his thoughts. "I came from
nowhere. My father was a sharecropper, and I didn't have the
opportunity to get much formal training when I was growing up. It
wasn't until I left the farm and went to Atlanta that I was able to
get any real education. I was a man when I finished college, a
grown man with my wife and three children.

"I wanted my children to have all the things I had not had. I
prayed for the Lord to let them do the things I could not do. This
young man here became a minister, and I wanted him to have the
best training available, so he was able to get his Ph.D."

Then Daddy King talked about the struggle over the years and how difficult it had been for him and Mamma King to live with the knowledge that what Martin was doing was so dangerous. He talked of the threats the two of them had been subjected to. He said, "You don't know how it feels when some stranger calls you on the phone and tells you that he wants to kill you, or kill your son."

By now we were all crying, and Daddy King, standing there so big and kind, not bitter at all, said, "I have to talk about this because even though I feel so proud tonight about what is happening here in Oslo, I also must be humble. I don't want to get puffed up with pride; I am not that kind of person. So I have to continue to pray so that the Lord will keep me humble. The Devil is busy out there, and we have to pray that God will keep my son safe."

We were crying because we had all come such a long way and because Martin was at last receiving the recognition which he had been denied.

Two days later, December 10, 1964, Martin received the Nobel Prize. We had quite a time getting him ready. He had to wear formal dress, striped trousers and a gray tailcoat. While several of us were working on the ascot, Martin kept fussing and making funny comments about having to wear such a ridiculous thing. Finally he said, "I vow never to wear one of these things again."

He never did.

But I must confess that when he was finally dressed, he looked very handsome—so young and eager and excited, almost like a boy going to his first dress-up party.

The ceremony was held in Aula Hall of Oslo University, a long and narrow auditorium decorated with hundreds and hundreds of small white flowers. The stage was low and very deep, with an orchestra filling the back of it and the rostrum in front. The hall held about seven hundred people, and it was crowded to capacity. We sat in the front row with the Nobel Committee. I kept thinking of the several thousand people gathered outside who, because Martin had been escorted through a back entrance, did not even catch a glimpse of him.

Then King Olav came in, with Crown Prince Harald and an aide. Everyone stood up, and the orchestra played the Norwegian

national anthem. The King's party sat in special chairs close behind us, and the ceremony began. After Dr. Jahn presented the
prize, the gold medal, and the scroll, Martin responded:

I am mindful that only yesterday in Birmingham, Alabama, our children, crying out for brotherhood, were
answered with fire hoses, snarling dogs, and even death.
I am mindful that only yesterday in Philadelphia, Mississippi, young people seeking to secure the right to vote
were brutalized and murdered.

Therefore I must ask why this prize is awarded to a
Movement which is beleaguered and committed to unrelenting struggle; to a Movement which has not won the
very peace and brotherhood which is the essence of the
Nobel Prize. After contemplation I conclude that this
award, which I receive on behalf of the Movement, is a
profound recognition that nonviolence is the answer to
the crucial political and racial questions of our time—the
need for man to overcome oppression without resorting
to violence.

I accept this award today with an abiding faith in
America and an audacious faith in mankind. I refuse to
accept the idea that man is mere flotsam and jetsam in
the river of life which surrounds him. I refuse to accept
the view that mankind is so tragically bound to the star-
less midnight of racism and war that the bright daylight
of peace and brotherhood can never become a reality.

As I sat listening to Martin, I tried to remind myself of Daddy
King's words about humility. Yet I could not help myself. I was
proud of Martin and of what he stood for. I was proud that his
work, and that of his associates, had made better the lives of so
many of our countrymen. I was proud that black people all over
the world had felt renewed courage and hope because of this man,
my husband.

"Forgive me, Lord," I prayed silently. "Forgive me if I am filled
with pride. But that's how I feel. I am so proud of Martin and what

he has tried to do that I am worse than puffed up. I feel as if might burst. Lord have mercy."

The thunder of applause as Martin finished startled me from a reverie.

We went back to the suite together so we could be by ourselves and reflect on what all of this meant. We were all very emotional and each of us felt we must say something. This tribute from his friends meant as much to Martin as the formal ceremony which had preceded it. When my turn came, I talked about what my role had been—simply giving support to Martin over these years. I explained what a great privilege it had been, what a blessing, to be a co-worker with a man whose life would have so profound an impact on the world. It was the most important thing I could have done, and I had wanted to do it. I said, "This great experience has given me renewed faith. I will continue to give what support I can to my husband, and to the struggle."

Someone produced champagne and gave a toast to Martin. We were all becoming a little overwrought. Daddy King said with a smile, "Now I want to give a toast to the person who really is responsible. I want to give a toast to God."

Daddy King was, of course, a teetotaler, and he obviously did not understand the meaning of "a toast to God." It was so sweet and funny that we all burst out laughing. The web of emotion was broken, and we got back to normal.

The next day, Martin gave the Nobel Foundation lecture in Aula Hall. Then he went to Stockholm for the great reception for all the other Nobel Prize winners, who had received their prizes in Sweden.

While we were in Sweden, Martin and I attended a ball that the African students in Stockholm gave to celebrate the independence of Kenya. It was a very colorful affair, with many students present, the Africans among them wearing their native costumes.

We and other members of our party were received as special guests, and the committee wanted Martin and me to dance the opening selection together. We had not danced publicly since our college days in Boston. Martin had told me then that, as a Baptist, when he became pastor of a church we would not be able to dance anymore in public because it would be distasteful to the older members of the congregation. We never had, and Martin was quite reluctant to dance now.

Daddy King was not with us that evening, but I do not think he would have minded. There was a time when Baptists felt very strongly about young people dancing together. But Daddy King grew with the times, and he even told his congregation from the pulpit that the young people were going to dance. Pounding his fist down on the pulpit, he said, "I know how you feel about this, but you're going to have to accept it. It is better to provide a place for them to dance here than for them to go somewhere else."

From Stockholm we all went to Paris. By then Martin was completely exhausted. All the excitement, the many speeches he had to make, the receptions, the press conferences, and, most important, being always at the center of things had worn him down. He wanted to hide away and rest, but his efforts, as usual, were unsuccessful. In Mississippi the accused murderers of James Chaney, Andrew Goodman, and Michael Schwerner, three civil rights workers, had been arrested, and reporters swarmed into our hotel wanting a statement. Martin needed sleep so badly he had resorted to a sleeping pill and had gone to bed; but he had to get up and work on a statement. It was a painful reminder that, in spite of the glory of the past few days, so much remained to be done.

Our trip home was glorious. The strain was over, the tension eased; and, for the moment, we put away our solemn thoughts and enjoyed the fireworks. New York gave Martin a hero's welcome. Fireboats on the Hudson River jetted streams of water. Mayor Robert Wagner received Martin at City Hall and gave him the Medallion of Honor, the highest award the city could give. Martin was the first African American to be so honored. Even this gesture had a certain irony for us. Where is the key that can unlock the heart of a city like New York, which imprisons its minorities in ghettos, which shuts doors to decent educational opportunities for children of certain racial and national backgrounds, which erects bars to employment, which shackles the human spirit day after day, year after year, and decade after decade?

The next day, representing the state government, Governor and Mrs. Nelson Rockefeller entertained Martin and the other members of the King family at a luncheon in their New York apartment. Though such receptions seem common enough now, when Martin met the Governor it was a breakthrough for African Americans.

Martin also spoke directly to the people of Harlem about his experience in receiving the Nobel Prize. He said, "For the last several days I have been on a mountaintop, and I really wish I could just stay on the mountain, but I must go back to the valley. I must go back, because my brothers and sisters down in Mississippi and Alabama are sweltering under the heat of injustice. There are people starving in the valley, and people who don't have jobs, and people who can't vote."

Martin and I had been invited to the White House in accordance with the tradition for Nobel laureates. Instead, he used the occasion to discuss with the President and the Vice-President the continuing deprivation of voting rights and job opportunities.

When we arrived at Atlanta airport we were met by a large number of people, most of whom were Ebenezer members. We were driven directly to our church for a reception which had been carefully planned for us in Fellowship Hall. It did not have the glamour and the splendor of the other receptions Martin had been given, or was to be given, but it had the special qualities of sincerity and humility inspired by genuine love. These were the home folk who had shared with his parents the agonies and joys of his childhood, youth, manhood, and maturity. They had watched his development from Auburn Avenue, where he was born, to Boston University, where he received his Ph.D. at twenty-five, to Montgomery, where he began his public career in the ministry, seeing the accolades of the world showered upon him. Finally they were sharing with him, perhaps as no other group of people could, this pinnacle of recognition, the Nobel Peace Prize. Martin was for them a true servant of God. I felt glad for those souls whom God had allowed to see this day. Aside from the prize itself, this was for my husband the most meaningful of all testimonials.

Perhaps the most surprising tribute to Martin in connection with the Nobel Prize was the testimonial banquet for him held in Atlanta. Aside from the custom of neglecting a prophet in his own country, there was, of course, the problem of race. There was a strange mixture of feeling in the white community. Some white people were very proud that a hometown man had won this great honor and felt a sense of identification with him. Others were still afraid to honor him because he was such a controversial figure.

To make it more complicated, Martin and the SCLC were engaged in a controversy with the Scripto Company, which had one of the largest factories in Atlanta. The predominantly black workers, several of whom were members of Ebenezer, wanted to have a union and to improve their working conditions. Martin felt that the workers were right, and SCLC supported them. Various ministers marched in the picket lines, and Martin also picketed the Scripto plant for several days.

As a result, there was considerable controversy in the white community as to whether Atlanta should take any official notice of my husband's winning the prize. Liberals were strongly for it, as were all the white people friendly to us. Atlanta has always prided itself on being the most liberal city in the South. As former Mayor William Hartsfield expressed it, "Atlanta is a city too busy to hate." Many Atlantans felt that the world was watching to see how they would treat their most distinguished fellow citizen. They wanted to have a tribute in which the whole city, black and white, would respond. For this they needed the backing of city leaders and the business community.

Certain important businessmen were said to be opposed to such a ceremony, and apparently it took some time to bring them around. At one point the testimonial committee was having so much difficulty that Martin said he did not care whether they had the affair or not. Eventually invitations were sent out for a banquet to be held at the end of January 1965 at the Dinkler Plaza Hotel.

When we arrived at the hotel that night we beheld a beautiful sight. The big ballroom was filled with fifteen hundred people, and several hundred had to be turned away. There were blacks and whites from all levels. Judges and top-ranking industrialists were sitting at the same tables with cooks and porters, all mixed up deliberately. The audience was about sixty-five percent white and thirty-five percent black. It seemed as though everybody in Atlanta was there—completely integrated. Ten years, five years, even one year before, such a sight would have been unthinkable in a southern city.

The testimonial committee had been co-chaired by Rabbi Jacob Rothchild; Don McEvoy, director of the Conference of Christians and Jews; and Dr. Benjamin E. Mays, then president of Morehouse College.

The dais speakers and guests, headed by Mayor Ivan Allen, were a beautiful combination reflecting the city's determined efforts to make this a special welcome for Atlanta's returning hero.

My three oldest children were there. Bernice, who was only a baby, was of course at home. It was wonderful for the children to see this occasion, the first ever like it in the South, and to hear so many nice things said about their father. When they were introduced to the audience, Yoki, with much poise, stood up and waved to everybody; Marty responded with a little bow. Dexter, who was only four, was supposed to stand on his chair so that he could be seen, but instead, a typical little boy, he slid *under* his chair.

At the end of the ceremonies, after all the beautiful tributes had been paid, we all joined hands and sang "We Shall Overcome." It was tremendously moving—the spirit of it. We *had* overcome a major barrier for a southern city. We felt, for that night at least, it was really "black and white together" in Atlanta.

Then the most unexpected thing happened. After the singing, Mr. James Carmichael, the president of Scripto, came up to Daddy King, and said to him, "Reverend King, I know how you feel tonight. I am a father myself and I can share your feeling of pride in your son at this time. I just could not hold back the tears. Anything this meaningful should be preserved, and I have requested a tape recording of this ceremony."

Of the many tributes Martin received that night, that, I think, was the most extraordinary.

2

"You are just as good as anyone else"

We spoke in Oslo of the long road we had come; but no one who has not traveled it could possibly envision how very long it was. Martin and I both had a heritage deeply rooted in southern soil. I had grown up in the rural South while he was a product of the urban South; consequently, our backgrounds were dissimilar. I was born in a modest house on my grandfather's farm, twelve miles out in the country from Marion, Alabama.

My father, Obadiah Scott, whom everybody calls Obie, built the house in 1920, the year he and my mother, Bernice McMurry Scott, married. It was an unpainted frame structure which had once been papered on the inside, but by the time I can remember, the paper was fairly worn off. There were two large rooms—a kitchen and a bedroom—and a front porch. The bedroom was heated by an open fireplace. There were two double beds, one dresser, and a wardrobe. One of our prized possessions was a Victrola which stood on the floor, and we had an unusual collection of records. I remember such treasures as Clara and Bessie Smith recordings, sermons, and jazz recordings, as well as popular songs and hymns.

The kitchen was of unfinished pine with plain floors. Mother cooked on a big wood-burning iron stove, equipped with a food warmer and hot water tank which was also a source of heat for the kitchen. There was a rough carpenter's kitchen table, and several chairs with cane seats. In the back of the room, there was a "safe"—

a chest similar to a china closet. Though the furniture was simple, it was on a very large scale for our small house. It is a family joke that Dad has always bought the biggest of everything that he could find.

We were fortunate to have a well in the backyard which furnished water the year round. Many other people had to "tote" water from the nearest stream or spring. When the drought season came, sometimes the springs and even the wells would dry up. I remember my cousins climbing up and down the steep hill to their house with buckets of water for their large family. As a child, I would watch them and feel very grateful for our well. When we wanted to wash, water was heated outdoors in a big iron pot over a fire. We had two large tin tubs and a rub board with which we washed the clothes.

My grandfather Jeff Scott was born in 1873. He and my grandmother Cora Scott worked long hours in the field and sold pine timber in order to get together enough money to acquire the farm they both longed for. The struggle drove Cora Scott to an early grave, but by the time I knew my grandfather, he owned three hundred acres of land and was an important man in that rural black community. Whatever Jeff Scott said, people listened to. Jeff Scott either led or played an important role in everything involving the uplift of the people in our community. He was the preacher's steward and chairman of the board of trustees of our church, the Mount Tabor A.M.E. (African Methodist Episcopal) Zion Church, and also superintendent of the Sunday school. His positions as preacher's steward and president of the Rising Star Burial Society required him to travel a great deal to church conferences and burial association meetings. All the blacks in Marion called him Mr. Scott. Of course, members of his own family called him Uncle Jeff or Cousin Jeff, and almost everyone in Marion was related in some way or other.

My father was one of thirteen children, and when my grandmother died, at the age of forty, Grandfather married Fannie Burroughs and had twelve more children. At sixty-eight Grandfather Scott was killed in an automobile accident and his death left a real leadership vacuum in our small community.

I often wish that I had known my grandmother Cora, especially since I carry a part of her name. It was said that she was the real inspiration behind the success of Jeff Scott. She was a woman of unusual strength and drive. When I was growing up, my mother often told me that I reminded her of Grandmother Cora.

Though he was harder to know than Grandfather Scott, I think my maternal grandfather, Martin McMurry, was a very interesting man. He was part American Indian and was born just before the Emancipation Proclamation. Short of stature, with a very sturdy frame, he was fair skinned and as he grew older he looked more and more like an Indian, with his straight black hair and bold features.

Grandfather McMurry would be considered semiliterate by modern educational standards. He said he went to school "about two days in his life," but he taught himself to read the Bible, and that was all he ever read. He never tried to read the newspaper, but he had a library of reference books that interpreted passages in the Bible. He became such an authority that people would say, "If you want to know anything about the Bible or a passage of Scripture, ask Brother McMurry." His vocabulary was extensive.

I remember him very well, a strong man even in his old age. When he was over seventy he would walk the twelve miles to Marion from his three-hundred-acre farm and back in a day. He was unyielding and very strict and believed that children should be seen and not heard. When we used to visit him we had to play very quietly if he happened to be indoors reading or meditating. If we made a noise he would come out and threaten to whip us. I wish I had talked to him more, but we were afraid of him. Grandfather McMurry was well respected in the black as well as the white community, if you can use that word for the kind of respect that white people had for blacks at that time. Of course, they never thought of us as real people, as equals.

Both of my grandfathers were leading men in the community. But Martin McMurry lived close to the soil, never owned an automobile, and seldom traveled outside a fifteen-mile radius. Thus, his activities were confined to our immediate community and church. On the other hand, Jeff Scott regularly traveled all over the country in his automobile, attending and speaking at meetings of the various organizations he headed or was affiliated with, as well as in connection with being an insurance salesman. He was deeply concerned with the religious, civic, business, and political aspects of the life of our community. His world reached far into the larger community of the overall South and the nation.

My grandmother McMurry was a very gentle woman, a typical, loving, and indulgent grandmother. She was of average height with fair skin and curly hair. A good seamstress, she made most of our clothes while we were growing up. She loved flowers and had a beautiful garden on which she spent a lot of time. My mother and she were very close—Mother was the baby of the family and would turn to her own mother whenever she needed help.

My father is also an unusual person, as you had to be to get anywhere at all in those days if you were black. A born leader, he was a good combination of both his parents. I often wonder how he and Daddy King ever made it, for all the cards were stacked against them.

They were both born at the beginning of the century, which, in the South, was the very worst period of the repression of African Americans since the days of slavery. After the Civil War, when African Americans were made free by the Emancipation Proclamation, and given the vote and legal equality by the Fourteenth and Fifteenth amendments to the Constitution, things were better for a while. Black people did vote, and they enjoyed a certain amount of freedom. Then the federal occupation troops were pulled out, and the white southerners began the process of eroding African-American rights. They were a little careful at first, but in the 1880s and 1890s, with very conservative federal governments in office, the local governments really clamped down. It was then that several of the southern states put the "grandfather clauses" in their constitutions. Under these rulings, no one was eligible to vote unless his grandfather had been a voter. Of course, most of our grandfathers had been slaves, so that effectively disfranchised almost the entire black population.

Another device to keep blacks from voting was the high poll tax. It cost two dollars to vote in Alabama, but if you were, for example, thirty years old the first time you voted, you had to pay all the back taxes from the time you were twenty-one—in this case, twenty dollars, a large part of the annual income of many people at that time. This trick was almost as effective as the grandfather clauses, because very few black people could afford to pay that much to vote. In 1940, in Marion and the surrounding countryside, where we lived, there were about one thousand whites and two thousand blacks. But even as late as 1955 only about a hundred and fifty black people were registered to vote.

That was not the worst of it. After the *Plessy* v. *Ferguson* decision of the Supreme Court in 1896, legalizing segregation, or "separate but equal" facilities, the Jim Crow laws passed by the white legislatures went to horrible—and ridiculous—lengths. They made it illegal for blacks and whites to eat together in public; to sit together in theaters, buses, or trains; to use the same comfort stations or water fountains; even to enter public buildings by the same door. It was as though the blacks had some contagious disease.

And yet, we worked in their houses, prepared their food, nursed their children, and were intimately associated with them in every domestic way. The whole idea was to impress upon the black people that we were an inferior race; to reduce us, not to slavery again, but to being less than men. African Americans, no matter what their positions or how much education they had, were never called "mister" or any other title. They were addressed as "boy" or "girl" even if they were old and gray. They were supposed to say, "Yes, sir," and "Yes, ma'am"—even to teenage whites. It was all deliberately aimed at instilling the slave mentality in our people. Unhappily, the whites succeeded all too frequently for many years. How sad it made me feel to see some of our people who had been so badly treated. When they spoke to a white person, their backbones seemed to crumple, they seemed diminished. After we became involved in the Movement, Martin would say to his oppressed brothers and sisters, "We can straighten up our backs and walk erect now. We are walking to freedom in dignity."

During those earlier years, any African American who stood up like a man was considered "uppity." If he went too far, or even if he merely tried to assert his legal rights, he was in grave danger of disappearing. The authorities never investigated. A black man's life was worthless. Of course, in any direct clash or an accusation by a white woman against him, the black man was almost invariably lynched. One of my great-uncles was lynched. A "kindly" white woman came and told his wife what had happened. When she went out looking, she found his body hanging from a tree. After they had strung him up, the lynch mob must have used him for target practice. His body was full of bullet holes.

The system of slavery and consequent segregation, as practiced in the United States, is arguably the most vicious and evil sin against humanity anywhere. It created within the white man a false sense of superiority, while instilling in the black man a false sense of inferiority. Racism, as we define it today, is deeply rooted in these inhuman practices.

It is a wonder that my own father did not end up in a swamp because of his obvious self-respect. His additional and unforgivable crime was that he worked too hard and got ahead—ahead of some of the poor whites. When he and my mother were married, he had a steady job in one of the local sawmills earning three dollars a day. By the time I was born, he had saved enough money to buy a truck and was hauling logs and timber for the local sawmill operator. He had also learned the barber's trade, and in the evenings and on weekends there might be a line of men outside our house waiting to have their hair cut. Mother would help him by also cutting hair when there were more customers than my father could handle. Because of the Depression he began what was called "truck farming." On our piece of land, we raised corn, peas, potatoes, and garden vegetables. We had hogs, cows, and chickens. Because Daddy was away working all day, Mother, my sister Edythe, and I tended the crops. We started as soon as we were big enough to hold a hoe—I was six or seven. My sister Edythe, my brother Obie, and I tended the garden and the crops. Mother assisted us when there was a lot to do. My father hired someone to plow the fields, but we planted the corn, hoed it, and gathered it, fed the chickens and hogs, and milked the cows. We did not sell the produce—we and the animals ate it. Even if we had not needed it, living on a farm without growing things was unthinkable.

Later, when I was about ten, I worked in the cotton fields with the hired hands. I hoed and chopped the cotton—that is, I thinned out the rows so that there was a hoe's width between one stalk and the next. In the fall we picked cotton. We hired ourselves out to make money to help with our school needs. If you made four or five dollars in the course of the season, that was pretty good money in those Depression days. I remember one special year when I made seven dollars picking cotton. I was always very strong, and I made a very good cotton-picker. Martin used to tease me about it, years later, saying that was why he had married me. He would say, "If you hadn't met me, you'd still be down there picking cotton!"

So we all worked, but Daddy worked harder than almost anyone for miles around. While both of my parents shared the feeling that we must learn how to work, my father seemed to have a passion for keeping busy. He used to chide us about getting up early, saying, "When I was growing up at home, we ate breakfast every morning by lamplight. If you don't have anything to do, just get up and sit down. I won't have lazy people in my house."

Like most people who had debts, when the Depression hit, my father suffered badly. He was still paying for his truck and could not earn enough to make his payments. A white man, whom we shall call John Thomas, took up his payments, but held the mortgage on his truck. He was "the Man" of my childhood, a great exploiter of blacks. Imagine, in the twentieth century, hundreds of people were living on this man's plantation and working for him. He owned the general merchandise store where they bought their food on credit, yard goods, and all the other things they needed. Thus, when they got paid at the end of a season, most if not all of what they had earned they owed to him. He also owned a share in the lumber company for which my father worked.

Mr. Thomas knew that my father was a good, steady worker, so he made the payments on the truck. Then Daddy worked for him, not as a sharecropper, but hauling lumber and logs. Mr. Thomas never paid him quite what was owed, but my father knew it was useless to complain. In addition, Thomas sold us gasoline and oil for the truck, food staples, and other essentials at high prices. The interest he charged on the loans he had made to my father, as well as other indebtedness, completely tied Daddy to him.

My father's paycheck from the lumbermill would be sent to Mr. Thomas, who would then deduct what he wanted from it. What he wanted was all of it; and because Dad was heavily in debt, this was what he got during the worst years of the Depression.

Although he got no money to take home from his regular job, my father derived some income from hauling lumber for other people on weekends and sometimes during the night. But even this got him into trouble with the poor whites. He was the only black who owned a truck. This brought him into competition with the whites, and they resented him. Sometimes they would stop him on a lonely road and curse him and threaten to kill him—and there was always a good chance they might do it. He was not a big man, only about five feet seven, but he had a lot of courage. He never ran away, and I am sure that is why he survived. He would stand up to them quietly and respectfully. My father used to say, "If you look a white man in the eye, he can't hurt you."

Daddy knew it was dangerous. After receiving so many open threats, he bought a pistol and carried it in the glove compartment of his truck, but I don't think he would have shot anyone. It would have been against all his principles. Many times during these years when he left home to go into the deep woods to haul lumber, he'd say to Mother, "I may not get back."

I learned very early to live with fear for the people I loved. It was good training, for I have lived that way most of my life. My father, in his bravery and his refusal to be beaten down, is very much the same kind of man my husband was.

There was a curious destiny entangling my father and John Thomas. One day, about 1937, when my father was driving his truck, he collided with Mr. Thomas' car. I don't know whose fault it was, but the car was completely smashed and Mr. Thomas was knocked unconscious. Though two of his helpers were slightly wounded, Daddy was not hurt at all, but he was terribly worried. If Thomas had died, they would have put him in jail for manslaughter, no matter what the rights of it, and he would not have had much chance for a fair trial.

But Thomas recovered. He saw to it that my father did not have to serve any time. He considered that Obie was one of his hard-working "good niggers"—he was reliable, didn't drink or steal—and took care of him in a condescending, paternalistic way. But my father had to pay for the car. Though he had been doing pretty well and was steadily paying off his debts, it took my father several years to pay that new debt to Thomas. Finally the day came when he went down to make the final payment. Mr. Thomas looked over his books and commended Obie for working so hard. Then he said, "Let's see. Oh, here's another hundred dollars you owe me."

My father knew this was not true; he had kept very careful records. But in order to avoid trouble, he agreed to pay it. This meant another two weeks' work before he was out of debt. He came home to us one night with forty dollars in his pocket. My little brother, Obie, and I were waiting anxiously for him. (Edythe was away at school.) We were going to town, to Marion, and it was almost time for the stores to close. Mother was lying down. Daddy came in and he said, "Bernice, wake up! I can take you to town now and buy you what you want."

It was a glorious occasion, because while we'd been in debt we had to get everything at John Thomas' store. Now we all got into the truck, and my father drove us to town. It was a great feeling for us, and how much greater it must have been for him to feel that once again he was a man who could run his own affairs. From 1939 until he finally stopped working in 1991, he ran his own business and paid his bills; and, if he needed money, he went to the bank on his own name and collateral.

When I was very young and growing up, I was protected from the extreme hardships of segregation, though I was always aware of being deprived of the rights to which I was entitled. We lived on that big farm, and up the hill were my Scott cousins and all my half-uncles and half-aunts from Grandfather Scott's second marriage to play with. There were also my cousins Willie and Ruth McMurry, who were just about our age. It was an all-black community of three generations of land ownership. This factor, perhaps more than anything else, helped to instill in us racial pride, self-respect, and dignity which inevitably gave us the proper self-image.

My first experiences of social life were happy too; they centered around the Mount Tabor A.M.E. Zion Church. Most of the congregation were kinfolk, so it was almost a family affair. Church-going on Sunday was the great occasion of the week. People came from long distances, sometimes in farm wagons or walking; very few had cars. All of them put on the best clothes they owned. The men wore suits when there was a regular service. The women wore hats. I wore braids, and I remember my mother and sister fussing over them on Sunday mornings. Little girls in my church seldom wore ribbons, but on special occasions, like Easter or Children's Day, when we had new clothes, we might have had ribbons to match our dresses.

When we could not get a ride in my father's truck, we children would start walking early to get to church for Sunday school. Mount Tabor was about four miles from where we then lived, but we were used to walking. Though we ourselves did not, other people often carried their shoes, so they would not get muddy or dirty from the unpaved roads. They also carried a rag to wipe their feet before they put their shoes on at the church. Others wore old shoes on the road and changed before they got to church.

Grandfather Scott would open the Sunday school service by singing a hymn. We had a prayer in the large group—about thirty-five people—then went to our classes, where we were told Bible stories and taught the Catechism. *Who made you? God. Who is God? God is a spirit. Where is God? God is everywhere. What can God do? God can do everything. Does God know everything? He knows everything that we can think, say, or do....*

After Sunday school there was a recess, and the older people began to arrive for the church services. To my eyes, when I was a small child, it was quite a big church. It was a frame structure with white paint peeling off because it was painted only once every ten years or so. There was an elevated pulpit with a railing around it where members of the congregation knelt for communion. The pews were rough, homemade wooden benches, though they were varnished. The church was heated by a big potbellied stove, and on very cold days people clustered around it to keep warm. Kerosene lamps, looking much like the electric fixtures which replaced them some years later, hung down from the ceiling on long cords. The men and the women usually sat in different aisles, with the young people in the middle aisles between them. Though I don't remember anyone speaking about it, it was rare for a man to sit with his wife. There were even separate waiting rooms on each side of the foyer for the two sexes.

Mount Tabor Church was a "two-Sunday church." Since it could not afford a full-time minister, it hired a preacher to come twice a month. Two-Sunday churches are still fairly common in the South. On the odd Sundays my grandfather Scott conducted the usual Sunday school service, with prayers and readings from the Bible, and, of course, hymns. During the second service after Sunday school, Grandfather McMurry, who had a fine high baritone voice, would "line the hymns," as it was called. That is, he would start off alone, on perfect pitch, setting the meter, and the choir and the congregation would join in. Grandfather Scott would lead a prayer and maybe call on one of the brothers to read the lesson. Then he might give a little talk. There would be more hymn singing—"Amazing Grace" and "Holy, Holy, Holy," all the Methodist hymns. Of course, a collection would be taken up.

On the Sundays when the minister preached, there were leaders who were supposed to collect from their group members. Twenty-five cents a person was the proper amount, but that ran too high for large families, and ten cents apiece was quite common. Except for what was paid to the bishop and for foreign missions, the money went to pay the pastors—and some people thought they were not worth what they got.

Our church was one of the three leading churches in our district, which included three counties in the black-belt area. Because Mount Tabor was considered a strong church, some of the better ministers were sent to us to pastor. In general, though the ministers were well meaning, they were often poorly educated and ill prepared to serve the political and economic needs of their people. However, they laid a strong psychological and social foundation for coming generations. The churches they built were often the only institutions owned by black people. Without them, our modern movements would have been much more difficult.

On the Sundays that the minister came, he would conduct the regular A.M.E.Z. service and then preach a sermon. If he was dull, some of the congregation went to sleep. Once in a while, one would come who preached a rousing sermon. People would become emotional and shout "Amen!" or "Yeh!" or "Preach!" Still, the Methodists were not as emotional as the Baptists, and our members would make jokes about the "carryings-on" of the Baptists. This church atmosphere was the cultural haven which gave birth to the concept called "soul." Soul music was the music of the black church almost a century ago—a mixture of African and American folkways in the context of the Christian religion.

Seldom if ever did the preachers of that period deal directly with the plight of their people. Occasionally, when some black person had been beaten or otherwise badly treated by whites, there would be a reference to it from the pulpit. The preachers' role was to keep hope alive in nearly hopeless situations. "God loves us all, and people will reap what they sow," they would tell us. "So, just keep on praying, especially for our less fortunate brothers. The Bible teaches that. So, don't worry, someday God will straighten things out."

They never preached what we would now call "the social gospel," neither did they discuss from their pulpits the rights of blacks or the issues of segregation. It was too dangerous.

This attitude was in some ways true of the men who gathered at our house to have their hair cut, or got together at the country store to discuss some injustice done to one of their brothers. They would talk about how unjustly blacks were treated, some of them saying what they would do if it had happened to them, but there it ended. They felt it hopeless to openly protest in those days. That was the way things were, though they hoped that things would get better.

But to me, as a child, church was a warm and heartening experience; with my grandfathers leading the community, and all my family there, it was the largest and most important part of my world.

Even before my sister and I started school, my parents began to instill in us a desire for education. We had a few books in the house which were read and reread. Among the ones which I remember, Mother used to read stories to us about Rumpelstiltskin and the Little Match Girl. We learned "Mary Had a Little Lamb," "Humpty-Dumpty," and other nursery rhymes.

Mother had only a fourth-grade education, which she got going to school three months a year, "minding cows" and working in the fields the rest of the time. She married when she was sixteen, and began to have children. She used to say, "I never was a child; I've been a woman all my life." When I first remember her, she must have been still in her early twenties. When she did her hair in braids, she too looked like an Indian. Unlike my father, who is openhearted and openhanded, my mother is reserved and cautious with strangers, especially white people. "You can't trust any of them," she said, though she does have white friends now whom she likes. But once she accepted you as a friend, she opened her heart. Despite her lack of education, she had a good mind and a lot of practical wisdom and understanding of life. She seemed more resentful of the injustice done blacks than my father, who says that people are bad because conditions make them that way. He chooses to think the best about people. My parents realized how much they had missed by not going through school, and my mother was determined that her children would get an education.

My early schooling was greatly affected by the system of segregation. These impressionable years are so important in laying a solid foundation. Our elementary school was at Heiberger, a crossroads village nearer than Marion, but still about three miles from home. Rain or shine, we walked there and back each day, and I remember that the buses carrying the white children to their school would rattle past us in a cloud of dust or a spatter of mud. I remember resenting that.

Our school was an unpainted frame building with one big room in which one hundred or more children were taught in the first through sixth grades. Later, it was partitioned into two rooms and painted inside and out. There were combination wooden benches and desks that had been built by a local carpenter. Sections of the wall were painted black, and these served as blackboards. The toilets were outdoors, and the room was heated by the usual wood-burning stove.

We had two black teachers, and they were dedicated women. They probably had junior college training, though in previous years you had only to pass an examination to begin teaching—in black schools. Some people who passed had only an eighth-grade education. Mrs. Mattie Bennett is one teacher who stands out in my memory as especially dedicated. Mrs. Bennett encouraged both Edythe and me because she saw that we were eager to learn. I think she worked a little harder with us than with the other children—though perhaps part of her gift as a teacher was that she made us feel that way.

Every so often, the county supervisor, a black woman, would come around to inspect our school, and we would be on our best behavior to impress her. Our teacher was eager to demonstrate the talents of her pupils. As song leader, I was always asked to lead songs. Sometimes I sang solos or recited poetry.

Despite efforts by African-American parents to protect their children from the dreadful hurt of segregation and discrimination, sooner or later, all African-American children lose their racial innocence. Some incident suddenly makes them realize that they are regarded as inferior. White children may suddenly refuse to play with them, or they find out that they have to sit on the hard wooden seats in the hot, crowded balcony at the movies, as we did, instead of in the comfortable orchestra. I always smile a little when I hear white people talking nostalgically about the corner drugstore. I remember, when I was a very little girl, having to go to the side door of the white-owned drugstore with the other black children to buy an ice cream cone. I would have to wait until all the white children were served, and then, no matter what flavor I asked for, the man would give me whatever he had too much of. Of course, we paid exactly what the white kids paid.

Black children realize very early that there are places that they cannot go. When that time comes, they go to their mothers and ask, "Why?" Every African-American mother says, "You are just as good as anyone else. It's just the way things are." With his deep hurt, the child realizes that his mother is trying to explain without explaining, and that she wouldn't have to tell him that if there weren't some problem. And it is hard for a child to believe, when everything is rigged to prove it is not so.

When I went to my own mother with this eternal question of black children, she too said, "You are just as good as anyone else." And then she said very forcefully, "You get an education and try to be somebody. Then you won't have to be kicked around by anybody, and you won't have to depend on anyone for your livelihood—not even on a man."

Today it is still very true that black children have to be prepared for discrimination. They are not always going to be treated as equals. I think one of the problems that we face today is that we have not prepared our children for the racism they will encounter. Young people are very, very cynical and very bitter because they did not expect to find what they have found. They thought the battles had been won. One of the failings of the Movement was that, while we taught people to fight against the system, and how to respect themselves, we didn't teach young people that they would have to fight all over again. As long as we have a democratic system we are going to have to work to protect our freedom and self-respect. And that is for blacks or whites or whatever color. Freedom is never guaranteed forever; you have to fight for it.

My parents taught us to think of education as the first step on the way to freedom. This was particularly true when I was growing up. Mother said to me, "You want clothes and other things now, but once you have an education, if you still want these things, you can get them. The most important thing now is to get an education."

The time came when I fully realized how very different our school was from the white children's school. The facilities were certainly separate, but they were extremely unequal. The whites had a fine brick building. Though I never set foot in it, I was sure there were separate classrooms for each grade, and all sorts of equipment we never had. I know there was a library. We had no library and very few books. We had to buy our regular textbooks, while the white children were given their books free. They went to school nine months a year; we went for seven months—in Mother's time, it was only three months. Under these conditions, how could the achievements of black children be equal to those of white children?

Yet, going beyond all that, we were, in some respects, luckier than many of the supposedly integrated children in the ghetto schools up north. In many instances, at least what we were taught was planned for us by our own people, *by* blacks *for* blacks. Many of our schools even had courses in black history. The children of the northern slums were educated under a mass-produced system designed for the majority of white students, which was totally irrelevant to their experiences and which they could neither identify with nor adapt to; and nobody cared whether they did or not. Herein lies the source of black student unrest on many white college campuses today. I think that black schools should be open to white people as well, but I do feel the predominantly black institutions need to be supported and should flourish. There is so much history wrapped up in those institutions that must be preserved. But not as museums; the schools have to continue to be relevant to the modern world. Schools shouldn't be an excuse for black people to get together to feel good. They should be places where students are challenged to work hard and where their history and culture are preserved. Today's students could learn a lot from the lives and struggles of the great leaders of some of the black schools; they are true role models. Hearing about their courage, wisdom, and spirituality is one thing that could inspire young people and keep them from becoming embittered.

By late 1937, things were looking up a little for the Scott family. We moved into a bigger house that Daddy rented. It had six rooms. At first, we had to share the house with another family, some cousins who lived in a separate section but used the same kitchen. That did not work very well, and a year and a half later they moved out. Edythe was just coming into the "courting age," and my father bought a new set of furniture for the living room of which we were very proud. It was the first time we had a living room and the first time my sister and I ever had a room of our own.

But the pattern of segregation was strong enough to come into our fine new house. I remember the time my father asked a white man to a meal. He was a friend as well as a business acquaintance. We had an argument about whether Daddy should eat with this man. My father thought he should not, but Mother said, "Obie, this is your own house. He is coming as your guest. You should sit and eat with him." Edythe and I strongly supported her.

"No," my father said. "No, I wouldn't feel right doing it."

The white man ate alone.

My elementary school took me through the sixth grade. Then Mother arranged for Edythe and me to go to a much better school ten miles away in Marion—one that was as good as any school, white or black, in the area. Lincoln High School was a semiprivate school when we went there, but it began as a private school. The American Missionary Association started it shortly after the Civil War, when there were no schools for blacks in the South. The association sent white missionary teachers down to teach the former slave children. By the time I went to Lincoln, the faculty was integrated—about half white, half black—but of course the students were all black. All the white teachers were northerners, except for one southern woman. They were dedicated people who were concerned about us and our development as human beings. Black and white teachers lived together in a spirit of brotherhood in the dormitories provided by the school.

The white people in Marion generally despised our northern teachers, whom they called radicals and "nigger lovers." They considered the school's integrated housing facilities scandalous, and the teachers were fairly isolated in the community. Of course, a few of the townspeople made friends with the teachers—there are some good people in every situation.

The faculty at Lincoln was brave and dedicated, and the school had a strong tradition of service to humanity which was communicated to its students. I feel that the chance to go to such a school made a real difference in my life. As I look back now, so many things that happened to me when I was much younger seem to have been preparing me for my life with Martin. Going to the Lincoln School was one of the most important of these.

It was quite a sacrifice for our parents to send Edythe and me, and later my brother Obie, to Lincoln. The tuition was four dollars and fifty cents a year for each of us, and that was a lot of money for them to pay. In addition, we had to board with a black family in Marion, because it was too far from home to walk. A farmer not only lost a helper when he sent his child away to school, he also had to raise the money for room and board. But there was no alternative. The nearest black high school was twenty miles away, and you had to furnish your own transportation. On the other hand, the white children in the area were bused in to Marion High School.

My sister was the first child I knew in our immediate community to go to high school, though my father had attended Lincoln for one year in his own youth. By the time I was a junior at Lincoln, the county agreed to provide some of the funds to transport black rural students to school. The parents also contributed. My father converted one of his trucks into a bus, and my mother drove the children from our area to and from school every day. After that time, I was able to live at home.

Lincoln opened the world to me, especially the world of music. I was taught to play the trumpet by Frances Thomas, who gave me free lessons on her trumpet. Miss Olive J. Williams of Harrisburg, Pennsylvania, a Howard University graduate, was our music teacher, and my ideal. She had her singing group tackle works like Handel's *Messiah*, which was very unusual for a black woman teacher at that time. I doubt whether any other high school in the South was attempting such challenging works. We all had to learn to read music, and those who were particularly interested could go much further. I learned to play the flutaphone and performed on it in school programs. Of course, I sang—I always sang. Miss Williams gave me my first formal voice lessons and I performed vocal solos, and also sang solos with the choruses. I learned to play the beginning repertoire of all new pianists. Later, on my own, I learned to play hymns, gospel songs, and spirituals. When I was about fifteen, our church asked me to serve as choir director and pianist—we had a piano by that time— and I trained the Junior Choir. The young people of my age were a fine group, and there were some very good singers among them. We did special programs, and one of them was the origin of the format I used for my Freedom Concerts many years later. I would choose a song such as "Does Jesus Care" and write a narration to go with it. It would tell about some of the problems we as Christians face, and would ask whether anyone cares about us. "But Jesus does care. He cares when no one else seems to and our hearts are in despair." Then I would lead the singing of the song.

In Marion, I ran into much more racial feeling than I had ever personally known. When we walked to school, the white teenagers would come down the street all abreast and try to knock us off the sidewalk. If we stood our ground, they would call us "dirty niggers" and we would call them "white trash." Sometimes it looked as if there would be a fight, and I was a little frightened, but as a group we had more courage, and we stood our ground. We never really came to blows.

During this period, I also took a job doing housework for a white woman in Marion. She expected me to say, "Yes, ma'am," every other word and to use the back door. I never did either. I was not submissive enough, and I did not last long in her employment.

My father was having troubles too. By now he owned three trucks, but as he prospered, feeling against him among the poor whites grew stronger. They harassed him, and sometimes they complained to the police that he was a reckless driver. They would do anything to get him into trouble.

On Thanksgiving night in 1942, one of our undertakers, Hampton D. Lee, telephoned Edythe and me in Marion to tell us that our house had burned down. The authorities did not investigate at all, supposedly because we lived outside the town limits. However, really no one cared about what happened to black people. We never definitely found out how the fire started, but it was quite suspicious. All our beautiful furniture was gone, and we had to go stay with Grandfather McMurry. My mother felt abandoned, especially because her mother had died a short time before. She said, "Now I don't have anyplace to go with Mamma gone."

Still, my father was not discouraged. He went to work the next day as usual, and by spring he had saved enough money to buy a sawmill. The logger who worked in the mill was white, and after my father had owned the mill for about two weeks, the logger came to him and said he wanted to buy it. My father said, "No, I don't want to sell."

The logger answered, "Well, it won't ever do you no good."

The next Monday when my father went to his sawmill in the woods, he found only ashes. Some white people who were friendly toward my father felt very sorry for him and suggested that he ask for an investigation. But Dad knew it was no use. He went back to work, hauling lumber for other people with his truck and turning his thoughts toward other ventures.

My father is such an amazing person. He never became bitter, despite all these incidents, all the humiliations and harassment by the whites who wanted to keep him down because they saw their own jobs imperiled, and because they did not want *any* black man to rise above "his place."

Yet, my father would say, "There are some good white folks." Many years later people accepted him as a substantial person, and he could say, "Nobody hates me. I have paid all my debts. My credit is good. That is because of the way I have conducted myself. I haven't an enemy in the world." And it is true. I know his example helped me not to hate; that, and my own deep belief in Christian principles.

At Lincoln School, Edythe sang alto in a musical group called the Lincoln School Little Chorus, which was well known in Marion for its beautiful singing. Frances and Cecil Thomas had just come to teach at Lincoln, and they had contacts with various midwestern colleges. They arranged for the Little Chorus to make a tour. One of the colleges the chorus sang at was Antioch at Yellow Springs, Ohio. And that is how Edythe's life and mine were completely changed.

Two years after this concert tour, Edythe was to graduate from Lincoln as valedictorian of her class. At about that time Antioch

College decided to invite black students to apply for admission and to offer scholarship help to a limited number who could qualify. They remembered the fine young students who had come from Alabama to sing for them two years before, and a letter came to our school principal offering a scholarship. Edythe and several other students applied, and Edythe was awarded a year's scholarship to Antioch, including tuition, room, and board. Thus, in the summer of 1943, she was the first black student to go to Antioch on a completely integrated basis.

That it was far away was a main attraction for Edythe. She and I both wanted to get out of the South, to go north, because we thought we would enjoy a greater degree of freedom there. In our lack of sophistication, we did not realize that there were special problems we would have to face there, too.

Edythe's letters home were generally favorable. She was very excited about Antioch and the overall program there. She wrote a lot about the academic freedom and how Antioch stressed giving the students free choices and making them assume responsibility for their actions. There were no housemothers, or rules about what time a student had to go to bed. In some exams, certain teachers used the honor system.

Edythe wrote about how wonderfully warm and friendly the white students were. She said, "Oh, you'd just love it here, Coretta."

I think she omitted the negative things because she did not want to discourage me. She felt the good in Antioch outweighed the bad. I found out later how difficult it was for her to be the first representative of her race at the college. The other students thought she should know all the answers about race relations. They talked to her about this subject all the time. Later she admitted she got awfully tired of discussing the problems of blacks at breakfast, lunch, and dinner. There were other difficulties that are hard to define. For example, my sister is tall and attractive; she has a little of that striking Indian look of my mother's family. Some of the young men at Antioch liked to talk to her because she was intellectually stimulating. She would have lunch with them, and they were attracted to her, but they did not have the courage to ask her out formally. In all the time she was at Antioch, Edythe dated only one white fellow on two occasions.

I was not aware of any of these problems, and I could hardly wait to get to Antioch. When I was in twelfth grade I applied for and got a partial scholarship. It was for four hundred and fifty dollars, and my parents had to pay another two hundred dollars in fees, plus my transportation, but by then they could manage to scrape the money together.

I was tremendously excited. My first year at Antioch was made easier for me by the fact that Edythe was still there. I had always looked up to her. We are very close, and she has been a great influence on my life ever since I can remember, but particularly when we were together in college. She has a quick, brilliant mind and the power to express her thoughts in a dynamic manner. I got into the habit, in those days, of letting her speak for me, since I was still shy and inexperienced in this new situation. If a question was asked, I would wait for Edythe to answer. It was not until my sister had gone to take her senior year at Ohio State that I came into my own.

Despite all Edythe's glowing letters, I did not really know what Antioch would be like. When I got there, the first thing I noticed was the friendliness of the people I met. You sensed it at once. Everyone spoke to everyone else; if you were an Antiochian, they accepted you right away and attempted to make you feel at home immediately. It was not until later, when I had more experience, that I realized that there was, even there, a color bar. People were nice to me and tried to be friendly, but I could sense that in the backs of their minds was the feeling of race superiority bred in them through generations and by all the myths about black people they had acquired. It was then that I became aware that Antioch students, too, were products of a society infested with racism. I must admit, however, that on the whole Antiochians tried hard to overcome their prejudices.

Often they would say naive things, always beginning with "Of course, *you're* different, Corrie." But then they'd ask me the kinds of questions I couldn't help resenting: Why were blacks boisterous? Immoral? Why weren't there more black students qualified for Antioch?

What they couldn't understand was that not everyone wants to be a pioneer. There were black students who *were* qualified and who could afford Antioch but who would not *want* to come because they might be isolated or subjected to special treatment. Also, many African-American parents hoped that their sons and daughters would find suitable wives and husbands at college. That was most unlikely at a school like Antioch in the mid-1940s, which had only token integration.

The student body, though preponderantly white, represented a cross section of the country, though it seemed a sizable number were Jewish young people from New York. In my class there were three black students—myself, another girl, and one young man. Counting the African Americans in Edythe's class, we were six altogether. One of the things I did not like was the unspoken expectation that I would date the black fellow at the proms and social events. That was not what I wanted, to be "socially segregated" in this way. Quite deliberately, I refused to date him. I guess it was a little self-conscious of me, but through all the years we were there, I never dated him because I did not want to acknowledge that covert assumption.

It was not until my junior year that a white student asked me for a date. He was Jewish, a good musician, and he had a fine mind. We had a great deal in common and we went steady for a year, until he graduated.

I roomed with two white girls—that took quite an adjustment for all three of us. There was no animosity, just a matter of getting used to the situation, and eventually it worked out very well.

At first, I had a difficult time with my studies. Although I had been valedictorian of my class and had maintained an A average in my senior year, like most southern students I had such an inadequate educational background that even Lincoln had not prepared me properly. I had to become what they used to call a "grind." I studied very hard and had little or no time at first for the outside reading that meant so much in the intellectual life of the place, though later, when my schedule changed, I read a tremendous mount. In my second semester, I enrolled in a remedial reading course. In a sense, I made more progress than some of the students who came with more advantages, because I had so far to go to catch up.

Then, an unfortunate thing happened. I was the first black to major in elementary education. This required that I teach a year in the Antioch private elementary school and a year in the Ohio public schools. I was becoming more and more interested in music, so I taught music the first year at the Antioch school. The second year, I was supposed to teach in the public elementary school. However, the Yellow Springs School Board was very reactionary, and the supervisor of practice teaching at Antioch would not allow me to push the matter when I was turned down. She was the type who openly said, "God did not intend the races to mix." The Yellow Springs schools were integrated, but the faculty was all white, and she told me that if I forced the issue it would imperil the whole Antioch practice-teaching program.

I appealed to the president of Antioch. He was quite new to the school and was no pioneer in race relations. As a matter of fact, it was said that he had a black dog called Nigger. After I told him my story, all he said was, "Well, Corrie, what do you want us to do about it?"

"You might appeal to the school board," I suggested. But, on the teaching supervisor's advice, he refused to act.

So I was given two options. Either I could go to Xenia, Ohio, and teach in a segregated black school there, or I could teach another year at the Antioch school. I said, "I will not go to Xenia because I came here from Alabama to be free of segregation."

I taught in the Antioch school but I was terribly disillusioned and upset. I had support from my faculty counselors, Walter Anderson and Mrs. Jessie Treichler, who were both very close friends of mine.

Finally, I pulled myself out. I said to myself, "Now, I am going to be black the rest of my life, and I have to face these problems. So I'm not going to let this one get me down. I'll have to accept a compromise now, but I don't accept it as being right. I'm going ahead in a more determined way than ever, to do something about this situation. I don't want those who come after me to have to experience the same fate as I did." Many years later, after I had left Antioch, all students majoring in education were given the opportunity to practice teaching in Yellow Springs public schools. Though I could not change the system, I knew that I had to stand up for what I believed in. In the end, my efforts helped those who followed me.

From that incident on, I was even more motivated than before. Antioch had a chapter of the NAACP and a Race Relations Committee and a Civil Liberties Committee. I was active on all of them. From the first, I had been determined to get ahead, not just for myself, but to do something for my people and for all people.

I took to my heart the words of Horace Mann, who founded Antioch. In his address to the first graduating class he had said *"Be ashamed to die until you have won some victory for humanity."*

Sometimes I am asked what I think Antioch did for me. It did a great deal beyond the fine education I received. For one thing, it taught me how to get on in a white community. Even its hypocrisies, like the lack of support given me against the Yellow Springs School Board, taught me not to expect too much, and to make allowances for, without condoning, the inbred things white people have difficulty with. It also reinforced my idea that one ought not think too much about material things such as clothes. At Antioch the importance of clothes was downplayed. If I had gone to another kind of school, even to some black colleges, I might not have been able to manage financially, since I would have had to spend much more money on clothes.

The total Antioch experience helped me to reaffirm and deepen the values which I had already acquired during my childhood and adolescence, in my parents' home and at Lincoln High School. Though they were born "disadvantaged," my parents always aspired for the best. My father used to say that he always stood at the head of his class, and he encouraged us to do our very best, no matter what the task. Especially were we encouraged to excel in our studies.

What did Antioch do for me? The college's emphasis on service to mankind reinforced the Christian spirit of giving and sharing which had been taught to me by my parents, particularly my father. The embodiment of this spirit in the dedicated lives of our teachers was a further inspiration to us.

Antioch was a place which offered many opportunities for development. Even as a student, I had the unusual experience of appearing on a program with the then world-famous baritone Paul Robeson, who commended my voice and encouraged me to continue my voice studies. By the time I left Antioch, I knew I wanted to develop my voice to its fullest potential. This made it imperative that I consider training in a conservatory of music.

Antioch gave me an increased understanding of my own personal worth. I was no longer haunted by a feeling of inadequacy just because I was an African American. I enjoyed a new self-assurance that encouraged me in competition with all people of all racial, ethnic, and cultural backgrounds, on their terms or on mine. Antioch—the total experience of Antioch—was an important element in preparing me for the role I was to play as the wife of Martin Luther King, Jr., and for my part in the Movement he led.

"A very promising young man"

3

"A very promising young man"

I left Antioch in 1951, with the feeling that this unique experience had been invaluable preparation for whatever career I chose to follow. The knowledge, tools, techniques, and insights which I had acquired in this intellectually stimulating climate served to compensate for the deficiencies in my educational background, as well as to broaden and enrich my whole life. This was the foundation upon which I felt that I could build a career in music. Somehow, I had always had a strong desire to develop all my talents, as well as every aspect of my personality, in order to make the greatest contribution possible to society. Embodied in this attitude was the belief that each individual's life is purposeful and that he has a special role to play; that he has a responsibility to himself, to his fellowman, and to his Creator to give back to society in proportion to his ability and opportunities.

Two Antioch faculty members for whom I had the greatest respect, Walter Anderson and Jessie Treichler, encouraged me to pursue my musical training at a conservatory of music. Part of my dream had always been to study and graduate from a conservatory of music. Jessie was my everything at Antioch. She was assistant to the president and she was also a counselor for the students. If she had not been so supportive when I got depressed and frustrated I might not have stayed at Antioch. I would go to her office in tears literally, and just about ready to give up for the moment. I would eave her uplifted and ready to go on. I probably would not have given up in any case, because I am a strong person, but I felt she knew exactly what to say to lift me up and to point out my strengths. Soon I would feel better and then I would say, "I do have what it takes."

Dr. Anderson, at that time Antioch's lone African-American faculty member, was one of those exceptional, multitalented individuals, remarkably gifted as a musician. He was at home with Bach as well as bop. He became my second music idol, after my music teacher at Lincoln High School. A graduate of Oberlin Conservatory, he advised me to apply to a list of what he considered the five leading music conservatories in the country.

In the end, the choice was between Juilliard in New York and the New England Conservatory in Boston. I had strong reservations about the possibility of adjusting to living conditions in New York. My last job experience had been in New York City—I worked in a branch of the New York Public Library during a semester off from Antioch—and, as a student, I found it difficult living there. There is no doubt that New York City represents the mecca of culture and achievement in America, but as a struggling student, I feared that I might be crushed by the impersonal, competitive quality of New York life. I reasoned that Boston was culturally as advanced as New York City, but easier to adjust to. By the time I had reached these conclusions, I received word that the New England Conservatory had accepted me. I decided to go there.

Professor Anderson was the one who directed me to the New England Conservatory of Music. If it had not been for Walter I might not have met my destiny.

Mrs. Jessie Treichler assisted me in applying for scholarship aid. She wrote at least a dozen letters of recommendation to foundations and individuals, applying on my behalf for financial assistance to enable me to further my music training. One of the letters which Mrs. Treichler wrote was to the Jessie Smith Noyes Foundation.

The foundation replied to me that its grants were already awarded for the next year, but if a chosen applicant decided not to use a grant, it would be given to me. On that uncertain note, I went home to Alabama to visit my parents and to get ready for school. Although my father could have afforded to send me to the conservatory, I decided not to ask him. I had been dependent long enough. I would go to Boston whether or not I had a scholarship.

As I was leaving, my father asked me, "What are you going to do if you don't get that scholarship?"

"I'll get a job," I said. "I'll work and go to school part-time until I'm able to go full-time."

I left Alabama with my train fare and a little money to cover expenses. In passing through New York on my way to Boston, I called home to discover that a letter had been received from the Jessie Smith Noyes Foundation that awarded me a grant of six hundred and fifty dollars to study at the New England Conservatory of Music. My prayers had been answered!

Meanwhile, Jessie Treichler had written about me to a Mrs. Bartol who was a patron of Antioch living in Boston. She lived in a big old house on Beacon Hill.

When I reached Boston, Mrs. Bartol was very kind to me. She said I could live in her house and have breakfast for seven dollars a week. Surely that was reasonable, but it was more money than I could afford to pay. The grant would just pay my tuition and the fees at the conservatory. I would have to work for the money for my board. Nevertheless, I decided to enroll full-time at the conservatory.

My first days in Boston were very difficult. The fifteen dollars I had when I arrived was almost gone. Though I did not want to take a regular allowance from my parents, my mother had promised to send me money from time to time, but the money had not arrived. I was almost out of funds, but I was determined to save twenty-five cents for my carfare to the conservatory the next day. That was something I would not give up. So I bought some graham crackers, peanut butter, and fruit, and had that for dinner.

The following morning I got my breakfast as usual at the Bartol residence. After that I became somewhat frightened, and I didn't know what I was going to do. Then, as an answer to my problem, I got a phone call from Mrs. Bertha Wormley. I had met Mrs. Wormley through Anne Tanneyhill of the National Urban League

n New York City. They had been collegemates and were still
friends.

Now Mrs. Wormley was calling to ask me how I was and whether
I needed anything. The mail had already come for the day, with no
letter from home, and I knew I was in trouble. Still, it was very hard
for me to bring myself to ask Mrs. Wormley for money. I was too
proud, and it was very embarrassing. Finally I realized that there
was nothing else for me to do.

Bertha Wormley did not hesitate one minute. She worked at the
State House around the corner from where I lived, and she said,
"You just come on by here on your way to school, and I'll have it
ready for you." When I assured her that I would pay her back as
soon as I could, she said, "Oh, we'll let our grandchildren worry
about it."

After I left her to go to school, I sat on the subway and opened
the envelope she had given me. In it was fifteen dollars. I sat on the
train, tears streaming down my face, thinking, "There are such
good people in the world! When you are most discouraged, someone like Mrs. Wormley comes along to restore your faith."

To this day, she has not accepted the fifteen dollars I found in the
envelope she gave me that morning, but I can never forget the
kindness of one woman who barely knew me, but who wanted to
help a young girl trying to make something of her life.

Mrs. Wormley was a special person, yet she shared the spirit of
many blacks of that day—and this—who have achieved some
degree of success and who form a sort of chain to help the younger
people of their race. Think of how complicated the chain was that
led me to her—yet how strong.

After this incident, my counselor from the conservatory, Mrs.
Jean Demos, and I had a talk with Mrs. Bartol to see if I could work
for her. She agreed to let me clean up my room, the two other
bedrooms on the fifth floor, the hall, and the two stairways that
went down from that floor. It was a double house with a passage
running between the two parts. Two white students lived in the
other bedrooms. Mrs. Bartol had a cook and two Irish maids who
taught me how to scrub those floors the way they did, on my hands
and knees with sponges and cloths—a really thorough job.

That work paid for my room and breakfast, but I still needed money for my other meals and extras. So I persuaded Mrs. Bartol to pay me a little money to wash the pillowcases and towels on Saturdays. Luckily, I did not have to do that too long, for in November the Urban League got me a part-time job with a mail-order company. Of course, all these details of my economic problems are important only because they are typical of the painful struggle of young African Americans, even today.

In my second semester, for an ironic reason, I got a grant from the state of Alabama. Because the state wanted to keep its schools segregated, such grants were made to African Americans who wanted to get the professional training for which there were no facilities in Alabama's black colleges.

Developing my voice was the most important thing to me then, and even to this day, with everything else that has enveloped my life, it still remains very important to me. I was determined to get the best training I could, but voice lessons were terribly expensive. Luckily, I did well at the conservatory and was awarded an additional one-hundred-dollar scholarship. This was applied to my fees.

I was on my way toward a chosen career, working toward my goal.

I feel very strongly that I was *sent* to Boston, directed there, because it was in Boston that I met Martin Luther King, Jr. Neither Martin nor I believed in destiny, in the sense of predestination that one cannot change. But we both felt that God guided our lives in the way that He wanted us to serve, so that we might be the instruments of His creative will.

I believe that there is a plan and a purpose for each person's life and that there are forces working in the universe to bring about good and to create a community of love and brotherhood. Those who can attune themselves to these forces—to God's purpose—can become special instruments of His will.

From the time I was very young, I had strong hope, not only about success for myself but also about serving humanity. Now, I feel that I was being led to Martin Luther King, Jr., to fulfill this hope with him. And even though we were both very young in Boston and even though our courtship was not too different from a thousand others, it was all leading us where we were going.

Of course, I had no premonition of this at the time; quite the contrary. I had not planned to get married for a long time. I was deeply interested in developing my voice and my potential in music; and by now I had reason to think that I had enough talent to achieve some success. I wanted to give myself an opportunity to find out if this was so. At the least I would have the satisfaction of having developed what talent I had to its full capacity. Whether or not it was ever used professionally, I knew I would be a happier person for having done so.

All these years I had waited, and now I was here in Boston in this environment where I was absorbing music. Everything about it seemed so right. I was very happy.

Martin Luther King, who changed all this, came along in my second semester.

We met through a mutual friend at the conservatory named Mary Powell. She was a little older than I was and was married to a nephew of Dr. Benjamin Mays, the president of Morehouse College in Atlanta. I was attracted to her because she was very intelligent and mature and we shared a similar southern background. Most of the students at the conservatory were younger than either of us—and had just graduated from high school.

Of course, another reason we became friendly was that there were very few African Americans at the conservatory. By the time I had left Antioch, there were about thirty black students, but at the conservatory there were only about fifteen or twenty, including part-time students.

Think of the waste that pitifully small figure represents! White people always marvel at the number of African-American performers in jazz and popular music, and then they say, with great surprise in their voices, "Why, I bet so-and-so is almost good enough to play in a symphony orchestra!"

How naive and unsophisticated America has made its white population, and how unconsciously cruel. First-rate black performers, with extraordinary talent, either were not able to get professional training at first-rate institutions or, if they had the training, were not able to find the jobs. How many symphonies, do you imagine, had any blacks playing in them, for example, in 1951, when I was studying?

One of the worst evils of segregation was the waste of this creative force and the ruin of the lives of talented men and women who happened to be black.

The problem was not exclusive to the conservatory. There were only a limited number of black students in the entire Boston area. Though there were no signs posted, as there were in the South, we certainly did not feel completely welcome at many white restaurants and nightclubs in the Boston area. Because of this, most of our social life was conducted at a few "southern-style restaurants" or at parties in private homes. Naturally, for all these reasons, black students were thrown together and, naturally too, there was a lot of matchmaking going on in the group.

Mary Powell was a bit of a matchmaker herself, though, as I later learned, Martin had nudged her into the role. One day late in January 1952 she said to me, "Have you heard of M. L. King, Jr.? (In those days everyone called him M.L., and in his own family that was always his name.)

When I answered, "No," Mary began to tell me about him. "Dr. Mays tells me that he is a very promising young man," she said. "He is at Boston University taking his doctorate. He is a Baptist minister, ordained in his father's church, the Ebenezer Baptist Church in Atlanta. He has been preaching at churches around Boston and is very brilliant. I want you to meet him."

The moment Mary told me the young man was a minister I lost interest, for I began to think of the stereotypes of ministers I had known—fundamentalists in their thinking, very narrow, and overly pious. Genuine piety is inspiring, but many of the ministers I had met went around wearing a look of sanctity that they seemed to put on like their black suits. The fact that young King was a Baptist also prejudiced me. In the African Methodist Episcopal Zion Church we felt that baptism by sprinkling was adequate. I remember hearing my father and mother discuss with their Baptist friends whether it was necessary to be immersed in order to be saved. I thought I would never want to become a Baptist because I did not think it was necessary to be baptized by immersion.

However, that was not the thing that mattered; it was just one of those minor prejudices that came to the surface. I was really thinking of the Baptist churches—and my own church too—as being overly emotional. Though I was deeply religious, I was moving away from fundamentalism. After I left Antioch I decided that I wanted to identify myself with a church or religious body that was more liberal than the kind I was brought up in. I intended to investigate the Quakers and Unitarianism. I was, in fact, dissatisfied with organized religion as I knew it and sought to find a faith with which I could identify totally.

For this and other reasons, I did not attend church regularly when I first went to Boston. I was the only black living in the Beacon Hill section, and I did not feel comfortable going to the churches in that area. I said to myself, "I can worship in my room."

Mary Powell had known Martin Luther King, Jr., in Atlanta when he was at Morehouse College and she was at Spelman. They met again in Boston. They ate at the same restaurant, the Western Lunch Box, near the conservatory, where black students attending the various institutions of learning often gathered. It specialized in southern cooking—we would call it soul food now. I did not go there much because I lived far away on Beacon Hill.

One day Martin said to her, "Mary, I am about to get cynical. I have met quite a few girls here, but none that I am particularly fond of. Do you know any nice, attractive young ladies?"

She mentioned two girls, one of whom Martin had already met, and then he asked, "Who is the other one?"

"Coretta Scott," Mary said, and began to describe me. According to Martin she gave me a good character reference: a very nice girl, intelligent, pretty—all those things. But she warned him that she did not think I was religious enough, that I did not often go to church. Later he told me that this did not bother him, that he did not want for a wife a fundamentalist or anyone too set in her beliefs. He asked Mary for my telephone number, and after some of Martin's powerful persuading, she gave it to him.

When he called me and said, "This is M. L. King, Jr.," I didn't recognize who he was. He quickly said, "A mutual friend of ours told me about you and gave me your telephone number. She said some very wonderful things about you and I'd like very much to meet you and talk to you."

I began to remember then and I said, "Oh, yes, I've heard some very nice things about you also." That was all Martin needed to begin talking, very easily and smoothly. I had never heard such talk in all my life. He said, "You know every Napoleon has his Waterloo. I'm like Napoleon. I'm at my Waterloo, and I'm on my knees."

I must admit I enjoyed the fun. We had a long conversation in which he asked me about my studies and told me a little about his work under Professor Edgar S. Brightman.

Finally he said, "I'd like to meet you and talk some more. Perhaps we could have lunch tomorrow or something like that."

I found that I was free from twelve to one between classes the next day, and Martin said cheerfully, "I'll come over and pick you up. I have a green Chevy that usually takes ten minutes to make the trip from B.U., but tomorrow I'll do it in seven."

The next day I waited for him on the steps outside the conservatory, on the Huntington Avenue side, in a cold January drizzle, with a scarf on my head and my coat buttoned up tight. The green car pulled up to the curb, and as I walked down the steps I could see the young man sitting in the car. My first thought was "How short he seems" and the second was "How unimpressive he looks."

I have been quoted as saying that when I first met Martin I thought "he was a typical man—smoothness, jive. Some of it I had never heard of in my life. It was what I call intellectual jive." There was nothing typical about Martin the man, but when we first met that is how he came across to me.

Martin drove me to Sharaf's Restaurant on Massachusetts Avenue, where we had lunch, cafeteria style. I took off my coat and scarf. I still remember everything I was wearing that day. I remember the shoes I had on and the light-blue suit and the black coat. Martin looked at me very carefully. At that time I was wearing bangs that had a natural wave, and my hair was long. He liked that and said so. I was rather self-conscious but tried not to react too much, to remain as poised as I usually was.

It was a little difficult, for in those few minutes I had forgotten about Martin being short and had completely revised my first impression. He radiated charm. When he talked, he grew in stature. Even when he was so young, he drew people to him from the very first moment with his eloquence, his sincerity, and his *moral* stature. I knew immediately that he was very special.

We got our lunch and sat down at a table and began to talk. This young man became increasingly better looking as he talked, so strongly and convincingly. With a very masculine self-possession, he seemed to know exactly where he was going and how he was going to get there. In our discussion, I must have made some reasonably intelligent comments, for he said, "Oh, I see you know about some other things besides music."

Then we had to go back to the conservatory. In the car, Martin suddenly became very quiet, and he said, "Do you know something?"

"What is that?" I asked.

Very quietly but intensely he said, "You have everything I have ever wanted in a wife. There are only four things, and you have them all."

Somewhat flustered, I said, "I don't see how you can say that. You don't even know me."

"Yes, I can tell," he said. "The four things that I look for in a wife are character, intelligence, personality, and beauty. And you have them all. I want to see you again. When can I?"

Still trying to keep my poise, I said, "I don't know. I'll have to check my schedule. You may call me later."

I know it sounds strange that Martin should talk about marriage so soon in our relationship. However, Martin was ready to get married and was quite consciously looking for a wife. He already knew exactly where he was heading in his life and had formed a pretty good idea of the kind of wife who would fit in with that life. I do not mean to say that he was cold and calculating, without any romantic ideas. That is certainly not the case. What is true is that

Martin was remarkably mature for his age. He knew the sort of person he himself was, and the sort of woman he needed. It was as if he had no time for mistakes, as if he had to make up his mind quickly and correctly, and then move on with his life. Our courtship had this quality, but so did the rest of Martin's life until the end. Think of all he did by the time he was thirty-nine!

When I got home to my room after our first meeting, my intellect hoped that Martin had not really meant what he said about marriage, for I did not want anything to stop me, to stop my career, and my emotions told me that this might. I was not a young girl. I had thought myself in love before, but things did not work out, and I had resolved not to become emotionally entangled again until I was absolutely certain. "The next man I give my photograph to is going to be my husband" is the way I put it to myself.

With Martin I had all my defenses up, but in my heart I knew they were not too strong. I did not know what to think about him. He seemed so serious, so deeply sincere in what he said. I argued with myself that men always flattered you and pretended to be in love, when they were just playing a game. But even though I had the feeling that the career I had wanted and worked for so hard might be jeopardized, I had no intention of not seeing him again. I rationalized it by telling myself that he was such a fine young man, that I would wait and see what happened.

Martin telephoned me the next day and suggested that we meet Saturday night. I explained that friends of mine were giving a party in Watertown on Saturday night, but the young man who was supposed to escort me was uncertain whether he could make it. If he could not, I told Martin he could join us. Martin was willing to wait and see. I noticed that.

We drove to the party in Martin's car. On the way, we went by the conservatory to see Mary Powell. Martin said to her, "Mary, I owe you a thousand dollars for introducing me to this girl." Though I was still resisting intellectually, that was very nice to hear.

Our arrival at the party caused quite a stir among the other girls. They said to him, "Oh, so you are M. L. King, Jr. Oh! We've heard so much about you."

Martin seemed pleased at the attention they gave him, but I suspect it was because he wanted to impress me. He was always very popular with the girls and was completely relaxed and free and un-self-conscious. He explained his popularity by saying, "You know women are hero-worshipers." There is no question in my mind that he was the most eligible young black man in the Boston area at that time.

He had taken me to the party, and I was his girlfriend. He treated me with respect and consideration, but he was thoroughly enjoying his success—the swooning and all that. I was very calm, never letting it appear that it bothered me at all; because, of course, I had no claim on him. I never said a word. I just observed, and I could not help being affected.

That same night when he brought me home, I could see things moving—closer and closer.

The next day, Sunday, Martin brought his friend and roommate, Philip Lenud, to meet me. Philip was from Birmingham, Alabama, and had been at Morehouse College in Atlanta with Martin. Like Martin, he was the son of a Baptist minister, and was a minister himself, at that time the pastor of a church in Everett, Massachusetts. Philip made quite a fuss over me, and I felt he approved of Martin's new girlfriend.

From that day forward Martin pursued me—not that I ran very hard. We had wonderful times and talks together, some of them quite serious. Martin had a scholarly mind, and as he told me about delving into philosophy, I realized the depth and breadth of his learning. He had studied the great German philosophers, among them Kant and Hegel and Nietzsche. He was influenced by Hegel and hated Nietzsche, whose *Will to Power* almost brought Martin to despair of his hope of influencing the world through the power of love, though it served as an antidote for Hegel's easy idealism.

Of the more modern thinkers, Reinhold Niebuhr interested him, and Walter Rauschenbusch's *Christianity and the Social Crisis* left an indelible impression on his mind, though Martin thought him "a victim of the nineteenth-century cult of inevitable progress."

Martin had, of course, read Karl Marx, who, he said, had convinced him that neither Marxism nor traditional capitalism held the whole truth, but each a partial truth. "I could never be a Communist," he said. "My father is a thoroughgoing capitalist, but I could not be that either. I think a society based on making all the money you can and ignoring people's needs is wrong. I don't want to *own* a lot of things."

Martin told me that the turning point in his thinking on how to reconcile Christian pacifism with getting things accomplished was when he heard Dr. Mordecai Johnson of Howard University give a lecture on Gandhi at Friendship Hall in Philadelphia. He was so fascinated that he went out and bought all the books he could find on Gandhi and nonviolence and read them at Crozer Theological Seminary. He also read Thoreau's essay "Civil Disobedience." Though I don't think he had as yet consciously considered applying the Gandhian technique of nonviolence to the African-American Movement, the idea began germinating in his mind. Later he wrote, "Christ furnished the spirit; Gandhi showed how it would work."

Even at the time we were courting, Martin was deeply concerned—and indignant—with the plight of the African-American in the United States. He talked about black people being freed from oppression, though never in terms of violence. He believed in nonviolent militancy and in redemptive love. He believed ardently in Christ's words about loving your enemies. Even if you get beaten by not defending yourself, he said, somehow your suffering helps to redeem the other person and to purge your hatred of that person. He said, "The chain of hatred must be cut. When it is broken, brotherhood can begin."

There is going to be much talk of love in this book, so it is time to describe the kind of love Martin meant, as he himself later defined it. It is curious that in so rich a language as English there is only one word for all the different kinds of love. Martin said many times, though it bears repeating here, that the Greeks had three words for it! First there was *erōs*, which in Platonist philosophy meant the yearning of the soul for the divine and now has come to mean aesthetic or romantic love. *Philia* meant reciprocal love, as between friends or men and women. "No one," Martin said, "could be such a fool as to expect a person to feel that kind of love for his oppressor."

The third kind of love was *agapē*. This meant understanding, redeeming goodwill toward all men. It was disinterested love in which the individual sought not his own good, but the good of his neighbor. It was not weak or passive, but love in action. Love of this sort is not sentimental; it is active. If you love you do something about that love. You care about the problems in society and so you seek to address them. You care about human beings and so you will go to any length to try to help them. This was the kind of love Martin aspired to give his enemies. If, because of the defect in the English language, he sometimes sounded mild, just remember that his was a militant life and a militant love.

Another aspect of his liberal thinking was his attitude about details of ritual. When I mentioned that I would not like to become a Baptist because I did not believe immersion was necessary, he said, "You would not have to be immersed. There is no saving efficacy in water."

That was when he was talking about marrying me, which he did much of the time from that very first day. He was quite evidently looking for a wife in Boston; and yet he was in an ambivalent position, because, as Mary Powell had told me, he was engaged to a girl in Atlanta. Quite early in our friendship Martin told me about her himself.

She was, he said, a fine girl whose parents were very close to his. Their "engagement" was more an assumption on the part of their families and of themselves that someday they would marry than a formal arrangement. His father "was very keen on it," Martin told me. "My father wants me to marry, and he will help me to take care of my wife as long as I'm in school. But I am going to make my own decisions; I will choose my own wife."

He made it clear that I was his choice, though he was concerned about my attitude toward the career I was preparing for. Martin had, all through his life, an ambivalent attitude toward the role of women. On the one hand, he believed that women are just as intelligent and capable as men and that they should hold positions of authority and influence. But when it came to his own situation, he thought in terms of his wife being a homemaker and a mother for his children. He was very definite that he would expect whomever he married to be home waiting for him.

At the same time, Martin, even in those days, would say, "I don't want a wife I can't communicate with." From the beginning, he would encourage me to be active outside the home, and would be very pleased when I had ideas of my own or even when I could fill in for him. Yet it was the female role he was most anxious for me to play.

There were also other considerations he had thought about. He would say, "I must have a wife who will be as dedicated as I am. I will be the pastor of a large black church in the South. That's where I plan to live and work. I want the kind of wife who will fit into that kind of situation. Can you adjust yourself to 'Aunt Jane'?"

By "Aunt Jane," Martin meant the good but uneducated parishioner who does not know the difference between, as he put it, " 'you does' and 'you don't.' " He always had a strong love for the people and a very strong sympathy for the underdog, for the masses, as he would have said. Of course, I had grown up among women like "Aunt Jane" and had no qualms about adjusting to them. For I felt that no matter how far I had gone and might go, I would never forget my origins or look down upon the kind of people who were my own. I tried to reassure Martin.

Martin saw me as a young lady who was studying music with deep cultural appreciation, and to whom the aura of Antioch clung. He was concerned that it might have so far removed me from the people that I would not be able to make the necessary adjustment. It is, really, sometimes difficult for African Americans who have had this experience to go back into an all-black community and find a balance. Inevitably, you adopt white men's standards, and you unconsciously begin to act as they would expect you to act rather than being yourself.

Martin was concerned about me because at that time he did not know of the early struggles I had gone through in order to survive. He did not yet know I was from such a culturally deprived background. I felt that because I had this kind of background and

dentification with the masses, I would have no problems. I had not
forgotten my heritage.

And that is how it proved to be. Martin and I never had serious
differences of opinion about racial matters or economics, or the
difficult and terrible and glorious things that so unexpectedly
befell us.

But it took me a long time to make up my mind. I had such a
dissimilar plan for my life, and as I have said, I did not want to
marry a minister. But he was so different from the stereotype I had
envisioned. He was good—such a very good man. His conscience
was a formidable thing that kept him on the path he thought was
right. If he ever did something a little wrong, or committed a
selfish act, his conscience fairly devoured him. He would, throughout his life, really suffer if he felt there was some possibility that he
had wronged anyone or acted thoughtlessly. When this happened,
if it were possible, he would always make apologies and seek
forgiveness. He felt that having been born into what was a middle-
class African-American family was a privilege he had not earned,
just as he felt the many honors heaped on him in the later years
were not his alone. He would constantly examine himself to determine if he was becoming corrupted, if he was accepting honors too
easily. He was very sensitive about having people do things for him
because of his position. He was extremely grateful for any help he
got. He was a truly humble man and never felt he was adequate to
his positions. That is why he worried so much, worked so hard,
studied constantly, long after he had become a world figure. These
qualities enabled him to continue to grow.

But he was also so alive and funny, and so much fun to be with.
He was a great tease; how he loved to tease me when we were
courting by pretending to like some other girl until I rose to the
bait, my eyes spitting fire. How he would laugh at me then!

He loved to dance and was a good dancer. He loved people and
enjoyed parties and, especially, good conversation. He loved music
too. I remember the first concert he took me to at Symphony Hall
in Boston. I was touched that Martin, who knew how much music
meant to me, would think of that kind of date. The great Polish
artist Artur Rubinstein was the pianist, and this was the first time I

ever heard him play. In spite of my great love of music, I had attended no concerts with famous artists until I went to Antioch. When I did, it was a great pleasure for me.

As Martin made comments on the various selections, I thought at first that he wanted to impress me that he knew about music too. But I soon realized that I was not being fair. He was so genuinely pleased to be able to take me to this concert, which I could not otherwise have afforded; he was so happy in my pleasure that I stopped being watchful. We shared the concert together and enjoyed it very much.

Another way that Martin began to groom me for my role as the wife of a Baptist minister was in my clothes. In those early days he was very fastidious about his appearance, while I had been first told by my mother and father, and then indoctrinated in the Antioch attitude, that clothes don't matter. I had a good coat and some nice dresses, but I took no great pains about my appearance. I might comb my hair in the morning and seldom touch it again all day, nor retrace my lipstick.

Very gently Martin would make suggestions. "Perhaps you'd like to go to the ladies' room and comb your hair." "You look so pretty with lipstick on." "Why don't you buy that pretty red coat we saw in Filene's window?" and such things as that. I finally saw what he was aiming at and began to be more concerned about my personal appearance.

But with all the fun we had, and his charm and his growing love for me, I still was not sure. As we began to talk more seriously about marriage, I asked myself again and again, "Is this really what I want?"

Finally I thought, "If I am serious about a commitment to service, how better could I serve than as a minister's wife?" But I still had to convince myself.

I prayed earnestly to God, "Oh, Lord, help me to make the right decision." I knew this was the most important decision of my life, that it had to be the right one. This process of careful thought and prayerful meditation went on for about two or three months.

One thing that worried me was that I knew Martin's big problem in deciding whom to marry was his great love and respect for his father. Whatever he might say about deciding for himself, I recognized that his father might be the determining factor, because of the strong influence he had on his son. I wondered whether, if his father said no, Martin would give in to him. Mary Powell had told me that she believed Reverend King, Sr., wanted his son to marry the girl in Atlanta, and she doubted that Martin would make the final decision himself. As I fell more deeply in love with him, this worried me a great deal. It seems strange, but a dream helped me to decide.

In my dream Martin's father, whom I had never met, was there, and the girl in Atlanta was also there. Martin's father was smiling at me, and somehow I knew he approved of me. I woke up with a great feeling of relief. It seemed a miraculous kind of thing.

I was wrestling with this problem throughout April and May. I realized that I did want marriage and a family. Without those things my life would be incomplete. It was not until later in the fall that I finally decided that because I really loved Martin, I would go ahead and marry him and let the question of my career take care of itself. However, I was determined to go on and get my degree. I would finish that much, so I would have a sense of accomplishment, even though I would not have the kind of career I had planned. I decided I would be open to developing a relationship with Martin to see whether he was someone I could live my life with and then whether or not I was truly in love.

It may seem unusual for a girl in love to think things out so thoroughly, though I did not consider it so. This was, and still is, my way of dealing with problem situations. I have always faced my problems and dealt with them. In addition, my decision did not concern only me. I worried about whether if I were discontented and had conflicts Martin's promising career would suffer.

Another thing that helped me to decide was that Edythe came to Boston that summer. Though I did not confide in Edythe how serious I was about Martin, the fact that she liked him very much was a good mark in his favor.

I did not tell Martin of my decision right away. Instead, I made up my mind to stay in Boston and study for most of the summer instead of going home. We continued to see each other constantly.

In July he was going back to Atlanta, and he asked me to visit him there. I had to pass through Atlanta on my way to Alabama, so I could do it easily enough. But to test him, to see if he really wanted me or not, I said, "No. I don't think I will."

He was very upset. He said, "If you don't want to come—just forget everything. Forget it. Forget the whole thing." Later we used to laugh about his ultimatum.

I realized that if this thing was going to work out between us, I would need to meet his family—his father and mother—and see his church. I also wanted to determine for myself if it was a situation I could adapt to and be happy in, and if I could have a real place in Martin's life.

Martin drove home in his car. I had to have my tonsils removed, so I waited in Boston until August first for my final checkup, and then took the train. When I came to Atlanta I was very much on guard, watching everything. Though I had tentatively made up my mind, I was still overtly resisting. There was no commitment.

My first visit to Atlanta was not an unqualified success. I was to stay with Mary Powell, who was home for the summer. When I stepped off the train, Martin and Mary were there to meet me. We drove out of the station into the mass of traffic on Peachtree Street. Then we went several blocks, turned a couple of corners, and stopped. Martin's mother got into the car. I had not expected to meet her so soon, and was put a little off balance. Mrs. King was a short woman, meticulously and fashionably dressed. She could be a little hard to know at first, not unlike my own mother. Even so, I was somewhat nervous. When Martin said, "Mother, this is Coretta Scott," her greeting was polite but casual.

We drove first to the Kings' big yellow-brick house on Boulevard. It was a lovely home, and it gave me a new view of Martin's background, and some new problems. I did not understand then that the King family was entirely wrapped up in the Ebenezer Church and its congregation. When I saw their comfortable home, all I could think of was the well-known, rather closed social life of the black middle class of Atlanta. I had heard about their clubs and social functions and their "exclusiveness." I was a little concerned about how the family would react to me, an outsider, as well as how I would like the atmosphere.

I realized later that the Kings were dedicated people who judged others on their own merits and that my early fears were unnecessary. I met Martin's father for the first time that day. He was a big man, bigger than I expected. One could feel his strength of character as well as his physical power. He was gentle and courteous, but he too was casual. As he said long afterward, "I didn't pay much attention to Coretta that first time. I wanted Martin to marry another girl, and I wanted him to get married soon. There were so many girls who liked him. They were pushing him. I was afraid he would get tied up with one we did not like."

I spent the night at Mary Powell's house, and the next day, Sunday, we all went to Ebenezer Church. It was a modest-sized, handsome building on Auburn Avenue. The unpretentious interior was finished in off-white with polished woodwork that had a golden tone. There were lovely stained-glass windows. Behind the pulpit the white-robed choir sat in tiers of seats. They sang very beautifully. In the pews and the balcony, which overhung a third of the main floor, there were seats for seven hundred and fifty people. I was told that Reverend King had brought the membership of Ebenezer up from a few hundred, when he first was called to its pastorate, to nearly four thousand.

In summer, to give his father a rest, Martin took over the responsibilities of pastoring and preaching, and he preached the Sunday I was there. As always, his sermon was both interesting and moving. After church we all got together at the Kings' home. I met his brother, A.D., Naomi, his pretty young wife, and their little girl, Alveda, a charming child who called me Coco and took a great liking to me.

A.D., also a minister, graduated from Morehouse and the Interdenominational Theological Center in Atlanta. During his pastorate in Birmingham he was very active in the Birmingham Movement. Later he accepted a pastorate in Louisville, Kentucky, where he organized the Kentucky Leadership Conference and gave invaluable leadership to it. He died in 1969.

Naomi was also an Alabamian. Many people said then that there was a striking resemblance between the two of us. When I first knew her, Naomi appeared gentle, sweet, and sympathetic. Later, I was to learn that she combined all the qualities of a strong and loving wife and mother: kindness, compassion, and unselfish devotion to her loved ones.

I had met Martin's sister, Christine, when she was visiting him in Boston during the spring holidays. She greeted me on this occasion with warmth and friendliness. (Christine, a graduate of Spelman College and Columbia University, is now a professor of reading at Spelman.)

We went to church again that evening. I noticed how easy and loving Martin was with the members of the congregation and how they accepted him as a leader, despite his youth. Watching him at Ebenezer, it was impossible not to be proud of him.

Afterward, Martin had to pay some visits to church members, and I went back to Mary's house. I stayed with her family a day or two more and then went on to Marion to visit my family.

Martin promised to come to Marion to see me in my own home, but something interfered and he did not come. However, he asked Mary Powell and me to drive back to Boston with him. My mother did not like the idea. She said, "If I were you, I'd just go on back the way you had planned. You have your ticket. Go back on the train as you planned, without stopping at Atlanta."

We argued about it gently. Finally I made my own decision. "I'll go back to Atlanta and ride up with them," I told her.

Mother was not too happy about it. Of course, she had not yet met Martin and so could not understand my going to so much trouble to ride back to Boston with him.

Martin and Philip Lenud had taken a little apartment together on Massachusetts Avenue, in a predominantly black section of Boston. It was near the conservatory and I stopped in nearly every afternoon. Once, during the summer, when Edythe was there, Martin had said half seriously, "Coretta, how good a cook are you?"

Edythe and I went to his apartment one Sunday afternoon and I cooked my specialty, banana pudding, and Martin's favorite cabbage smothered in bacon; my sister did creole pork chops. Of course, we had corn bread and tossed salad. Martin and Philip ate it all appreciatively. When we finished, Martin teased me and said I had passed the test. Though I didn't like the idea of a "test," I felt pretty good.

In November, Martin's father and mother came to Boston to visit him. That brought things to a head. At Martin's suggestion I continued to drop by almost every afternoon while they were there. Daddy King began to realize that there were no other girls around. He started asking Martin about the girls he had known before he had met me and found that they just did not exist anymore as far as Martin was concerned.

He talked to me about it one afternoon, with Martin sitting right there. He said, "Coretta, do you take my son seriously?"

I said, "No," but I thought he was referring to something Martin had just said.

He said, "I'm glad to hear you say that. You know, I don't understand this young man. He's gone out with some of the finest girls—beautiful girls, intelligent, from fine families. We love people and we want to be nice to everyone, but we don't know how to act. He gets us involved, and then he just seems to lose interest. Those girls have a lot to offer."

By this time I was getting a little irritated, and I said rather sternly, "I have something to offer too."

Reverend King seemed to pay no attention, but he remembered that. After that, whenever I achieved recognition in any way, like doing a successful concert, or helping Martin in a difficult situation, Daddy King teased me, saying, "Coretta, I have something to offer too." And he added affectionately, "You know, that's right. You sure do have something to offer!" It became a family joke.

But there in Martin's little apartment he did not seem to notice. He went on to tell me all about the girl in Atlanta. "A fine family . . . a very talented . . . wonderful personality. We love that girl. I don't know what M.L. is going to decide. But I'm glad to hear you say you don't take him seriously, because unless you know my son better than I do, I would advise you not to."

I said to myself, "I think I do know him better than you do." All that time Martin had not said a word. He just sat there grinning like an embarrassed schoolboy. He did not want to hurt his father by going against him. He was amazingly respectful, thoughtful, and considerate of Daddy King's feelings. Yet he was completely his own man. He made his decisions, and his father would hear about them. And his father would come around.

But I sat there thinking, "Why don't you *say* something?"

At last Martin got up and went to the other room, where his mother was. He told her about me. And he said, "Coretta is going to be my wife." But he did not tell his father.

When Martin drove me home, he was displeased with me because he feared I had not made a good impression on his father.

I said, "It was difficult for me, hearing about what great personalities your other girls had. I could not pretend to like it. I can't be insincere."

Daddy King came around sooner than we expected. Only two days later he suddenly slammed his big hand down on the table and said, "You all are courting too hard. What's this doing to your studies?"

Martin said, "I'm going on to get my doctorate, and then I'm going to marry Coretta."

Reverend King turned to me and asked, "What about you, Coretta? How are you getting on at the conservatory?"

"I'm getting on all right, but it *is* difficult."

"That's what I thought," said Reverend King. Wham went his hand on the table again. "Now you two had better get married."

Only later did Daddy King tell me his thoughts about me. He told me how concerned he was that Martin had made the wrong choice and how Christine had said, "She's a fine girl. You must accept it, for Martin is going to marry her."

Daddy King also said that he was influenced by the fact that his little granddaughter Alveda was so fond of "Coco" and kept asking about her. "If that little girl loved you, I thought, you must be a fine girl, and then in Boston I really got to know you and decided that you were."

Once, in my presence, Daddy King said to a group of people, "I don't believe there was any girl who could have fitted into Martin's life as Coretta did. No other could have gone through what she did with him and afterward. She has been a source of strength to me—to the whole family. I will never forget her saying throughout the years to me, 'Dad, you've got to understand what it all means. It will be all right.' "

After Martin's parents left Boston we discussed marriage in a serious way. We tentatively decided that at Eastertime we would announce our engagement in the black newspaper *Atlanta Daily World*. We would be married in June after the school year ended.

Martin went home alone for Christmas—I could not afford to go home. He had to convince his father still another time and persuade him that I was the right one. Finally his father gave in. He said, "I can see that is your choice. I agree to it because I respect your opinion and your choice."

Meanwhile I wrote to Edythe that I was probably going to marry Martin and asked her if she thought I was doing the right thing. When her reply came, I had already made up my mind, but she further confirmed my decision. Though I do not have her letter, I can remember what she said: "Don't have silly doubts, Coretta. You know how difficult it is to find a stable, intelligent, dedicated man. Martin has these qualities in an unusual way. If you love him, go ahead and marry him. You won't have the career you dreamed of, but you'll have a career. You will not be marrying any ordinary young minister."

After that I decided to switch my major at the conservatory from performing arts to musical education with a voice major, so I could teach wherever we lived instead of having to travel all over the country giving concerts. Martin had said, "When I come home I want my wife to be there." When I decided to marry him, I said to myself, "Regardless of what happens after I marry Martin, I will adjust myself to these conditions, whatever they may be. Wherever Martin lives, I will live there too. Whatever he does, I will be involved in it."

And I think that having made that decision—the most important in my life—is what made all the rest possible, the amazing and wonderful and terrible things that came later in our lives. At that point, though, I was still holding in abeyance my final judgment on whether or not I had made the right decision. I thought I had, and everything pointed in that direction, but I still was not sure. That confidence, that absolute knowledge that my destiny was as the wife of Martin Luther King, awaited me in the city where the rest of the world also began to learn about my husband: Montgomery.

4

"You must stand up for your rights"

Martin and I were married by Daddy King on the lawn of my parents' home on June 18, 1953. It was not the house I grew up in, but one my father had recently built in Marion, next door to his general merchandise store. I decided not to have a typical wedding with a formal white gown and all the rest, but rather to have a small private wedding and wear a pastel, waltz-length gown.

With the Antioch attitude of disdaining materialism, I would not even choose a pattern for my silver or china. As I look back on it now, I really had some nerve, and I don't know why I did not understand that there was a practical aspect to those gifts: I had to go on and buy the same plates and silverware later on.

All the King family came from Atlanta, as well as some of the deacons and trustees of Ebenezer, and some Atlanta friends. Edythe and I drove into Marion to meet them all on the day of the wedding. My father was somewhat surprised and mentioned the old custom that the bride and groom are not supposed to see each other before the ceremony. Though I laughed and said I didn't care about such conventions, I did have a twinge of superstition and was concerned about whether people would think me a bit forward.

Soon the "motorcade" from Atlanta arrived, led by Martin. He and I went immediately to the courthouse to get the license, and then all of us drove the nine miles to our house.

None of the Kings had ever met my parents, and I was unnecessarily concerned about whether they would form a favorable impression of our home in the country. All my training at Lincoln and Antioch, and even my knowledge of Martin and his family, ought to have kept me from feeling that way, but of course I couldn't help wondering if they had been so conditioned by middle-class values that they might be concerned with such superficialities. Also, I wanted the Kings to accept me and my background for what they were.

I did not want to appear to be trying to "impress" the Kings. In fact, I was very much against that attitude. Still, I wanted so much for the families to get along well, and I wanted them to be comfortable together. I really think that my prospective in-laws had not been expecting to find in a country area so comfortable and nice a house as ours was by that time. Certainly, my parents were people of such obvious character and with such high standards that there was no question of their being accepted. I suppose those are not uncommon worries of prospective brides or grooms.

I was silly to have worried. The meeting between the families went off very well. Martin rushed into the house saying, "Hello, Mother," as he kissed my mother. That really did it! Then Reverend King came in, looking so tall and dignified that my mother seemed awed. But he was so gentle and kind that she soon got over that feeling. The two mothers had a lot in common.

We had the usual country-style dinner, part of which I had cooked myself, with a variety of southern dishes with their special country flavor. I was doing a dozen things at once. Christine and my sister, Edythe, went out and picked some vines and flowers to decorate the wedding arch, and though I seem to have needed to manage everything myself, I allowed them to do that. Then Daddy King took Martin and me aside for the little talk he always gave young couples before they were married. We sat on chairs outside my father's store. I don't remember too much of what he said because my mind was on so many things, but I do recall that he said to me, "Coretta, if I were you I would not marry M.L. unless I could not help myself. M.L., I would not marry Coretta unless I could not help myself. I preach because I can't help myself, and when you get married you should think of it like that, as something you are impelled to do. Think about this for a few moments and decide if this is the way you feel."

Martin and I had long ago decided that, and it was easy for us to reassure Daddy King.

We were both very tired. Martin had driven almost straight through from Boston, and I had been arranging so many of the details of the wedding that I was nervous and on edge. We had ordered a grass mat, and when it was not delivered in time for the seven o'clock ceremony I got upset and unfairly blamed my father. I was so concerned about having everything go perfectly.

My father said, "Why don't you just hold off the ceremony for a little while?"

I blew up then and answered in a very angry tone, "Daddy, I'm not going to wait. The wedding is going to come off exactly as scheduled."

Daddy King looked at me very sternly. He told me later that he had been surprised to discover that I had a temper.

Then the guests began to arrive, and I went to my room to put on the wedding dress I had bought in Boston. It was a gown of pale blue lace and net, and I wore gloves and shoes of the same color. Christine had designed my veil, with a crown made of flowers.

In spite of all my worries, it was a lovely wedding. Edythe was my maid of honor, and A.D. was Martin's best man. We stood under a little arch we had built in the garden, and Daddy King performed the short, simple service. At our request, he left out the bride's promise to obey. He didn't object to this departure from custom because by this time he had learned that, on some issues, the thinking of young people was different from his.

After the wedding there was a reception. Martin, who was usually so congenial, was so exhausted he almost fell asleep on the receiving line. Then we motored in to Marion; I asked him to let me drive because I was afraid he would go to sleep at the wheel. As a matter of fact, he slept all the way to town. We spent that night at the home of friends, Mr. and Mrs. Robert E. Tubbs. Mr. Tubbs was the undertaker my mother's family used. In later years Martin would say jokingly, "Do you know, we spent our honeymoon at a funeral parlor."

I suppose it does sound funny, but one has to realize there were no hotels with bridal suites for African Americans in that part of the country. Furthermore, the undertaker played a special role in rural black life, somewhat comparable to the friendly protectiveness that an older doctor might assume in a small community. When we needed extra chairs for a party, or to get a telephone message to a family without a phone, or the use of a car, it was the undertaker we called.

On Friday we went to Atlanta. The Kings gave a reception for us that evening so that Martin's friends could meet me. Everybody had a very special feeling for Martin, and naturally they were concerned about the girl he had married. The people who came greeted me warmly and welcomed me.

On Sunday Martin preached at Ebenezer, and I joined the Baptist Church. I had discussed this before with Daddy King, who said, "If you don't want to be immersed, it is not necessary in order for you to become a Baptist. As far as I am concerned, you don't need to be immersed. But, since Martin is going to be a pastor, there might be an objection by some of the church people; I think maybe you should do it."

At this point, I no longer had any conflict about sprinkling versus immersion, and I was willing to go through with this ritual as a matter of course.

Our wedding was unusual in another way too: We did not have a traditional honeymoon. After joining the Baptist Church on Sunday, I went to work on Monday. We lived in the Kings' house all that summer, because we were going back to school in Boston in the fall. Our honeymoon was delayed for five years.

In Atlanta I learned more about Martin's family and his growing up than he had ever told me. His father had come from a small town outside Atlanta called Stockbridge. Martin's grandfather, James Albert King, had been a sharecropper on a plantation in this little town in the country outside Atlanta. He never had a hance to get ahead. He was the victim of an agricultural system inexorable as the seasons and far less rewarding. In those days, sharecroppers, Martin's grandfather among them, bought their seed on credit from the plantation owner. They also bought from him all the other things they needed—household supplies, food, clothing—everything on credit. At harvesttime, before the crop was equally divided, the year's debts had to be paid. But there never seemed to be enough money to get out from under. James King might work hard all the year and still end up owing four hundred dollars to the owner. The next year it was the same: He toiled and reaped and dug, and his digging buried him always deeper. What was so unfair about the system was that the sharecropper paid *all* the expenses, but he had to *share* the profits with the plantation owner. The landlord advanced the sharecropper whatever he needed and then did his own bookkeeping and his own reckoning of what had to be subtracted from the benefits.

Once when Daddy King was quite young he was present at the annual reckoning between his father and the plantation owner. The calculations were rapid and bewildering. "So many bales of cotton sells at one hundred dollars per five-hundred-pound bale, equaling an amount which, divided by two, equals another amount. Here's your bill, so you owe me fifty dollars."

Daddy King had a keen mind for business. He said to his father, "Papa, don't forget to figure in the cottonseeds." The seeds had sold for enough to clear the debt. The white man barked back to his father, "Now, listen, you take care of that boy. Because if you don't, I will." James King said quietly, "No, it won't be like that," and he sent his boy away. But as Daddy King was leaving, he called back over his shoulder, "Remember the seeds, Papa."

People often wonder whether the spirit of nonviolence flowed naturally to Martin from his parents and grandparents. Daddy King tells this story about one incident when he was a small boy. One day his mother gave him a pail and told him to fetch some water. He had filled the pail and started back home when a white man stopped him and said, "Hey, boy, give me that water." Daddy King said, "I can't. My mamma told me to bring it to her."

The white man insisted, "Boy, I said give me that pail."

Daddy King replied, "I'm not gonna do it."

The white man pulled him close, tore his clothes off, stripped him until he was naked, and beat him. When Daddy King went back and told his mother what had happened, the first thing she said was, "You must swear to me that you will not tell your papa about this, because if you tell him, he'll kill that white man."

She then picked up a club and went out and beat the man herself. Apparently the shame of it caused him to say nothing about the incident, and it seemed to blow over. However, in the community, the story got around, and Martin's grandfather, when he heard it, got a gun and went after that white man. At one point, the Kings were driven off the land for a time. They were hunted, and they lived in the woods for weeks, until finally the crisis blew over. As you can see, the spirit of nonviolence was not inherited from Martin's family. What is also amazing is how young Martin's father was when he was taught, "You must stand up for your rights."

James King had ten children, of whom his son Martin Luther was the second. Daddy King had a miserable youth because of the family's extreme poverty and because, in a life without hope, his father sought refuge in drink. I think that watching his father struggling with this problem was one of the reasons Daddy King turned out to be so strong a teetotaler.

The job that was especially Daddy King's all during the time he was growing up was currying the mules. At the Stockbridge school the other children would tell him he smelled like a mule, and most likely he did. He would answer, "I may smell like a mule, but I don't think like one." However, this aroma of his honest labor made him shy with the girls and very self-conscious.

Later he would say, "You know, I've got a mule complex. I vowed when I left the country: I'm not going to be a slave, and I'm not going to plow another mule."

When Daddy King was sixteen he left home and started walking toward Atlanta with his only pair of shoes slung over his shoulder. As he went past the plantation owner's brick house, he told himself, "Someday I'm going to have a brick house as big as that—bigger.

omeday I'm even going to be a director of a bank like that man." ventually my remarkable father-in-law did both, and a lot more esides.

At that time his chances looked small. He had only a sixth-grade ducation from the little plantation school in Stockbridge, but he ad a football player's build, a good brain, and a spirit as strong as is body. He worked hard all day—as a mechanic's helper, as a ireman, and at whatever other jobs he could get. At night he went o school. He was fervently religious and began preaching—"because I couldn't help it." His eloquence in the pulpit was inpired by a powerful faith and a deep love of people.

Martin's father was pastoring at two small churches outside Atlanta when he met Alberta Christine Williams. Her father, the Reverend Adam Daniel Williams, was the well-known pastor of Ebenezer Baptist Church on Auburn Avenue, a position he had hen held for over thirty years. Alberta was a small young woman who was then teaching school after having studied at Spelman College in Atlanta.

Spelman was considered the best black women's college and is still a fine school with a rich curriculum and an excellent staff. As a matter of fact, I believe the road to integration should be a two-way street, and with the difficulties of college placement these days, more white families ought to consider fine black schools such as Spelman and Morehouse.

After graduating from Spelman, my mother-in-law went to Hampton Institute in Virginia and then returned to Atlanta to teach. She and the young Martin Luther King fell in love and were married, with the Reverend Williams' blessing. The young couple moved into the Williamses' big wooden Victorian house on Auburn Avenue. With the black-owned Citizens' Trust Company, the Atlanta Life Insurance Company, real-estate firms, and other businesses, it was the main business street of the African-American community in Atlanta.

A little later, Reverend Williams asked his son-in-law to join him as assistant pastor. Then, in 1931, Reverend Williams preached his thirty-seventh-anniversary sermon. He died of a heart attack that same week, and Reverend King became pastor at Ebenezer.

Reverend Williams' wife, Jennie, Martin's grandmother, continued to live with the Kings as their three children were born—
Christine, Martin Luther, Jr., and Alfred Daniel. Martin would tel
me of his grandmother's wonderful spiritual qualities and also o
her soft heart. When Daddy King would whip Martin for some
thing he'd done, Martin would take his punishment without
word, determined never to cry, even when he was quite young. Bu
in the background, always, was his grandmother Williams, tear
streaming down her face, unable to bear the punishment.

Even with his family and church responsibilities, Martin's fathe
kept studying. He graduated from high school and went on t
study at Morehouse College. He finally got his degree there whe
his children were growing up. Second only to Reverend King'
religion was his ambition to make something of himself. In addi
tion to his church work, he kept on with his business pursuits. H
eventually became a director of the Citizens' Trust Company, an
had an interest in other businesses. He always said, "If I could kee
from preaching, I'd make a better businessman than a minister.
He was prominent in civic as well as religious affairs, becoming
trustee of Morehouse College, Atlanta University, and Morri
Brown College.

Daddy King had always been a great penny-saver. Even afte
Martin and I were married his father carried thrift to an extrem
we would often joke about. If chickens were on sale somewhere i
town, he would drive across the city to save ten cents, ignoring th
cost of the gasoline he used, for the pleasure of a bargain. H
would complain about our paying to have our car washed, saying
"You should wash it yourself."

Martin, the sociologist, would answer, "Daddy, I have a theor
about that. You know society is based on the division of labor, an
if I wash my own car it means somebody else doesn't have a job."

His father would smile and say, "You go ahead, son. Spend you
money! If you go broke, I guess I'll always have a dime in m
pocket for you." He meant it too. He may have been thrifty, bu
particularly where his family was concerned, he was very generous

Martin's mother was extremely fashionable and well dressed an
had a keen sense of humor—I think Martin inherited it from he

She had many wonderful stories to tell. One of my favorites is of the time, one Sunday morning, when she and Daddy King were driving through the country trying to find a small church at which he'd been invited to preach.

They stopped an old black man walking down the road and asked him for directions. He said, "Let's see, now. To get to that church, you go down this road about two miles, then turn right . . . No, that's not right. What you do is, you turn around and go up to the crossroads, then turn left and . . . No, that's not right, either. Let's see . . ." He scratched his head and said, "You know, I reckon I don't know *where* that church is."

The Kings thanked him for his trouble and pulled away. Suddenly they heard someone calling, and looking back, they saw the old man huffing and puffing down the road to catch up with them.

They stopped, backed up the car, and waited while he tried to catch his breath and then listened expectantly.

He panted out, "I just wanted to say . . . I just wanted to tell you . . . I just saw my brother, and I asked him . . . and he don't know where that church is either."

Mamma King had enormous energy and dedication to the church and its members. Throughout the years, when the rest of the family was busy with other matters, it was Mamma King who would call at one o'clock in the morning—or six—to discuss a wonderful idea for a young people's group, or for a special church program.

Her influence on Martin was enormous in the example of her quiet strength, temperament, fastidiousness, and high moral standards. Her talent and love of music were a blessing to the whole family as well as to Ebenezer.

As to Daddy King, of course he loved all his children—but he adored Martin. Shortly after Martin's death he said, "There was always something special about M.L. Even before he could read, he kept books around him. He just liked the idea of having them. He learned to recite the Scriptures before he was five, years before he could read the Bible for himself. His grandmother Williams was a religious woman and was an inspiration to the child. When he was

only six years old—and very small for his age—he used to sing
hymns from memory.

"We took him to a Baptist convention about that time. His
mother played the piano, and M.L. sang his favorite gospel song, 'I
Want to Be More and More Like Jesus.' When he finished,
people were shouting and crying. But the boy didn't get puffed up,
he just went and sat down, very quiet and humble.

"M.L. liked to listen to good preachers before he was old enough
to understand them. If he heard that some outstanding man was
going to speak, he would ask me to take him. I remember after one
such occasion when he was only about ten, he said, 'That man had
some big words, Daddy. When I grow up I'm going to get me some
big words.' As soon as he could read, he lived in dictionaries, and
he made that saying come true."

Daddy King's stories about Martin make him sound rather
precocious and too good to be true, but he was not like that at all.
He always had a playful sense of humor and liked practical jokes.
As a child he was small, but very strong and quick, good at sports.
When he got older, he was quarterback of the football team at
Morehouse College, because in spite of light weight, his compact
body and tremendous spirit made him very hard to stop. He also
loved to play basketball, and he was a strong swimmer. Though he
liked tennis, he seldom got the chance to play, because during the
years he had the time, most tennis courts were segregated. Even
after he became a leader of the Movement, he used to play basketball with the staff of the Southern Christian Leadership Conference, and he delighted in teaching our sons—to my despair
sometimes. Occasionally, on rainy days, when Martin was in town
and he happened to be at home, you could hear me saying over and
over, "Martin, please don't play ball in the house."

The boys and he would look at me with pitiful expressions, and
my husband, quite logically, would ask, "Where else is there for us
to play?" I never did think of a satisfactory answer for that question.

Martin was always eager to work. When he was very young his
family put a coal furnace in their house. He soon learned to fire it,

to bank the fire at night, and to get up early mornings to open the damper, put on the coal, and haul out the ashes.

My husband learned about segregation early in his life. Some white children with whom he used to play lived near the King home in Atlanta. When Martin was six he went to the black elementary school, and his friends went to the white school. That was when their parents decided to draw the color line. Quite suddenly they told Martin he could not come to play anymore, "because we are white and you are colored." In tears he rushed home to his mother. She took him on her lap, and because he was so intelligent, she told him the story of his people. She explained about slavery and how, after it was ended, the white people still thought they were superior and kept apart from the blacks, and how they made the segregation laws so that blacks would still feel like slaves. She told him that this happened to our people every day of their lives. Mamma King ended with the black mother's old refrain, "You're just as good as anybody else."

Another incident of early discrimination that Martin would recall was the time in his boyhood when a black fraternal organization, called the Elks, sponsored an oratorical contest in Valdosta, Georgia, a good distance from Atlanta. Martin traveled to the competition with his teacher, and he won the prize as second-best orator. Naturally he and his teacher were feeling pretty good as they started back home, but their happiness was short-lived. Though there were seats on the bus to Atlanta, none happened to be in the black section, and the two of them were forced to stand for the long journey. Martin said the irony struck him then—that his prize meant nothing to white people, that because he was black there would be no seat for him.

Unlike many African-American boys and girls, Martin was very fortunate. The circumstances of his life protected him from the worst of the suffering of segregation and, most important, he had his father's example to guide him. Daddy King had fought Jim Crow from boyhood on. He had a tremendous sense of his own dignity. "When I stand up," he said, "I want everyone to know that a *man* is standing there." He seldom rode in buses because African

Americans were forced to ride in the back seats; but even before he could afford this luxury, he would say, "Even though the law may force me to ride in the back, my mind is always up front."

Daddy King was a leading figure in the local chapter of the National Association for the Advancement of Colored People and the Atlanta Negro Voters League, and he was a member of the Interracial Council of Atlanta, which played a great part in keeping peace between the races and ameliorating some of the worst abuses of segregation. He led the fight to desegregate the elevators in the courthouse long before his son was old enough to join the struggle. One of his outstanding achievements was his fight to equalize salaries for black teachers, which he won. Later on, when Martin became involved in the national Movement, it was Daddy King who was most active in the Atlanta struggle.

When he was a little boy, Martin had many opportunities to see his father in action. Once they went into an empty shoe store and sat down in the front seats. The clerk said politely, "If you will move to the back I'll be glad to help you."

Daddy King's temper rose. "You will wait on us here or we won't buy any shoes."

"I can't do it," the clerk said.

Daddy King took Martin's hand and left the store. As they walked down the street, he rumbled in his deep voice, "I don't care how long I have to live with this thing, I'll never accept it. I'll fight it till I die. Nobody can make a slave out of you if you don't think like a slave."

On another occasion, now well known, when Martin was riding in the car with his father, a policeman stopped them and said to Daddy King, "Boy, show me your license."

Pointing at Martin, Daddy King said in his powerful voice, "Do you see this child here? He's a boy. I'm a man."

Martin said the policeman was so shattered that his hand shook as he wrote out the ticket.

Martin started his education at the nearby elementary school, but was soon transferred to Atlanta University's private laboratory school. Both of them were segregated, of course. In eighth grade he entered Booker T. Washington High School, with five thousand students, the only black high school in Atlanta at that time. There he skipped ninth grade and at the end of the eleventh grade took and passed the entrance examination for Morehouse College. However, Martin was always the first to point out the inadequacy of the education he received in Atlanta's segregated schools. Even though he had special abilities and did not come from a "deprived" background, he entered Morehouse reading at an eighth-grade level. Imagine what happened to many of the others, without Martin's advantages.

Morehouse is one of the leading black colleges in the United States. African-American families who send their boys there feel about it as white families would feel about Harvard. It has a very high standard for qualification and an excellent course of study. Some of the outstanding men who have graduated from More-house or been associated with it are Mordecai Johnson, former president of Howard University; Benjamin Mays; Howard Thurman, former dean of Marsh Chapel, Boston University; and Robert Johnson, executive editor of *Jet*. The tradition has continued with Lerone Bennett, Julian Bond, Spike Lee, and others. Martin matriculated there in 1944 at the age of fifteen. In later years he often talked about how important the college had been in his life.

When Martin first went to Morehouse he intended to become a doctor or a lawyer. His interest in intellectual matters and his strong social consciousness, together with his normal youthful rebellion against tradition, had decided him against the ministry. He was strongly motivated toward religion but was opposed to the emotionalism of the church he knew, and he believed in a relevant social gospel which few ministers preached at that time. Even at that young age, Martin intended to dedicate his life to improving the condition of the black masses, but he thought he could do this more effectively in a profession outside the ministry.

By the time he went to college Martin realized that he had led a far more protected life than most children. The Kings had a wonderful family relationship, and all through his childhood

Martin knew his parents would support him all the way. Whenever he had an assembly recitation to do in school, or was going to sing in the choir or play football—anything—Mamma and Daddy King were sure to be in the audience rooting for him. Daddy King always felt that it was his duty to be present whenever one of his children was doing something special. If he could not go, Mamma King would attend.

With his growing social consciousness, Martin wanted to learn at first hand what life was like for really underprivileged people—"to learn their problems and feel their feelings." He was also anxious to pay some of his expenses on his own, rather than always having to call on his father. That year, instead of taking a summer job in one of the white-collar black businesses, he chose to do hard manual labor. He worked handling baggage for the Railway Express Agency, and he took another job on the loading platform of the Southern Bedspring Mattress Company. The job was exhausting for him physically, and Daddy King wanted him to quit, but Martin persevered. In these jobs he not only became intimately acquainted with his fellow laborers, but he found out what it was like to work under white bosses. The foreman of the Railway Express Agency often addressed the black workers as "nigger," and at the mattress company Martin himself suffered almost daily humiliation.

In the summer of 1945 Martin went with several other Morehouse men to work in the tobacco fields of Connecticut. Though it was hardly a glamorous job, my husband would later talk of the exhilarating sense of freedom he felt at being able to eat in any restaurant and to sit in the orchestra at the movies in Connecticut. Then, when the train on which he was coming home reached the southern states and he went to have a meal in the dining car, the waiter ushered him to a rear seat and pulled a curtain down in front of him. "I felt as though that curtain had dropped on my selfhood," Martin said.

In Connecticut his friends asked Martin to lead their devotions. I think it was from this experience that he began to feel an insistent call to the ministry. However, the decision that finally led to that path was largely due to the example of Dr. Benjamin E. Mays, the president of Morehouse College. In later years Martin often spoke of Dr. Mays as "my spiritual mentor." He was a graduate of Bates College and a member of Phi Beta Kappa, and had gone on to earn his Ph.D. and become president of Morehouse, the most prestigious position an African American could hold in the academic world. Martin was deeply influenced by Dr. Mays. If Martin had twenty phone messages when he returned to his office, the first call he made was to Dr. Mays. Martin discussed every major decision he made with his mentor. Though he made his own decisions in the end, Martin always wanted to know what Dr. Mays thought. It is a tragedy that so many black young people will not know the greatness of a Benjamin Mays. Too many people think that Martin was an exception, different from all other black people. He was exceptional; but he had great teachers and mentors too.

At Morehouse, listening to Dr. Mays preach, and also hearing another brilliant minister, Dr. George D. Kelsey, head of the theological department, Martin came to see that the ministry could be intellectually respectable as well as emotionally satisfying. When he accepted this fact, it opened the way for him to go into the church. The balance between mind and soul, intellect and emotion, was what he would strive to achieve.

Martin was seventeen and finishing his junior year at college when he went to his father and told him that he felt the call to the ministry. Concealing his delight behind an air of doubt, Daddy King proposed that Martin should preach a trial sermon before a small congregation in one of the smaller auditoriums of Ebenezer. But when word got around that young M.L. was going to preach, so many people came that they had to move into the main sanctuary.

The sermon was a great success. Martin had inherited his father's ability to preach, though he adopted a far more subdued style. His effort to demonstrate his ability, with obvious restraint, was compensated for by his youthful sincerity. Daddy King was bursting with pride, but he was humbly grateful to God. He got down on his knees that night and thanked the Lord for giving him such a son.

In 1947, at the age of eighteen, my husband was ordained and made assistant pastor of Ebenezer Church.

Martin graduated from Morehouse when he was only nineteen. There was no question in anyone's mind that he should go on to study theology and get a Ph.D. He was accepted by Chicago Theological Seminary, Colgate, Andover Newton, and Crozer Theological Seminary in Chester, Pennsylvania. Martin chose Crozer. When he told his father, Daddy King said, "You're mighty young to go to Crozer."

But of course Martin was not mentally young, as Daddy King well knew; he was anxious about whether the competition would be too keen. There, again, is that wonderful relationship between father and son—the deep love, the respect and admiration each had for the other, and the fact that though Martin never abruptly forced an issue, he fought in his own way and always ended by convincing most people that he was taking the right course. He was a very persuasive man, and when he used his powers with his father, Daddy King also would succumb. And so Martin went to Crozer.

When he got there, he really applied himself to his studies. Now he knew what he wanted to do with his life, and he was a serious student. At Morehouse he had not had the straight-A average he was to earn in his three years at Crozer. Perhaps the call had been standing in Martin's way, and now that his searching for it was over, he could move forward more surely.

He was determined to get the best training possible for the ministry, and this drove him to excel at school. He also had the energy and interest to attend lectures on philosophy at the University of Pennsylvania and to do a great deal of outside reading, including the life and works of Mahatma Gandhi, which he then read for the first time. He also found time for some socializing with black young people in Philadelphia. That he was popular with his classmates is shown by the fact that he was elected president of the senior class at Crozer—the first black student ever to have won that honor.

When Martin graduated in June 1951, he won the Pearl Plafker Award as the most outstanding student and was awarded the J. Lewis Crozer Fellowship for graduate study. Both Martin and his father were determined that he would get the best training possible for the ministry, and they felt that it was essential for him to have a Ph.D. in order to accomplish this.

He applied to graduate school, and Yale and Boston University both accepted him. He chose Boston University because he wanted to study under the proponents of the philosophy of personalism, professors Edgar S. Brightman and L. Harold DeWolf.

And that was how Martin had happened to be at Boston University in the fall of 1951 when I went east to study at the New England Conservatory of Music.

In September 1953, after our marriage, Martin and I went back to Boston, he to finish the residence requirements and write the thesis for his doctorate and I to finish my musical education at the conservatory. We rented an apartment in a very old house right around the corner from the one Martin had had when we were courting. It had four rooms—kitchen, bedroom, den, and living room. Martin worked on his research in the den and I studied in the bedroom, though in order not to bother Martin or the neighbors, I never practiced my singing at home but used the practice rooms at the conservatory.

I had an extremely heavy schedule. It was my last year, and I was taking thirteen courses to finish the requirements for my degree. My degree was to be in music education, with a major in voice. My second instrument was violin, but in order to qualify to teach music, I had to run the whole gamut: voice, piano, choir directing, orchestral arrangement and directing, and four instrumental classes—percussion, strings, woodwinds, and brass. I was not required to have the proficiency of a performer in all these instruments. The idea was to get enough experience with the different categories so that one knew the theory of each and could teach them.

Just having that many classes and also finding time to practice all those instruments meant a tremendous push that last year in Boston. Then, in my second semester, I did practice teaching at one high school and two elementary schools. My pupils were white, but though I was the first black in this situation, the children accepted me readily. I was very pleased when the principal of one of the schools, a reserved but nice New England woman, told my supervisor how successful I had been in getting the children to respond and participate in the music program.

I also sang in several recitals that year. In the spring I was featured in the premiere performance of the Cuban composer Amadeo Roldán's *Motivos de Son*, with the conservatory orchestra. Most of it was percussion, very modern and difficult to sing. I was happy to be chosen for the role, but for a new bride it was a very heavy schedule. I consoled myself with the thought that after our schooling was over, we would settle into a less hectic routine. Little did I know!

Martin was working very hard too. In addition to his studies and research, he often preached at the churches in and around Boston. He must have been growing into a more powerful speaker all the time, because his reputation as "a remarkable young man" is still remembered in the Boston area. Though he did a large part of his work in the university library, most of the time he was at home studying. Because I was so busy, Martin was wonderful about doing the housework. He did all the heavy cleaning and even the washing. We had a tub in the kitchen where I would put the clothes to soak. Then my husband would wash them when he took a break from his studies. Martin did the best he could, but he generally was unsuccessful. When we put the clothes up on the kitchen lines to dry, though I never told him, they looked like the "before" on TV commercials. I was very appreciative, but I would wish to myself that he had let me do the job.

On Saturdays we did the weekly shopping for groceries together, and Thursday was Martin's night to cook, because I had a six-o'clock class. He had learned to cook when he had the apartment

with Philip Lenud, and was quite proud of his ability. In addition
to smothered cabbage, he cooked pork chops, fried chicken, pigs'
feet, pigs' snout, and pigs' ears. I never liked pigs' ears, but Martin
liked them because—his father's son—he said, "They're good and
they're cheap."

He would also cook turnip greens, southern style, with ham
hocks and bacon drippings, and of course corn bread, though we
cheated on that by buying a mix. As is apparent, we liked soul
food—highly seasoned, overcooked, and delicious southern cooking. Though over the years, as we traveled more, other foods were
added to our menu, Martin always loved southern cooking best.
Sometimes you might drop into the pastor's study at Ebenezer, and
there would be my husband gnawing at a pig's foot while the
delighted parishioner who had brought him a jar of her specialty
sat proudly watching his enjoyment. Dear Martin! He always complained that our cooking was too fattening, yet it was exactly what
he loved, and with a plate of greens before him, he never could
remember his diet.

Though Martin helped so much in the house the first year we
were married, all the domestic work did not make him self-
conscious. He was too sure of his manhood. One of the difficulties
American black men must face is that the whole social system beats
down upon them harder than on the women. It is more difficult
even now for them to find good jobs than it is for their women. The
men are regarded with more suspicion and with more fear by
whites. In that period especially, any assertion of black manhood
was regarded by the ruling class as dangerous and was quickly put
down, sometimes—in the South, at least—with a rope around the
neck. With this background, it has been difficult, until very recently, for black men to take their natural place as the heads of
households and the protectors of their families. Where black men
have had to turn away from their responsibilities, it has been
because of the remorseless pressure of a hostile society, not because
of any innate character fault.

Martin had none of these inhibitions nor any of the psychological insecurities that seem to beset so many men in white America.
He always made me feel like a real woman because he was a real

man in every respect. After we were married he said, "I want my wife to respect me as the head of the family. I *am* the head of the family."

We laughed together at that slightly pompous speech, and he backed down. "Of course, I don't really mean that," he said. "I think marriage should be a shared relationship."

But he really did mean it. That was an adjustment I had to make, and I believe I made it very well. At the same time he encouraged me to express myself, he did not like the idea of my working. He wanted the major responsibility. He said, "I'm supposed to earn enough money to take care of you and the family." He was willing to have me teach or give concerts if I wanted to so I could be independent. In fact, I did work over the years, and later, when he was involved in the struggle, the money I earned was a big help. I always said that if I had not married a strong man, I would have "worn the pants." Martin was such a very strong man, there was never any chance for that to happen. He had such strength that he imparted this quality not only to me but also to other people who met him. This was particularly true of other men, who seemed to derive strength from their association with him and were drawn to him for it.

Of course, Martin achieved great public renown and respect, but in private also he was always the kind of man whom I, as a woman, could look up to and respect.

In addition to Martin's course at Boston University, he took a course on Plato at Harvard from Dr. Raphael Demos and studied the modern existentialist philosophers—Jean-Paul Sartre, Karl Jaspers, Martin Heidegger. Yet these studies were side excursions. My husband was wholeheartedly committed to the philosophy of personalism of which Boston University was the center and Dr. Brightman the chief exponent. When Dr. Brightman died in 1953, Dr. L. Harold DeWolf became Martin's mentor. Personalism appealed to Martin because of its emphasis on the individual. It holds, as Martin put it, "that the clue to the meaning of ultimate reality is found in personality." Long years after he left Boston he wrote, "This personal idealism remains today my basic philosophical position. Personalism's insistence that only personality—finite and infinite—is ultimately real, strengthened me in two convictions; it gave me metaphysical and philosophical grounding for the idea of a personal God, and it gave me a metaphysical basis for my belief in the dignity and worth of all human personality."

For his doctoral thesis, Martin chose to write *A Comparison of the Conceptions of God in the Thinking of Paul Tillich and Henry Nelson Wieman*. This was an interesting exercise, because Martin did not agree with *either* of their conceptions of God. Martin believed all his life that God is both infinite and personal—a loving Father who strives for good against the evil that exists in the universe. He believed, as I do, that we who dedicate ourselves to God are His instruments in that glorious struggle.

With all our hard work and high thinking, you might suppose that the first year of our married life was rather grim and that we had few happy times. You might think that—if you did not know Martin. True, we did not have much free time, but we made the most of every precious second.

I remember that in the early summer of 1954 my mother came to visit me in Boston for my graduation. We went out to an amusement park at the beach where they had all the hair-raising rides, roller coasters, a Ferris wheel, and a roller-skating rink. Martin rode all the rides, and he and Philip Lenud roller-skated until they were ready to drop, laughing and roughhousing and doing fancy turns and gyrations.

My husband had preached that Sunday morning, and Mother had been tremendously impressed with his sermon. Now he was having so much fun that she could hardly believe that it was the same serious-minded young man who had spoken so wisely and well a few hours before. "You know," she said to him, "you act like you are about four years old."

But that was the way he was all his life—playful—even to the very last day. In the midst of the most serious times, Martin would bring fun into our lives with his ability to see the humor in even the most difficult situations.

* * *

As it had been before we were married, our social life in Boston was still mostly among other southern blacks who were studying at the various colleges and universities. Blacks were isolated, which is why "integration" was so superficial in the Boston community. The neighborhood we had lived in before, and still were part of, was almost completely black, and though the centers of learning were at least nominally integrated, they were so big and impersonal that no special effort was made to bring African Americans into campus activities.

This isolation was partly due to the fact that in Boston there is a kind of coldness, a formality, that is so different from the South. Not that we ever spent time with white southerners, but among their own kind, at least, southerners seem more openhearted and hospitable. Martin and I realized that there was a possibility of mingling with whites if we wanted to make the effort. But it *would* have been an effort, because at that time the social climate was not sufficiently permissive for blacks and whites to feel comfortable enough to be together naturally, without effort.

The ministry was Martin's dominant interest, and we had to decide which church positions he should seriously consider. Here we disagreed. I wanted to go back south *someday*—it was our home, and we loved it—but not yet. Selfishly, perhaps, I wanted to breathe the freer air and the richer cultural life of the North a while longer and to enjoy the greater opportunities a northern city would give me for furthering my musical career. But our lives did not permit that luxury. Martin seemed to have the need to get on with his destiny. He felt that he should go south immediately. His intense dedication compelled him toward the harder rather than the easier solution. He had warned me of this long ago during our courtship, and now he said to me, "I am going back south. I am going to live in the South because that is where I am needed."

Though Martin's interest was broad enough to include all underprivileged peoples, whatever their race, he most certainly felt that his place was as pastor of a black church in the South. He wanted this because it would bring him into close contact with the people to whom he wanted to devote his life. For several days we thought and talked and prayed over this decision. Eventually I bowed to his wish without any great struggle, for when we married I knew that where he went, I would go.

Through the intercession of T. M. Alexander, Sr., of Atlanta, a friend of the King family, Martin was invited to preach by the Dexter Avenue Baptist Church in Montgomery, Alabama, which was then looking for a new minister to replace Dr. Vernon Johns, who had just left.

Dr. Johns has since died, but at that time he was in his fifties. My husband and his friends could sit for hours swapping stories about this outspoken minister who always gave his middle-class congregation a very hard time. According to Martin, Dr. Johns' main purpose was to rock the complacency of the refined members of the Dexter Avenue Baptist Church—in whatever way he could.

I must admit that, at first, I was not enthusiastic about the prospect. Having come from a town in Alabama only about eighty miles from Montgomery, I knew the situation there only too well. I knew, from my own life, that in this city, living in its memories of its glory as the first capital of the Confederacy, the stifling hood of segregation at its worst soon would drop over us. I also felt that Montgomery would offer me little opportunity or challenge in pursuing my musical interests.

Though I was opposed to going to Montgomery, I realize now that it was an inevitable part of a greater plan for our lives. Even in 1954 I felt that my husband was being prepared—and I too—for a special role about which we would learn more later. Each experience that we had was preparation for the next one. Being in Montgomery was like a drama that was unfolding. Martin and I and the people of that small southern city were like actors in a play, the end of which we had not yet read. Yet we felt a sense of destiny, of being propelled in a certain positive direction. We had the feeling that we were allowing ourselves to be the instruments of God's creative will.

As Martin was being made ready to be the leader and the symbol of the black Movement, so I was being prepared to be his wife and partner. It was in Montgomery that I became aware of the contribution I could make in sustaining and helping the Movement, and my husband, in what was to come.

5

"To overcome fear"

I first saw the Dexter Avenue Baptist Church on the first Sunday of July 1954. After graduating from the conservatory I had gone to stay with Mamma and Daddy King in Atlanta while Martin remained in Boston to finish his dissertation. That July weekend, on his trip to Montgomery, he took me with him to meet his new congregation.

Dexter was a fine, solid, Victorian brick church, standing on Montgomery's handsome public square. Right across Dexter Avenue was the Supreme Court Building, and diagonally across the square stood Alabama's State Capitol, with its classic dome and the pillared portico where Jefferson Davis had taken the oath of office as President of the Confederate States of America.

The "official" white southern square was an odd place for a black church, but Dexter had been built in Reconstruction days, when blacks were enjoying their brief freedom after the Civil War. At that time blacks owned various other properties in downtown Montgomery, but they were all eventually pushed out. Only Dexter remained, a kind of symbol of African-American aspirations to its congregation, all of whom now lived a long way off in segregated areas. Most of them came to church in automobiles; a few came in the segregated buses. It was a considerable inconvenience, but they were proud of their church and accepted its inconvenience gladly.

Dexter was not as large as Ebenezer. It seated only four hundred people, as compared to Ebenezer's seven hundred and fifty. Its congregation was small, but it was definitely affluent. Most of the members were college-trained; many held advanced degrees. There were physicians, teachers, college professors, and prosperous businesspeople in the congregation. Poorer blacks in Montgomery referred to it as "the big people's church."

In fact, in spite of Dr. Johns' prodding of their consciences, the congregation did not encourage mass participation in the services, nor did they make any attempt to attract people "off the streets." Of course, my husband's idea was that the church should welcome all people and that the ideal of Christian worship was people of all classes participating in it together. Soon after he came to the church, he became known throughout the black community as "the friendly pastor."

That first Sunday, Martin warned me that he would call upon me to speak. I prepared a speech but did not write it out, as I wanted it to seem spontaneous. At the time visitors were being welcomed, some other newcomers were introduced. Then Martin said, "I am going to ask Mrs. King to say a few words to the congregation."

I cannot remember exactly what I said, but I tried to tell the members how pleased I was that they had called my husband to be their pastor and that I looked forward to living in their community and working with them. I told them this would be a new experience for me, and I asked their prayers to help me to become a good minister's wife.

I seemed to have made a good impression, and when I met them after church, many spoke of how happy they would be when we came to Montgomery permanently in September. Some people commented on how young I looked.

That was a curious thing. Though Martin was only twenty-five, such was the force of his personality and the wisdom of his words that they did not think of him as young once they heard him speak. When someone said, "Doctor King has such a young wife," I answered, "Well, my husband is a young man."

I remember a little later Professor Mary Fair Burks, of Alabama State College, came to Dexter with Jo Ann Robinson, who was also a professor at the college. When she saw Martin, Professor Burks said, "You mean that little boy is my pastor? He looks like he ought to be home with his mamma." She thought he could not possibly have anything to say that would interest her, but when she heard him she was deeply impressed. As the years went by, my husband's power as a speaker grew and grew. Hearing Martin speak when he was inspired could change your whole life.

Martin had told me, after his first few visits, "I like this church. This is where I want to begin my ministry." Now that I had seen Dexter, it was my turn, and I said, "If this is what you want, I'll make myself happy in Montgomery. You will perfect your preaching and improve yourself in the ministry at Dexter, and I will learn to be a good minister's wife."

I seem to have known then, too, that though being pastor of the Dexter Avenue Baptist Church was very important, Martin's special qualities and special training were going to take him beyond this point, and that this experience at Dexter would be—for both of us—another step toward our destiny.

Some of Martin's most inspiring sermons were given at Dexter. They usually had a social message as well as a religious one, because of my husband's belief that a minister should also be a leader in social progress. I remember one occasion, some years later, when he said to me, "I'm going to preach on Sunday about how you deal with the problem of fear." In the South that was one of our greatest problems. Racists, and groups like the Ku Klux Klan, and even the police used fear as their weapon to keep blacks down. We talked it over, and he wrote out an outline. That sermon, called *Antidotes for Fear,* was later thought to be one of his best.

Martin took as his text I John 4:18, "There is no fear in love; but perfect love casteth out fear; because fear hath torment. He that feareth is not made perfect in love."

First Martin spoke of the many kinds of fear that troubled men and women in this period of change and "calamitous uncertainty"—fear of illness or economic disaster, fear of personal inadequacy in our highly competitive society. More terrible was the fear of death, even racial annihilation, in this atomic age, when the whole world teetered on "a balance of terror . . . fearful lest some diplomatic faux pas ignite a frightful holocaust.

"Some fears are normal and necessary," he said, like the fear of snakes in a jungle, but when they become neurotic and unchecked, they paralyze the will and reduce a man to apathy or despair. He quoted Emerson, who wrote, "He has not learned the lesson of life who does not every day surmount a fear."

How, then, to overcome fear? First, Martin said,

> we must unflinchingly face our fears . . . this confrontation will, to some measure, grant us power. . . .
>
> Second, we can master fear through one of the supreme virtues known to man—courage . . . courage is the power of the mind to overcome fear.
>
> Thirdly, fear is mastered by love. . . . The kind of love that led Christ to a cross and kept Paul unembittered amid the angry torrents of persecution is not soft, anemic, and sentimental. Such love confronts evil without flinching.

Then Martin showed that hatred between races and nations is rooted in fear; that most wars are caused not by hatred but by fear. Racial injustice in America, Martin said, was caused by white people's fear of blacks' advancing status. And he said,

> If our white brothers are to master fear, they must depend not only on their commitment to Christian love, but also on the Christlike love which the Negro generates toward them. . . . *The Negro man must convince the white man that he seeks justice for both himself and the white man.*

Finally, Martin said,

> Fear is mastered by faith. Without faith we are orphans cast into the terrifying immensities of space in a universe that is without purpose or intelligence.
>
> But though death is inevitable, we do not fear it. The God who brought our whirling planet from primal vapor

and has led the human pilgrimage for these many centuries can most assuredly lead us through death's dark night into the bright daybreak of eternal life. His will is too perfect and His purposes are too extensive to be confined in the limited receptacle of time and the narrow walls of earth. Death is not the ultimate evil; the ultimate evil is to be outside God's love. We need not join the mad rush to purchase an earthly fallout shelter. God is our eternal fallout shelter. . . .

That sermon, spoken from the short outline Martin had made, was an expression of my husband's courage, his love, and his faith. Throughout his brief remaining years he was to need all three.

Among the new friends we made in Montgomery, one couple became very close to us, the Ralph Abernathys. Ralph Abernathy, pastor of the First Baptist Church, was a young man as ardent as Martin for social reform. Before Martin made the decision to accept the call to Dexter, he had gone to see Ralph, to find out how another young minister was faring in Montgomery. Ralph had encouraged Martin to come, though I sometimes think that was because the two of them became friends instantly, and Ralph liked the idea of having Martin to talk to in Montgomery.

There is very little merriment for a young minister in a small southern city, and the evenings we spent with Juanita and Ralph Abernathy were times of happy relaxation. Later, of course, Ralph became my husband's best friend and close colleague in the Civil Rights Movement. Though we continued to work together publicly, after Martin's death, unfortunately, our relationship became strained.

The spring of 1955 was especially joyful for us. Martin was awarded his doctor of philosophy degree in systematic theology. Twenty-one years of intensive study had reached a culmination— though not an ending, for Martin continued to study all his life.

That spring I discovered that I was pregnant. Martin was, if anything, happier about this than about his degree. From the time he was very young he had talked about getting married and having a family. We were both excited and happy, especially because, at one point, there was some question about whether or not we could have children. Martin often talked about how he loved children and said that if we could not have any, we would adopt some. Now our marriage was complete. Rather excitedly, he said he wanted to have eight children. I did not agree with that! After thinking it over I said, "We'll compromise and have four"—and we did.

During my pregnancy Martin was very attentive and concerned. We were both a little anxious for fear something would go wrong, but I suppose you always have these anxieties about the first one, especially when the child is wanted so much. Martin wanted a boy first. He always referred to the unborn baby as his son. "My son," he would say. "I want my son to be named Martin Luther III."

In November I went to St. Jude's Hospital to have my baby. It was a Catholic hospital, of course, and was unusual because it was the only hospital in Montgomery where blacks could be treated decently. Then, though normally St. Jude's kept whites and blacks separated, if the hospital became overcrowded they would be put together, particularly in the maternity ward.

Our baby was born on November 17, 1955. She was a big, healthy girl weighing nine pounds, eleven and one-half ounces. It turned out, as it usually does, that Martin did not at all mind not having a son. She was such a lovable child; she was very close to his heart.

From the beginning she was large physically, and she also seemed very advanced. Eight or nine days after I came home, I said to Martin, "You know, we are going to have to be very careful with this child. I think she is going to be a very sensitive person." She had such an awareness, even as a tiny infant, that I had that feeling, and sensitive and intelligent she has turned out to be.

I chose the name Yolanda Denise, but my husband had reservations about it. He questioned whether people would call her Yolanda or would mispronounce the name. He was right. Her name is so frequently mispronounced that it bothered her when she was growing up.

There is a tendency among middle-class African Americans to

give their children unusual names. Perhaps they are seeking elegance or some special identification. I fell victim to this custom, rather than following the sensible practice of naming the baby after a member of the family. Later Martin said, "If we ever have another baby girl, I'm going to give her a simple name like Mary Jane."

When we did have another daughter, we called her Bernice Albertine, after her two grandmothers. Her name was not quite Mary Jane, but at least she was named for members of the family. As a child she was known as Bunny, but today Bernice prefers her full name. Yolanda is happy to be called by her full name or her nickname, Yoki.

Martin always said that Yoki came at a time in his life when he needed something to take his mind off the tremendous pressures that bore down upon him. When he came home from the stress and turmoil that he was suddenly plunged into, the baby was there cooing and cuddly and trustful and loving. There is something renewing about a small child—something he needed very much, because two weeks after Yoki was born, a seamstress named Rosa Parks refused to give up her seat on a Montgomery bus, and the Movement was born.

6

"We have taken this type of thing too long"

There is a spirit and a need and a man at the beginning of every great human advance. Each of these must be right for that particular moment of history, or nothing happens. In Montgomery, what Martin called the *Zeitgeist*, or the spirit of the time was there under the apparent passivity of the African-American people; the hour had struck, and the man was found. Yet what was done there could not have happened without a buildup of forces and an accumulation of suffering.

You could say that the modern Movement toward black freedom and equality really began immediately after World War II. For long years, "the slow fire of discontent"—Martin's phrase—had burned almost unnoticed under the crust of apparent peace imposed by a predominantly white society, not just in America, but all over the world; not just among blacks, but among Asians and all the other exploited races of mankind. The stresses and upheavals of a worldwide war cracked the power-imposed, smooth surface of society; the steam began to hiss through the vents all over the world; and the conscience of humanity began to stir.

In America, one of the first steps toward racial justice was taken on December 5, 1946, when President Harry S. Truman appointed a group of distinguished citizens as members of the President's Committee on Civil Rights.

The next big breakthrough came on May 17, 1954. I was preparing for my graduation from the New England Conservatory of

Music and Martin was working on his thesis in Boston when the decision was handed down. The Supreme Court reversed its ancient opinion that separate but equal educational facilities met the requirements of the Fourteenth Amendment to the Constitution. In a case brought by the attorneys of the Legal Defense Fund of the NAACP, *Brown* v. *Board of Education of Topeka, Kansas,* it declared forthrightly that "separate educational facilities are inherently unequal." Any African American could have told them that long ago!

In 1955 the Court followed this decision with another, ordering public educational facilities in the United States to be desegregated "with all deliberate speed"—an unfortunate phrase that slowed the process up. A further decision of the same Court, upholding the "pupil-placement" laws, allowed manipulation of the Supreme Court decision by southern school authorities.

Of course there were violent reactions in the South. Citizens Councils sprang up in an attempt to nullify the Court's decisions, and the Ku Klux Klan got out its sheets and hoods and paraded and set crosses afire. We used to joke in those days about which of our friendly neighborhood grocers or dry cleaners was a Klansman or a member of the White Citizens Council. As a matter of fact, we did learn that some of these tradesmen *were* involved in the council.

Martin's efforts to arouse Montgomery blacks to action were severely hampered, not alone by the white people's opposition, but by the state of the black community itself, which was sharply divided by class, education, and organization. In addition to the NAACP and the Montgomery branch of the Alabama Council on Human Relations, there were three other civil rights committees, all jealous of one another. Add to that the facts that many of the leading black intellectuals were afraid to move for fear of losing their jobs, many ministers hesitated to mix theology and politics, and the great masses of African Americans had not yet found the effective means to express their discontent in action.

Though nothing dramatic happened for a while after the Supreme Court decisions, the very fact that the decisions had been made gave black people hope.

* * *

Of all the facets of segregation in Montgomery, the most degrading were the rules of the Montgomery City Bus Lines. This northern-owned corporation outdid the South itself. Although seventy percent of its passengers were black, it treated them like cattle—worse than that, for nobody insults a cow. The first seats on all buses were reserved for whites. Even if they were unoccupied and the rear seats crowded, blacks would have to stand at the back in case some whites might get aboard; and if the front seats happened to be occupied and more white people boarded the bus, black people seated in the rear were forced to get up and give them their seats. Furthermore—and I don't think northerners ever realized this—blacks had to pay their fares at the front of the bus, get off, and walk to the rear door to board again. Sometimes the bus would drive off without them after they had paid their fare. This would happen to elderly people or pregnant women, in bad weather or good, and was considered a great joke by the drivers. Frequently the white bus drivers abused their passengers, calling them niggers, black cows, or black apes. Imagine what it was like, for example, for a black man to get on a bus with his son and be subjected to such treatment.

There had been one incident in March 1955, when fifteen-year-old Claudette Colvin refused to give up her seat to a white passenger. The high school girl was handcuffed and carted off to the police station. At that time Martin served on a committee to protest to the city and bus-company officials. The committee was received politely—and nothing was done.

The fuel that finally made that slow-burning fire blaze up was an almost routine incident. On December 1, 1955, Mrs. Rosa Parks, a forty-two-year-old seamstress whom my husband aptly described as "a charming person with a radiant personality," boarded a bus to go home after a long day working and shopping. The bus was crowded, and Mrs. Parks found a seat at the beginning of the black section. At the next stop more whites got on. The driver ordered Mrs. Parks to give her seat to a white man who boarded; this meant that she would have to stand all the way home. Rosa Parks was not in a revolutionary frame of mind. She had not planned to do what she did. Her cup had run over. As she said later, "I was just plain tired, and my feet hurt." So she sat there, refusing to get up. The driver called a policeman, who arrested her and took her to the courthouse. From there Mrs. Parks called E. D. Nixon, who came down and signed a bail bond for her.

Mr. Nixon was a fiery Alabamian. He was a Pullman porter who had been active in A. Philip Randolph's Brotherhood of Sleeping Car Porters, and in civil rights activities. Suddenly he also had had enough; suddenly, it seemed, almost every African American in Montgomery had had enough. It was spontaneous combustion. Phones began ringing all over the black section of the city. The Women's Political Council suggested a one-day boycott of the buses as a protest. E. D. Nixon courageously agreed to organize it.

The first we knew about it was when Mr. Nixon called my husband early in the morning of Friday, December 2. He had already talked to Ralph Abernathy. After describing the incident, Mr. Nixon said, "We have taken this type of thing too long. I feel the time has come to boycott the buses. It's the only way to make the white folks see that we will not take this sort of thing any longer."

Martin agreed with him and offered the Dexter Avenue Church as a meeting place. After much telephoning, a meeting of black ministers and civic leaders was arranged for that evening. Martin said later that as he approached his church Friday evening, he was nervously wondering how many leaders would really turn up. To his delight, Martin found over forty people, representing every segment of African-American life, crowded into the large meeting room at Dexter. There were doctors, lawyers, businessmen, federal-government employees, union leaders, and a great many ministers. The latter were particularly welcome, not only because of their influence, but because it meant that they were beginning to accept Martin's view that "religion deals with both heaven and earth. . . . Any religion that professes to be concerned with the souls of men and is not concerned with the slums that doom them, the economic conditions that strangle them, and the social conditions that cripple them, is a dry-as-dust religion." From that very first step, the Christian ministry provided the leadership of our struggle, as Christian ideals were its source.

Martin told me after he got home that the meeting was almost wrecked because questions or suggestions from the floor were cut off. However, after a stormy session, one thing was clear: However much they differed on details, everyone was unanimously for a boycott. It was set for Monday, December 5. Committees were organized; all the ministers present promised to urge their congregations to take part. Several thousand leaflets were printed on the church mimeograph machine, describing the reasons for the boycott and urging all blacks not to ride buses "to work, to town, to school, or anyplace on Monday, December 5." Everyone was asked to come to a mass meeting at the Holt Street Baptist Church on Monday evening for further instructions. The Reverend A. W. Wilson had offered his church because it was larger than Dexter and more convenient, being in the center of the black district.

Saturday was a busy day for Martin and the other members of the committee. They hustled around town talking with other leaders, arranging with the black-owned taxi companies for special bulk fares and with the owners of private automobiles to get the people to and from work. I could do little to help because Yoki was only two weeks old, and my physician, Dr. W. D. Pettus, who was very careful, advised me to stay in for a month. However, I was kept busy answering the telephone, which rang continuously, and coordinating from that central point the many messages and arrangements.

Our greatest concern was how we were going to reach the fifty thousand black people of Montgomery, no matter how hard we worked. The white press, in an outraged exposé, spread the word for us in a way that would have been impossible with only our own resources.

As it happened, a white woman found one of our leaflets, which her black maid had left in the kitchen. The irate woman immediately telephoned the newspapers to let the white community know what the blacks were up to. We laughed a lot about this, and Martin later said that we owed them a great debt.

On Sunday morning, from their pulpits, almost every African-American minister in town urged people to honor the boycott.

Martin came home late Sunday night and began to read the

morning paper. The long articles about the proposed boycott accused the NAACP of planting Mrs. Parks on the bus—she had been a volunteer secretary for the Montgomery chapter—and likened the boycott to the tactics of the White Citizens Councils. This upset Martin. That awesome conscience of his began to gnaw at him, and he wondered if he was doing the right thing. Alone in his study, he struggled with the question of whether the boycott method was basically unchristian. Certainly it could be used for unethical ends. But, as he said, "We were using it to give birth to freedom . . . and to urge men to comply with the law of the land. Our concern was not to put the bus company out of business, but to put justice in business." He recalled Thoreau's words, "We can no longer lend our cooperation to an evil system," and he thought, "He who accepts evil without protesting against it is really cooperating with it." Later Martin wrote, "From this moment on I conceived of our movement as an act of massive noncooperation. From then on I rarely used the word 'boycott.' "

Serene after his inner struggle, Martin joined me in our sitting room. We wanted to get to bed early, but Yoki began crying and the telephone kept ringing. Between interruptions we sat together talking about the prospects for the success of the protest. We were both filled with doubt. Attempted boycotts had failed in Montgomery and other cities. Because of changing times and tempers, this one seemed to have a better chance, but it was still a slender hope. We finally decided that if the boycott was sixty percent effective we would be doing all right, and we would be satisfied to have made a good start.

A little after midnight we finally went to bed, but at five thirty the next morning we were up and dressed again. The first bus was due at six o'clock at the bus stop just outside our house. We had coffee and toast in the kitchen; then I went into the living room to watch. Right on time, the bus came, headlights blazing through the December darkness, all lit up inside. I shouted, "Martin! Martin, come quickly!" He ran in and stood beside me, his face lit with excitement. There was not one person on that usually crowded bus!

We stood together waiting for the next bus. It was empty too, and this was the most heavily traveled line in the whole city. Bus after empty bus paused at the stop and moved on. We were so excited we could hardly speak coherently. Finally Martin said, "I'm going to take the car and see what's happening other places in the city."

He picked up Ralph Abernathy and they cruised together around the city. Martin told me about it when he got home. Everywhere it was the same—a few white people and maybe one or two blacks in otherwise empty buses. Martin and Ralph saw extraordinary sights—the sidewalks crowded with men and women trudging to work; the students of Alabama State College walking or thumbing rides; taxicabs with people clustered in them. Some of our people rode mules; others went in horse-drawn buggies. But most of them were walking, some making a round-trip of as much as twelve miles. Martin later wrote, "As I watched them I knew that there is nothing more majestic than the determined courage of individuals willing to suffer and sacrifice for their freedom and dignity."

Martin rushed off again at nine o'clock that morning to attend the trial of Mrs. Parks. She was convicted of disobeying the city's segregation ordinance and fined ten dollars and costs. Her young attorney, Fred D. Gray, filed an appeal. It was one of the first clearcut cases of an African American being convicted of disobeying the segregation laws—usually the charge was disorderly conduct or some such thing.

The leaders of the Movement called a meeting for three o'clock in the afternoon to organize the mass meeting to be held that night. Martin was a bit late, and as he entered the hall, people said to him, "Martin, we have elected you to be our president. Will you accept?"

Fear was an invisible presence at the meeting, along with courage and hope. Proposals were voiced to make the organization which the leaders decided to call the Montgomery Improvement Association, or MIA, a sort of secret society, because if no names were mentioned it would be safer for the leaders. E. D. Nixon opposed that idea. "We're acting like little boys," he said. "Somebody's name will be known, and if we're afraid, we might just a well fold up right now. The white folks are eventually going to find out anyway. We'd better decide now if we are going to be fearless men or scared little boys."

That settled that question. It was also decided that the protest would continue until certain demands were met. Ralph Abernathy was made chairman of the committee to draw up the demands.

Martin came home at six o'clock. He said later that he was nervous about telling me he had accepted the presidency of the protest movement, but he need not have worried, because I sincerely meant what I said when I told him that night: "You know that whatever you do, you have my backing."

Reassured, Martin went to his study. He was to make the main speech at the mass meeting that night. It was now six thirty and—this was the way it was usually to be—he had only twenty minutes to prepare what he thought might be the most decisive speech of his life. He said afterward that thinking about the responsibility and the reporters and television cameras, he almost panicked. Five minutes wasted and only fifteen minutes left. At that moment he turned to prayer. He asked God "to restore my balance and be with me in a time when I need Your guidance more than ever."

How could he make his speech militant enough to rouse people to action and yet devoid of hate and resentment? He was determined to do both.

Martin and Ralph went together to the meeting. When they got within four blocks of the Holt Street Baptist Church, there was an enormous traffic jam. Five thousand people stood outside the church listening to loudspeakers and singing hymns. Inside it was so crowded, Martin told me, the people had to lift Ralph and him above the crowd and pass them from hand to hand over their heads to the platform. The crowd and the singing inspired Martin, and God answered his prayer. Later Martin said, "That night I understood what the older preachers meant when they said, 'Open your mouth and God will speak for you.' "

First the people sang "Onward, Christian Soldiers" in a tremendous wave of five thousand voices. This was followed by a prayer and a reading of the Scriptures. Martin was introduced. People applauded; television lights beat upon him. Without any notes at all he began to speak. Once again he told the story of Mrs. Parks and rehearsed some of the wrongs black people were suffering. Then he said,

> But there comes a time when people get tired. We are here this evening to say to those who have mistreated us so long, that we are tired. Tired of being segregated and humiliated; tired of being kicked about by the brutal feet of oppression.

The audience cheered wildly, and Martin said,

> We have no alternative but to protest. We have been amazingly patient . . . but we come here tonight to be saved from that patience that makes us patient with anything less than freedom and justice.

Taking up the challenging newspaper comparison with the White Citizens Councils and the Klan, Martin said,

> They are protesting for the perpetuation of injustice in the community; we're protesting for the birth of justice . . . their methods lead to violence and lawlessness. But in our protest there will be no cross-burnings, no white person will be taken from his home by a hooded Negro mob and brutally murdered . . . We will be guided by the highest principles of law and order.

Having roused the audience for militant action, Martin now set limits upon it. His study of nonviolence and his love of Christ informed his words. He said,

> No one must be intimidated to keep them from riding the buses. Our method must be persuasion, not coercion. We will only say to the people, "Let your conscience be your guide." . . . Our actions must be guided by the deepest principles of the Christian faith. . . . Once again

we must hear the words of Jesus, "Love your enemies. Bless them that curse you. Pray for them that despitefully use you." If we fail to do this, our protest will end up as a meaningless drama on the stage of history and its memory will be shrouded in the ugly garments of shame. . . . We must not become bitter and end up by hating our white brothers. As Booker T. Washington said, "Let no man pull you so low as to make you hate him."

Finally, Martin said,

If you will protest courageously, and yet with dignity and Christian love, future historians will say, "There lived a great people—a black people—who injected new meaning and dignity into the veins of civilization." This is our challenge and our overwhelming responsibility.

As Martin finished speaking, the audience rose cheering in exaltation. And in that speech my husband set the keynote and the tempo of the Movement he was to lead, from Montgomery onward.

When we talked about it later, we pondered why, in Montgomery of all places, a movement started which had such tremendous repercussions; why here, at this moment of history, African Americans were able to unite peacefully in the cause of freedom. We found only one final explanation. Though some of the impetus came from the Supreme Court decisions, and some was due to the particularly unjust actions of the city bus company, these were not enough to explain it. Other blacks had suffered equal or greater injustices in other places and had meekly accepted them. I suggested that it was due to his own leadership and to his devoted co-workers, but Martin said, "No." There was no rational explanation that would suffice. Therefore we must accept something else. The birth of the Movement could not be explained "without a divine dimension." My husband devoutly believed that there is "a creative force that works to pull down mountains of evil and level hilltops of injustice." As we have seen, he regarded himself as an instrument of this force, and he said, "God still works through history

His wonders to perform." He believed that "God had decided to use Montgomery as the proving ground for the struggle and the triumph of freedom and justice in America." Martin's strong sense of history delighted in the appropriateness of "Montgomery, the cradle of the Confederacy, being transformed into Montgomery the cradle of freedom and justice."

That night, December 5, 1955, victory was far away; the struggle just beginning. After Martin's speech the mass meeting unanimously approved the demands Ralph Abernathy had drawn up, which had to be met before we would ride the buses again. They were very moderate: (1) Courteous treatment by bus operators must be guaranteed; (2) passengers to be seated on a first-come, first-serve basis—blacks sitting from the back forward, whites from front to back; and (3) black bus drivers to be employed on predominantly black routes.

On Wednesday, December 7, Martin headed a committee to meet with Mayor W. A. Gayle, the city commissioners, and bus-company officials to discuss terms of a possible settlement. He was very hopeful. The commissioners listened courteously and seemed inclined to accept our proposals on bus seating, which, in fact, were identical to those in other southern cities such as Mobile, Alabama, and Nashville, Tennessee. It is important to realize that we were *not*, at first, asking for blacks and whites to sit in the same seats. However, the attorney for the bus company, Jack Crenshaw, declared that the plan would be illegal under Montgomery's segregation laws. After the meeting, he gave his real reason when he said, "If we granted the Negroes these demands, they would go about boasting they had won a victory over the white people; and this we will not stand for."

In spite of the agreeable way in which it had been conducted, the meeting came to nothing, and we knew we were in for a long struggle. The white people were expecting the boycott to collapse on the first rainy day, but Martin realized that the way to avoid this was through skillful organization. The first order of business was to get our people to and from work with as little inconvenience as possible. On Friday, December 9, city officials informed the black taxi companies that mass rides were illegal and that they would be put out of business if they continued that practice. However, by that time a motor pool of volunteer drivers had been organized, and pickup stations selected throughout the city with dispatchers to match passengers and destinations. Hundreds of people volunteered to drive. At the boycott's peak there were over three hundred cars participating. There were many memorable and inspiring occurrences during that period. For example, one of the drivers was Mrs. A. W. West, who was on the board of the Montgomery Improvement Association. Every morning and afternoon this well-to-do, elderly, and elegant widow drove her green Cadillac back and forth from the black neighborhoods, filled with workers who had to get to their jobs. Eventually the MIA helped ten of the African-American churches to buy station wagons to supplement the car pool. The names of the sponsoring churches were painted on the car doors, and as they drove along, filled to capacity, the people sang hymns.

But with all we could do, thousands of people still had to walk. They walked magnificently and proudly. Somebody asked one old grandmother, coming down the street, if she was not tired. She answered, "It used to be my soul was tired and my feets rested; now my feet's tired, but my soul is rested."

Without meaning to, some white women helped us by driving down to pick up their black maids, to make sure they got to work.

Mass meetings were held twice a week at churches in the city, to keep morale up. Thousands of people attended them, some arriving hours ahead of time to be sure of getting a seat. Martin kept a firm hand on the orators to preserve the delicate balance between inspiration and rabble-rousing. By now he was consciously emulating the Gandhian technique, and many people outside of the South were beginning to realize that something new was taking place in Montgomery: Black people, on their own, were creating a new instrument of social change; they were building and developing a totally new kind of structure.

The organization, all on a volunteer basis, was remarkable. The various committees—transportation, negotiation, programs, fund raising—functioned surprisingly well. All the things we were doing cost a great deal of money, and at first it all came from

Montgomery blacks. Then, as news of our Movement spread, contributions came in from all parts of the country and from foreign places as far away as Tokyo and Switzerland.

The spirit of the black community was inspiring. There was a sort of contagion of enthusiasm. Groups from all levels were becoming involved. This was most unusual in Montgomery, where African Americans had been divided into cliques and classes and had not been able to unite on anything before. I truly believe that this beautiful demonstration of unity was in great measure due to Martin's leadership. People believed in him and had great respect for him as a leader. Because of his training and background, the intellectuals could respect him, and his genuine love of people emanated to the poorer people so they knew he was fully identified with them. He became a symbol of black unity, a link between the divergent groups.

While it primarily helped African Americans, my husband never allowed the struggle to limit itself solely to the needs of black people. He said, "What we are doing is not only for the black man, but for the white man too. The system that has banished personality and scarred the soul of the Negro has also damaged the white man's personality, giving him a false sense of superiority as it gives the Negro a false sense of inferiority. Segregation is as bad for one as for the other. So in freeing the Negro we will also free the white man of his misconceptions and his subconscious feeling of guilt toward those he wrongs."

Although I had no prominent place in the boycott, it was an exciting time and I found my role an important one. At first our house was the office of the MIA. The phone rang from five o'clock in the morning until midnight; and all day long, groups of people were meeting there. It was impossible to keep Yoki on any sort of schedule, and she learned to adapt with the rest of us. I never knew how many people Martin would ask to stay for dinner, but somehow I managed to feed them. Sometimes it seemed like a loaves-and-fishes miracle.

Then, as the days of December dragged on, and the white community saw we would not give up, things began to get really difficult. All efforts at negotiation broke down. The mayor and the commissioners joined the White Citizens Council, as a "lesson" to us. The sick telephone calls to our house increased. At any hour, day or night, the phone would ring and some man or woman would pour out a string of obscene epithets, of which "nigger son of a bitch" was the mildest. Often the women callers raved on about sex, accusing Martin and me of incredible degeneracies. Frequently the call ended with a threat to kill us if we didn't get out of town. As the leader and elected spokesman of the protest, Martin was the target for all the hate and frustration of the whites—as he knew he would be when he accepted the role.

But in spite of all the work and confusion and danger, the chaos of our private lives, I felt inspired, almost elated. By January Martin and I became convinced that this Movement was more than local. We felt that something was unfolding that was very important to the common struggle of oppressed people everywhere. I was very excited to be a part of a surge forward that was much bigger than Montgomery—of a nationwide Movement whose birth was taking place before our eyes. Later we began to see that it was not only a national but an international phenomenon, part of a worldwide revolution of humanity, asserting the individual's right to freedom and self-respect.

One night in January, recalling that I had not wanted to come to Montgomery, I said, "Oh, Martin, how happy I am to be living in Montgomery, with you, at this moment in history."

But we could not hold that high note all the time. The threats and the real danger sometimes were very depressing. One night at a mass meeting, Martin found himself saying without premeditation, "If one day you find me sprawled and dead, I do not want you to retaliate with a single act of violence. I urge you to continue protesting with the same dignity and discipline you have shown so far."

On another day Martin came home feeling very weary. He said later that he had looked at me and the baby and thought, "They might be taken from me, or I from them, anytime." Then in the middle of the night the telephone rang. An angry voice said, "Listen, nigger, we've taken all we want from you. Before next week you'll be sorry you ever came to Montgomery."

It was just another of the abusive calls, but Martin felt he could take no more. He went into the kitchen and made himself a cup of coffee and began to think calmly of the position we were in and what the alternatives were. With his head in his hands, Martin bowed over the table and prayed aloud to God, saying, "Lord, I am taking a stand for what I believe is right. The people are looking to me for leadership, and if I stand before them without strength and courage, they will falter. I am at the end of my powers. I have nothing left. I've come to the point where I can't face it alone."

Martin said to me, "At that moment I experienced the presence of the Divine as I had never experienced Him before. It seemed as though I could hear the quiet assurance of an inner voice saying: 'Stand up for righteousness; stand up for truth; and God will be at your side forever.' "

Martin said that after this experience, he rose up sure of himself again, ready to face anything.

When it became obvious that the boycott was not going to collapse, the city government decided on a get-tough policy. On one of those dreary January afternoons, Martin and I were eating dinner. Bob Williams, a dear friend who had been at Morehouse with Martin and was teaching music at Alabama State College, was with us; he spent a good deal of time at our house, acting as a sort of protector. Martin told Bob and me, "You know, someone told me that the police are planning to arrest me on some trumped-up charge."

"That would be a good thing," I said. "It would make our people angry and unite them even more. It would be a great mistake, one of the mistakes they will probably make."

Both men agreed with me, and Martin decided not to try to avoid arrest. He and Bob drove downtown to pick up the church secretary, Mrs. Lillie Thomas (as Mrs. Lillie Hunter, she was the office manager of SCLC), and then continued on to one of the parking lots that was a station for the car pool. Martin picked up three passengers and started out. At the edge of the lot a police-man stopped him and asked to see his license. As Martin was showing it, he heard another policeman say, "It's that damn King fellow."

When Martin left the lot, a motorcycle cop followed him. Of course, he drove very carefully, obeying all traffic rules. As he stopped to let his passengers out, the policeman pulled alongside and said, "Get out, King! You're under arrest for going thirty in a twenty-five-mile zone."

A patrol car pulled up and took Martin to the city jail. He was thrown into a dingy and malodorous segregated cell. Among the prisoners he recognized a teacher who had been arrested in connection with the protest. Others crowded around Martin, asking his help in getting them out. Martin said, "Fellows, before I can get you out, I've got to get out my own self."

Meanwhile, the news of his arrest spread like wildfire. There were five mass meetings going on that evening, and the arrest was announced at all of them. One of our devoted church members, Miss Viola Webb, came rushing down our block to tell me the news. She was shouting, "Mrs. King, Mrs. King, they got him. They've arrested Dr. King. Mrs. King, please get him out. Please do something."

I took the news calmly, because I had been expecting it, but I'm afraid Miss Webb thought I was unconcerned.

The first person to reach the jail was Ralph Abernathy. When he offered to post bail for Martin, the official in charge said, "You'll have to wait till tomorrow."

"I am pastor of the First Baptist Church of Montgomery," Ralph said. "Do you mean to tell me I can't sign a bond?"

"No, you can't."

"Can I see Dr. King?"

"No."

Pretty soon the deacons of the church and many other people began gathering at the jail. It must have looked ominous to the police. Nervously, the jailer hauled Martin out of his cell to a chorus from its inmates: "Don't forget us, Dr. King!"

Martin was fingerprinted and then was told, "All right, King. You're released on your own recognizance."

Martin told me later that he had been a little frightened that first time in jail. He had not even known where the jail was before, and he thought they might be taking him out to lynch him. He cheered up when he saw all his supporters waiting outside. One of the deacons drove him and Ralph around to each of the meetings, where the people were praying aloud to God to soften the jailer's heart and make him let their leader go. God had surely answered their prayers.

The following Saturday night there were thirty or forty threatening and abusive telephone calls. Finally, at two thirty I took the receiver off the hook so we could get some sleep. When I put it back on at about seven in the morning, it rang immediately and a voice said, "My boys told me you took the phone off the hook last night."

Angrily I answered, "It's my phone, and I'll do what I like with it."

In the background Martin was saying, "Oh, darling, don't talk like that."

He would always say, "Be nice. Be kind. Be nonviolent." But I was just too tired and worn out to be nonviolent with so little sleep and so much provocation.

That Sunday, from the pulpit, Martin told the congregation, "We're getting so many unpleasant telephone calls that we're taking the receiver off the hook at night because it's the only way we can get any rest. If any of you are trying to get me, you'll know why you can't."

Our church people were becoming very concerned about me and felt I should have someone stay with me while Martin was out at meetings. When Martin told me this, I said, "I'm not afraid to be alone. I'm happy staying by myself."

We had considered the possibility of someone bombing the house. However, though the front of the house was right on the street, it was in a closely populated area, and I thought that no one would run the risk of attacking from there. In the back, there was a deep yard with a fence around it, so that no one could really get very close. The baby and I slept in back, and I was fairly confident we would be all right. Though there had been bombings in remote country towns, I did not think anybody would try it in a densely settled neighborhood in the heart of the city.

However, Martin seemed so anxious that I agreed to call our

good friend Mary Lucy Williams, who was a church member, and ask her to sit with me the following night.

That was Monday, January 30, 1956. At about nine thirty in the evening I had put on a robe and Mary Lucy and I were chatting in the sitting room. I heard a heavy thump on the concrete porch outside. Had I not been anticipating an attack, I might have looked out to see what it was. Instead I said, "It sounds as if someone has hit the house. We'd better move to the back."

We moved fast—not through the hall, which would have taken us nearer the sound, but straight back through the guest bedroom. We were in the middle of it when there was a thunderous blast. Then smoke and the sound of breaking glass.

Mary Lucy grabbed me and started screaming. Her screaming frightened me, and I was shaken by the impact and the noise. I hurried to my bedroom, two rooms back, where Yolanda was in her bassinet. She was all right, and I automatically reached for the telephone. Then I thought, "Whom am I going to call? I'm not going to call the police in this instance."

Then the doorbell started ringing. My first thought was that it was the person who had thrown the bomb. I was trying to think of what I should do about the baby, and for a split second I got panicky. Then I shouted, "Who is it?" and a voice said, "Is anybody hurt?"

I went to the door and let in my neighbors. They were frightened and worried. All over our part of town people had heard the blast and came rushing. The windows had been blown into the living room. The floor was covered with broken glass. The porch had been split, and there was a small hole in the concrete floor. All the lights were off in the front rooms, and I got a bulb and screwed it into a socket so we could see.

Then I decided to call Ralph Abernathy's First Baptist Church, where the mass meeting was being held and where my husband was speaking. Mrs. Irene Grant, a member of the church whom I knew, answered and I told her that our house had been bombed.

I didn't think about telling her that the baby and I were safe, but I asked her to get some people to the house quickly. My thought was that our friends ought to come for protection. I did not want the police, because I could not be sure that they did not know about the bombing before I did.

I called some of our friends and finally reached Mrs. Euretta Adair, who asked, "Do you want me to come and get you?"

I remembered that when Mrs. Adair arrived, she stood looking into the bassinet and talking to Yoki, who was not even crying. By that time the house was full of white reporters, neighbors, all sorts of people trying to find out what was happening.

A call came from the First Baptist Church to find out if we were safe. I assured them that we were, and they decided not to tell Martin until he finished his speech. But my husband noticed people rushing about looking worried and sensed that something had happened. He called to Ralph Abernathy, "Ralph, what's happened?"

Ralph couldn't speak. Martin insisted. "Ralph, you must tell me."

"Your house has been bombed."

"Are Coretta and the baby all right?"

"We're checking on that now. We think so."

In his account of that terrible night, Martin wrote, "Strangely enough, I accepted the word of the bombing calmly. My religious experience a few nights before had given me the strength to face it."

He interrupted the speech to tell the people what had happened, and he urged them all to go straight home. "Don't get panicky and lose your heads," he said. "Let us keep moving with the faith that what we are doing is right, and with the even greater faith that God is with us in the struggle."

Then Martin rushed home.

By the time he got there a big angry crowd was around the house. The police were nervously holding the people back. Mayor Gayle and Police Commissioner Clyde Sellers had just arrived. Martin hurried into the house. It was so full of people he could barely get in. He saw me and he saw the baby, and I think he was relieved to know that I had accepted the situation so calmly. He said, "Thank God you and the baby are all right!"

I reassured Martin, and he kissed me and said, "Why don't you get dressed, darling?"

Suddenly I realized that I had been relaxing when this happened, and although all those people were in the house, I still had my robe on!

The situation outside the house was tense and dangerous. Though the crowd was singing, the people were angry and aroused. I remember hearing "My Country, 'Tis of Thee," but you could sense the heat of their anger. Many were armed; even the little boys had broken bottles. A policeman held back one black man who said, "You got your thirty-eight, I got mine. Let's shoot it out."

Later someone said tension was so high that if a white man had accidently tripped over a black man, it could have triggered the most awful riot in our history. The crowd was so wrought up that the white reporters were afraid to leave to file their stories. The faces of Mayor Gayle and Commissioner Sellers were deathly pale. They went up to Martin and expressed their regret that "this unfortunate incident has taken place in our city."

C. T. Smiley, chairman of Dexter's trustee board and principal of Booker T. Washington High School, the largest black high school in the city, was standing beside Martin. He said angrily, "Regrets are all very well, but you are responsible. It is you who created the climate for this."

More people were joining the crowd every minute. They stood swaying and muttering and shouting insults at the nervous police. At that point Martin walked out on the porch. In some ways, it was the most important hour of his life. His own home had just been bombed; his wife and baby could have been killed. This was the first deep test of his Christian principles and his theories of nonviolence. Standing there, very grave and calm, he dominated those furious people. He held up his hand, and they were suddenly silent—the crowd of angry men and women, of excited children and sullen, frightened policemen in a clump by the steps, all were absolutely still. In a calm voice Martin said, "My wife and my baby are all right. I want you to go home and put down your weapons. We cannot solve this problem through retaliatory violence. We must meet violence with nonviolence. Remember the words of Jesus: 'He who lives by the sword will perish by the sword.' We must love our white brothers, no matter what they do to us. We must make them know that we love them. Jesus still cries out across the centuries, 'Love your enemies.' That is what we must live by. We must meet hate with love."

Then my husband's voice took on the resonance and grandeur of its full emotional power as he said, "Remember, if I am stopped, this Movement will not stop, because God is with this Movement. Go home with this glowing faith and this radiant assurance."

Many people out there were crying. I could see the shine of tears on their faces, in the strong lights. They were moved, as by a holy exaltation. They shouted, "Amen." They shouted, "God bless you. We are with you all the way, Reverend."

One person asked, "What will become of you?" Martin replied, "I have been promised protection."

Mayor Gayle and his commissioner came forward. The crowd turned, began booing and threatening. The police made it worse by shouting, "Listen to the commissioner!" The crowd yelled furiously. Martin stepped to the edge of the porch, holding up his hand, and the noise suddenly stopped, as when the conductor of an orchestra holds his baton high. Martin spoke: "Remember what I just said. Let us hear the commissioner."

Commissioner Sellers said, "We are going to do everything in our power to find out who did this dreadful thing and bring him to justice."

Mayor Gayle added, "We are offering five thousand dollars reward for information leading to his arrest."

After that the crowd began to thin out, and the people went back to their homes. A white policeman's voice was heard in the crowd saying, "If it hadn't been for that nigger preacher, we'd all be dead."

7

"Don't you get weary"

When everybody had gone away, Martin, Yoki, and I went to the home of Mr. and Mrs. Joseph T. Brooks, longtime friends of the King family, with whom we had spent our first night in Montgomery. We went to bed in the quiet front bedroom with a distant streetlamp throwing shadows on the walls. We finally fell asleep.

A little while later, the telephone rang in the Brookses' bedroom. It was Daddy King calling to say he had been knocking on the front door, but no one had answered! Christine, Daddy King, and A.D. soon were back, and sometime later my own father arrived.

Earlier that evening I'd been afraid that my family would hear about the bombing and would think we'd been hurt. I had called Mr. Hampton D. Lee, one of the two undertakers in Marion, to ask that he get in touch with my father and tell him we were all right. Now my father came into the room, and the first thing he said to me was "I've come to take you and the baby back to Marion."

I listened to him carefully and respectfully, but I said, "No, Dad, I am going to stay here with Martin."

Daddy King had said as soon as he arrived, "Well, M.L., you just come on back to Atlanta."

When Martin objected, Daddy King said, "It's better to be a live dog than a dead lion."

Then my father tried to persuade him. He said, "They're after you, Martin. I think you ought to move into the background and let someone else lead for a while, and, Coretta, I've come here to get you and the baby and take you home for a few weeks till this thing cools off."

I answered my father, saying again, "Well, I think I'll stay here. I would not be satisfied if I went home. I want to be here with Martin."

Of course, Daddy King argued. He very strongly insisted on Martin's coming home for a while and getting away from things. He really wanted him to get completely out of the Movement. Though I had sounded so brave, I was torn. Martin and I both realized that there was a possibility of something happening to us. The house might be bombed again; the baby and I could be killed the next time.

Finally, at breakfast, Christine said, "Daddy, M.L. has to make up his own mind, and you have to let him decide on what he sees as the right thing to do."

Of course, we decided to stay.

Afterward Martin said to me, "Coretta, you've been a real soldier. I don't know what I would have done if it had not been for you."

Before Martin said that, I had not thought about my own reactions that night but had proceeded in a way that was most natural to me. I had always been a strong person, but I had not realized that Martin, so strong himself, *did* need me. I was very moved that he recognized this need.

As soon as our house was repaired, we went back to it, but we did take certain precautions. Bob Williams, who attended Morehouse with Martin and was now teaching at Alabama State College, came to sleep there every night—not that he slept much. He slipped his shotgun into the house without Martin's knowledge of it and sat up most of the night with his gun beside him. When Martin discovered this, he insisted that Bob take the gun away. As a matter of fact, a church member had brought a pistol to keep in our house, early in the struggle, but Martin could not reconcile a gun with his nonviolent principles. He got rid of the pistol, and after that we had no more weapons in our house. Even outside, if Martin ever heard that someone in the Movement was armed, he made that person get rid of his weapons. He would remind the person, "He who lives by the sword will perish by the sword." If my husband had not had that attitude from the beginning the Movement would have gone in a different direction. We would not have accomplished what we did, and an ocean of blood would have been spilled.

We did put floodlights outside our house, and the Dexter congregation insisted on paying an unarmed man to keep watch outside all night. They also paid for a baby-sitter for me, and Martin promised not to drive around at night alone; Bob Williams or one of the other men always went with him.

A few nights after our house was attacked, E. D. Nixon's house was bombed. After that, things quieted down for a short time, and in the middle of February I took Yoki to stay with my family for a few days, and then I went to Mamma and Daddy King's in Atlanta. Martin went to Fisk University in Nashville to give a series of lectures. While we were gone, a Montgomery attorney dug up an old state law against boycotts. The Montgomery grand jury was called, and brought an indictment against Martin and about ninety other leaders of the Movement. The police immediately began to make arrests. The moment he heard this news, Martin canceled the rest of his lectures and came to Atlanta to pick me up and take me back to Montgomery with him. He went back knowing that he would be arrested.

Daddy King was absolutely determined that this should not happen. So unafraid for himself, he was in a state of terror for his son. He gathered a group of friends, Atlanta's most eminent African Americans, to reason with Martin.

Martin listened intently to everything they had to say, and then he made his position clear. "I must go back to Montgomery," he said. "I would be a coward to stay away. I could not live with myself if I stayed here hiding while my brothers and sisters were being arrested in Montgomery. I would rather be in jail ten years than desert my people now. I have begun the struggle, and I can't turn back. I have reached the point of no return."

There was dead silence in the room; all those men knew he was right. The silence was broken as Daddy King burst into tears. He too knew that Martin was right; he had surrendered. He said, "Well, son, you know that whatever you decide to do, you can count on Daddy."

Everyone immediately turned to reassure Daddy King, telling him that things were not as bad as they seemed.

Dr. Mays said if a large fine was involved, he would pay it. He had been very moved by Martin's words, and his advice was that my husband must do what he felt he had to.

The night before this, Martin's mother and father had been trying to convince him not to go back to Montgomery. They were all very upset, and while the argument was going on, I had quietly slipped away to take Yoki upstairs. I sat alone with my baby, thinking about what this could mean for Martin and for the whole family. I realized that both Martin and I could be killed—I always thought in terms of both of us. I admit I had been depressed and nervous both in Marion and in Atlanta. Now I realized that I, as well as my husband, had to make a decision. I felt I must be as dedicated as he, if I were to stand with him.

Martin came upstairs, half teasing, saying, "Oh, Coretta, you left me down there all alone. You deserted me!"

I explained that I had just wanted to get Yoki away from the argument and the tension, which could upset her.

Then I said, "Martin, there comes a time in every person's life when he has to make a decision all by himself, when he has to stand alone. This is such a time in your life. You know what you feel is right, and I want you to know that whatever you decide to do, I will always be with you."

Shortly after the house was bombed I had a sudden realization of why Martin and I were supposed to be together and in Montgomery: I knew for certain why we had come. We were part of a Movement that was worldwide in its impact. We had been chosen for that destiny. Being in the right place at the right time gave me a great feeling of satisfaction and fulfillment. I felt that there was a larger force working with me and that I was not alone. I was no longer holding my decision to marry Martin in abeyance. I knew at that point that being with him, and participating in this

Movement, was the right thing for me. I was able to draw strength from my religious faith that if you are doing what God wants you to do you will be successful and fulfilled in the process. That does not mean that it will be easy, but it means that somehow you will be given the strength to do what must be done at the time when you have to do it.

I was excited about being in Montgomery. I was excited about all that was going on, and I felt that I was a part of it. I was making a contribution. Something was moving, evolving, going in a direction that we could not control. We started out with a one-day protest. Because of the resistance that we faced, it got longer and longer. Finally, when we realized that those in charge weren't willing to give in at all, we decided to go all out for integration. We did not know what the end would be, but we knew that there was going to be a continuation and that in many ways we were fortunate and blessed to have been chosen to be part of what was taking shape. We felt as if we were being directed and guided.

The decision to stay in Montgomery made, Daddy King determined to come with us. We left Atlanta in his car at six o'clock the following morning and reached Montgomery at about nine. Reporters and television cameras were waiting at the house—how they found out we were coming, I do not know.

Ralph Abernathy, who had been arrested, was out on bail and came over immediately. Martin went down to the courthouse with him and with Daddy King to surrender himself. The police booked Martin, fingerprinted him, and took a mug shot of him with a number hung on his chest like a criminal. Then he was released on bail.

The trial was set for March 19 before Judge Eugene Carter. I was there, of course, with Daddy King, Christine, A.D., and many of our friends. People were picketing outside the courthouse; some wore black crosses on their chests with the words "Father, forgive them."

For four days Martin sat in the defendant's chair while the state produced witnesses to prove that he had organized a boycott contrary to the laws of the state of Alabama; and our lawyers brought in witnesses to show, among other things, the intolerable conditions for African Americans on the buses.

On Thursday, March 22, both sides rested their cases. With hardly a pause for consideration, Judge Carter gave the inevitable decision, "Guilty." He sentenced Martin to pay a fine of five hundred dollars or serve 386 days at hard labor. The judge said he was giving Martin a "minimum" penalty because of what he had done to prevent violence.

Many people in the courtroom burst into tears, while others sat with bowed heads. Our lawyers immediately said they would appeal, though they knew it was not much use; and Martin was granted bail. As Martin and I walked out of the courtroom, dozens of friends followed us. Outside there was a great crowd shouting, "God bless you!" Then they began to sing, "We Ain't Going to Ride the Buses No More."

In *Stride Toward Freedom* Martin wrote: "I came to the end of my trial with a feeling of sympathy for Judge Carter in his dilemma. To convict me he had to face the condemnation of the nation and world opinion; to acquit me he had to face the condemnation of the local community and those voters who kept him in office. Throughout the proceedings he had treated me with great courtesy, and he had rendered a verdict which he probably thought was the best way out."

Our lawyers not only appealed the verdict against Martin; they also started proceedings in the federal district court to have segregation on the buses declared unconstitutional. The case was heard by a three-judge panel on May 6, 1956. Martin spoke of the great relief it was for us to be in a federal court, where there was an atmosphere less restricted by southern thinking.

Two weeks later, in a two-to-one decision, this federal court held that bus segregation was unconstitutional. The city attorneys immediately appealed the case to the United States Supreme Court. This meant that it would be months before there was any decision.

Meanwhile, the boycott went on with renewed enthusiasm. The attempt to break the Movement by jailing its leaders boomeranged. It raised the spirit of our people and brought them into even closer unity. One important person who came into Martin's life at that time was Bayard Rustin. Bayard offered to help in any way he could. Later he became very close to us and was tremendously helpful to my husband.

Many white liberals also came to see Martin: Among them were Alan Knight Chalmers and Reverend Glenn Smiley, a white southern member of the Fellowship of Reconciliation. Very important to our lives at this time was a New York attorney, Stanley Levison, who was introduced to us by Bayard Rustin. At that time they were both officers of an organization called In Friendship, whose purpose was to raise funds for people in the South suffering from economic reprisals. Stanley, as well as others in the group, helped the Movement financially, serving later as fund raiser for the Southern Christian Leadership Conference. But it was Stanley's counsel that was most valuable to my husband.

Bayard and Stanley were indispensable to Martin and the Movement in the early days. They established links to other people in the North. Bayard was enormously helpful in sharing his thinking on nonviolence with us. He had been to India, he studied Gandhi, and he was a pacifist already. Working with the Fellowship of Reconciliation, he had been active in the civil rights struggle in the dark years of the forties.

A few of our white friends in Montgomery stuck by us and paid dearly for it. There was the tragedy of Juliette Morgan, a white librarian who was a member of the Human Relations Council. She had written a letter to the newspaper comparing our Movement to the Movement in India and praising it. From that moment on, the white community completely ostracized her. The pressure and isolation finally grew so intense that she committed suicide by taking an overdose of sleeping pills. It is hard to express how sad we felt. Then there were Aubrey Williams and his wife—he had been head of the National Youth Administration under President Franklin D. Roosevelt—and Clifford and Virginia Durr. The Durrs suffered terribly for their support of the Movement and friendship with us. Mr. Durr's law practice suffered considerably, but they continued to attend the Human Relations Council meetings and she came to the mass meetings. Other white people like the Morelands and Smiths also continued to come to the council meetings. Mr. Smith was an architect and his wife's family owned a laundry chain in Montgomery. Robert Graetz, the white pastor of a black Lutheran church, became a member of the MIA executive board.

What a strange turn our lives had taken. From being the minister of a Baptist church in a small southern city, Martin found himself at the center of a Movement of national proportions. For me, the change was equally demanding. Our house was always full; privacy, from the first moment, was completely gone. Almost every meal became a huge production. Martin might leave a meeting and bring the eight participants home to eat with him. The reporters who waited at our house until Martin could get home couldn't be allowed to starve, nor the travelers who had come from all over the world. I learned to cook in quantity and to get used to the fact—hard on any woman—that the food would rarely be eaten at the moment it was ready, but might sit on top of the stove for hours on end, waiting for slow-moving history.

Then, too, Martin was away a lot. He was in great demand throughout the country as a speaker, and he accepted many of these invitations in order to raise the money the Movement so desperately needed and to bring word of our work to the rest of the country.

In July Martin spoke at the Democratic National Convention, telling the delegates that civil rights was "one of the supreme moral issues of our time" and militantly calling for a strong civil rights plank in the platform.

As autumn days came to Montgomery, the boycott still went on, but our people were growing weary. The thought of another winter of trudging through cold and slush was appalling, and white resistance to the Movement had heightened. African Americans were dragged out of the car pools and badly beaten. Black-operated filling stations, which had been supplying us with gas, were bombed, and their owners were under constant harassment. The Montgomery police would intimidate black people, just venting their hatred, which was like a contagious disease, poisoning society.

At this point the city fathers thought up the most dangerous of all challenges to us. On October 30, 1956, Mayor Gayle instructed the city's legal department "to file such proceedings as it may deem proper to stop the operation of car pools or transportation systems growing out of the boycott." Our lawyers tried to block such a move by asking for an injunction in the federal court. They were unsuccessful. A hearing was set for November 13; Martin and the other leaders were served with subpoenas.

It was in those dark November days that Martin preached one of his most beautiful sermons at Dexter on Sunday, November 4. It took the form of an imaginary letter from Saint Paul to American Christians, in which the saint exhorted us to guard against forsaking spiritual values for material wealth. The letter ended with the words,

> The greatest of all virtues is love. Here we find the true meaning of the Christian faith and the cross. Calvary is a telescope through which we look into the long vista of eternity and see the love of God breaking forth into time. . . .

Then Martin's voice rang through our church:

> And now unto Him who is able to keep us from falling and lift us from the dark valley of despair to the bright mountain of hope, from the midnight of desperation to the daybreak of joy; to Him be power and authority for ever and ever. Amen.

Martin spoke bravely in public, but at home, as the day approached for the hearing on the car-pool injunction, he was apprehensive. He said to me, "You know the people are getting tired. If the city officials get this injunction against the car pools—and they will get it—I am afraid our people will go back to the buses. It's just too much to ask them to continue if we don't have transportation for them. They will go back."

In trying to encourage him, I found myself saying, "You know, what I think is going to happen is that by the time they get this injunction, the Supreme Court will have ruled for us. I think everything is going to work out all right."

I don't know whether I really believed that such perfect timing would ever come about, but I wanted so much to comfort my husband, and these were the words I found, though I had no idea how prophetic they were.

Martin, as always, recovered his strength through prayers to God and through inspiration from the people. On the night before the hearing, he spoke to a mass meeting, telling the plain truth that an injunction against the car pool would almost certainly be granted. He told the people he did not know if he could ask them to do more; yet, if they did not, all our months of protest would fail. Then he said, "This may well be the darkest hour before dawn. We have moved all these months with the daring faith that God is with us in our struggle. The many experiences of days gone by have vindicated that faith in a most unexpected manner. We must go on with that same faith . . . we must believe that a way will be made out of no way."

When he came home that night, my heart ached for my husband. And for our people.

The next morning, November 13, 1956, we were in court once more before Judge Carter. As chief defendant, Martin again sat at the table with the defense attorneys; I was in the back of the courtroom with Ralph Abernathy and E. D. Nixon. The Montgomery attorneys told the court that the city had lost fifteen thousand dollars in taxes as a result of the reduction of bus travel and asked for compensation. They further alleged that the car pool was "a public nuisance" as well as a "private enterprise" operating without a license fee or franchise; they asked for an injunction against it.

The arguments droned on. We all knew that it was just a matter of form. Judge Carter was going to grant that injunction.

Then, at just about noon, there was a sudden stirring. Mayor Gayle and Commissioner Sellers abruptly left their seats, followed by two of the city attorneys. Several reporters were rushing around.

The Associated Press reporter handed Martin a slip of paper, and we were all straining to see. Martin read the note to the people at the table; then he came running back to me, his face beaming. "Listen to this," he said, and he read aloud, "The United States Supreme Court today affirmed a decision of a special three-judge U.S. District Court declaring Alabama's state and local laws requiring segregation on buses unconstitutional."

Many of the people heard Martin reading, and the word passed through the courtroom in a moment. Though court was still in session, there was great humming and half-whispered talk, and people were moving about. One old man shouted out, "God Almighty has spoken from Washington, D.C."

The Supreme Court decision was a crucial landmark, but more basic and more heroic was the influence of the long boycott. Without the unprecedented unity and the determined militancy of the black community of Montgomery, the segregationists would have found the means of evasion, as they had for decades past.

The decision did not mean an abrupt end to our troubles. It took over a month for the court order to reach Montgomery. Judge Carter had granted the injunction against the car pool, but now it did not matter at all. Martin promptly called a mass meeting. There were only about fifty thousand African Americans in all of Montgomery, including children, yet eight thousand people turned out that night. The meeting had to be held in two churches, with speakers traveling from one to the other. Martin announced that the MIA board recommended calling off the protest, but delaying going back to the buses until the order arrived from Washington. Bob Graetz read the Scripture, St. Paul's First Epistle to the Corinthians: "Though I have all faith, so that I could remove mountains, and have not charity, I am nothing."

He continued, "When I was a child, I spake as a child, I understood as a child, I thought as a child: but when I became a man, I put away childish things." At those words the whole audience rose to their feet shouting, cheering, waving their handkerchiefs. They knew they had come of age. The spirit that night was so high! Every speaker spoke well because he felt so good, and the people would applaud with fervor to show that the suffering and waiting had been worth it.

That same night the Ku Klux Klan rode. Forty or fifty carloads in their white robes and pointed hoods drove through the black section. Always before they had found the streets deserted, houses tight shut, lights turned off in terror. Not so that night. All the lights were on. Blacks walked along the streets or stood in groups, chatting casually; some sat on their front porches. As Martin said, "They acted as though they were watching a circus parade." Because they had marched together and achieved their first triumph, they were no longer afraid. And the Klan got the message. After a few blocks, the motorcade turned off and disappeared.

As we waited for the official order to come from Washington, we prepared ourselves for bus desegregation. Leaflets were issued telling people how to act. They were instructed to behave with courtesy, no matter how insulting white people might be. They were told not to sit next to a white if any other seat was available. Above all, they were not to boast of victory, for, as Martin said, "This is not a victory for Negroes alone but for all Montgomery and for the South."

We even held classes with chairs lined up like bus seats—roleplaying, we called it. Actors were chosen from the audience. One would play the bus driver; others pretended to be white, and the rest, black passengers. Some of the people playing whites were supposed to be courteous, others insulting. Those who were "playing blacks" were supposed to respond to the insults with courtesy, even with phrases like "I love you, brother." The acting sometimes got all too real. Occasionally a "white" went overboard and became too insulting, and had to be called off. Some of the blacks forgot to be nonviolent and started fights. Martin and the others would talk then about our responsibilities in securing the rights we had won.

Perhaps, today, this preparation sounds as if we were being too conciliatory, bending too far backward to avoid difficulties. But remember, all this took place almost forty years ago, in the deep South, at the very beginning of the modern Movement of black militancy. In fact, it *was* the beginning of that militancy, and it was the groundwork laid so carefully then in Montgomery that made the rest possible.

The virulent segregationists among the white community did not make things easy. Members of the White Citizens Council threatened that blood would run in the streets if the desegregation order was enforced. One letter to Martin threatened to burn down fifty houses, including his, unless he kept his people off the buses. In this state of affairs the day drew near.

In the midst of all this excitement, I was very busy on another project. Stanley Levison, Bayard Rustin, and Ella Baker, who would become the first executive secretary of the Southern Christian Leadership Conference, had planned a big concert at the Manhattan Center in New York on December 5, 1956, the first anniversary of the boycott, to raise money for the Montgomery Improvement Association. Mrs. Ralph Bunche and Mrs. Minnie Wilkens, the wife of the NAACP's Roy Wilkins, were among the honorary chairwomen. They had secured great stars like Duke Ellington and Harry Belafonte to perform. In fact, it was there that I first met Harry, who was to become one of our truest friends. From that point on, whenever we got into trouble or when tragedy struck, Harry always came to our aid, his generous heart wide open.

Among these great stars at the benefit concert, I was the featured performer. It was a frightening responsibility, especially because the Manhattan Center was jam-packed that night.

Accompanied by Jonathan Brice, first I sang a program of classical music, and then I told the story of Montgomery in words and song. For this presentation I used the format I had invented for my concert at Mount Tabor Church long ago, when I was in Lincoln High School. It was also the format I later used for my Freedom Concerts. I told the story of the Movement and wove the spirituals and the freedom songs into the narration which I had written.

I spoke briefly of the oppression suffered by many people through the ages and said that God had always sent deliverers to them as He sent Moses to the Children of Israel. I said, "Today God still speaks to the modern Pharaohs to 'Let My People Go.'

"It was a year ago today, on December 5, 1955, that the cradle of economic, political, and social injustice began rocking slowly but surely. For a year we have walked in dignity rather than ride in humiliation. As we walked to and from our jobs, we sang a song to give us moral support."

At this point I sang the spiritual

> Walk together, chillun, don't you get weary,
> Walk together, chillun, don't you get weary,
> Dere's a great camp meetin' in the promise' land.

Then I told the story of the old lady who had said, "It used to be my soul was tired and my feets rested; now my feet's tired, but my soul is rested."

Fran Thomas had come to Montgomery during the summer of 1956. She had been inspired to write a song based on those words.

I spoke of the threats and violence we had endured and our determination to keep on in spite of them. I sang an old spiritual in an arrangement by Bob Williams: "Lord I can't turn back, just because I've been born again."

My next song was another spiritual, "Keep Your Hand on the Plow," and I said, "We are going to keep our hands on the plow because we are determined that there shall be a new Montgomery, a new Southland, yes, a new America, where freedom, justice, and equality shall become a reality for every man, woman, and child. We have felt all along in our struggle that we have cosmic companionship—that God Himself is on our side—and that truth and goodness ultimately will triumph. This is our faith, and by this faith we shall continue to live."

At the close of the program I sang one of Martin's favorite songs, the beautiful spiritual "Honor, Honor":

> King Jesus lit de candle by de waterside,
> To see de little chillun when dey's truly baptized.
> Honor, Honor unto the dyin' lamb.
>
> O run along little chillun to be baptize',
> Mighty pretty meetin' by de waterside,
> Honor, Honor unto the dyin' lamb.

My friends told me that the audience had been very receptive, but I knew it myself, because I could feel the warm, responsive love between us.

We had a great Christmas present that year. On December 20, 1956, the Supreme Court order reached Montgomery. That day Mayor Gayle announced that he would obey the ruling and maintain order. At a mass meeting that night, Martin reviewed the long struggle and said, "Our faith is now vindicated." He announced the official end of the boycott and urged everyone to return to the buses on a nonsegregated basis the next day.

Then Martin made a final appeal for restraint and courtesy. "We must respond to the decision with an understanding of those who have oppressed us, and an appreciation of the new adjustment the court order poses for them," he said. "We must seek an integration based on mutual respect.

"As we go back to the buses, let us be loving enough to turn an enemy into a friend. It is my firm conviction that God is working in Montgomery. With this dedication we will be able to emerge from the bleak, desolate midnight of man's inhumanity to man to the bright and glittering daybreak of freedom and justice."

The next morning, at five forty-five, a little group gathered in our living room. Mrs. Rosa Parks, Ralph Abernathy, E. D. Nixon, and Glenn Smiley (who was white) came to ride the first desegregated bus with Martin. No one knew what would happen, in view of the threats and fury of the white extremists. Reporters and television people waited outside.

Like an anniversary of that memorable morning over a year before, the headlights of the six-o'clock bus flashed down the empty street as it pulled up at the bus stop. The men walked down the steps of our house and through the front door of the bus. The bus driver, smiling broadly, said, in almost a parody of the explorer Stanley's famous remark to Dr. Livingstone, "I believe you are Dr. King?"

Martin said, "Yes, I am."

"We are glad to have you with us this morning," the driver said.

Smiling too, his tenseness gone, Martin thanked him and sat down in a front seat beside Glenn Smiley. With a clash of gears and a puff of exhaust, the first bus pulled away as though nothing had happened.

Martin rode different bus lines most of that day. At his suggestion other ministers did the same, to be on hand in case of trouble. There was no real disturbance at first, only a few minor instances of rude behavior of whites to blacks.

However, it was too good to last. Fury and frustration built up among a few extremist racists. Some nights, buses were stoned and shots were even fired into them. Blacks were dragged off the buses and beaten up. One pregnant woman was shot in the leg. People were taunted and abused. One night someone fired a small-caliber rifle through our front door. Then, on a night in January, there was a concerted guerrilla attack. Ralph Abernathy's house and his church were dynamited. Bob Graetz's home was bombed; three other black churches were bombed, two of them completely destroyed.

Martin was deeply affected. On his twenty-eighth birthday, Tuesday night, January 15, 1957, he spoke at a mass meeting. He pleaded with his followers to receive the violence and to meet it with love. He said that only through love could we survive. After leading the audience in prayer, he intoned, "Oh, Lord, I hope no one will have to die as a result of our struggle for freedom in Montgomery. Certainly I don't want to die. But if anyone has to die, let it be me!"

The audience was in an uproar, shouting, "No! No!" Martin stood in the pulpit, moved by the response, and then went quietly to his seat.

But that was the worst night. There was one more eruption of violence on January 28. Bombs were fired, and a smoking pile of fourteen sticks of dynamite was found smoldering on our porch. Finally, the city authorities took a firm stand. There were strong editorials in the papers and statements by white ministers calling for peaceful acceptance of desegregation. An organization of white businessmen, called the Men of Montgomery, announced their unalterable opposition to the bombings. With the leading white citizens standing on record against it, the violence ended.

Had these same leaders taken this position earlier, much suffering could have been spared. Yet, it was the force of the nonviolent movement that finally brought them to accord.

And Martin's prayer was answered. Not one person died as a result of the Montgomery Freedom Movement.

8

"We want freedom—*now*"

Montgomery was the soil in which the seed of a new theory of social action took root. Black people had found in non-violent, direct action a militant method that avoided violence but achieved dramatic confrontation, which electrified and educated the whole nation. It identified the evil, it clarified the wrongs, it summoned the latent strength of the oppressed and provided a means to express their determination. Without hatred or the abject bending of their knees, the demand for freedom emerged in strength and dignity. Black people had been waiting for this, and instinctively they seized the new method and opened a new era of social change.

Our victory in Montgomery showed the South what could be accomplished by a united effort carried out in a legal, nonviolent way. My husband had become a hero to black people all over the United States. They had long been looking for a genuine and creative leader, and now they turned to Martin. He was conscious of the tremendous responsibility.

He would say to me, "I am really disturbed about how fast all this has happened to me. People will expect me to perform miracles for the rest of my life. I don't want to be the kind of man who hits his peak at twenty-seven, with the rest of his life an anticlimax. Neither do I want to disappoint people by not being able to pull rabbits out of a hat."

On the other hand, as I have said before, I have always felt that somehow Martin Luther King, Jr., was called to do the things he did, and that he subconsciously knew he did not have much time. When you look back on his early life, it seems to reveal that he was being prepared for the role he was to play. He went to college at fifteen and never paused in his breakneck rush for an education until he had earned his Ph.D. He was pastor of a leading African-American church by the time he was twenty-five. It was as if he was being readied for the moment in history when our people would need a leader. Martin was driven by a sense of urgency. Looking back now, I feel that he had to complete his life's work early because of his ultimate destiny of becoming a martyr, so that God's will and His creative purpose might be fulfilled.

Martin always felt that unearned suffering and personal sacrifice were redemptive. He stressed this in the Movement, to give his followers courage; and in his personal life, it was this belief that enabled him to endure.

With the victory of the buses, other movements, inspired by Montgomery, were starting up in places such as Tallahassee, Florida; Birmingham and Mobile, Alabama; and even Atlanta. These movements were headed by able men, most of whom were to work very closely with my husband in the years to come. The Reverend C. K. Steele, the dedicated and courageous president of the Tallahassee Movement and eminent pastor of the Bethel Baptist Church in Tallahassee, was to become the first vice-president of the coming southwide organization, and worked for civil rights until his death in 1980. Under the dynamic leadership of the Reverend Joseph E. Lowery, the Mobile Movement was founded and flourished, giving Mobile the image of the model city of Alabama. Joe Lowery was to eventually become the president of the Southern Christian Leadership Conference, the post he currently holds.

The Reverend Fred Lee Shuttlesworth early became a symbol of the southern struggle. A man of unusual courage, Reverend Shuttlesworth was president of the Alabama Christian Movement for Human Rights in Montgomery, a city that became the symbol of southern oppression. He was to become secretary of the new southwide organization and is still a member of the board of the SCLC.

Martin felt that all these activities should be coordinated and that the tide of the affairs of black men should be taken at the flood. He also wanted to broaden the base of our Movement. A group of us had talked about this in our home one day in December 1956, before that last flare-up of bombings and violence in Montgomery, and Martin proposed calling a conference of black leaders to meet and map out a general strategy for integration in the South. It was decided to call the meeting for January 10 and 11, 1957, in Atlanta. C. K. Steele and Fred Shuttlesworth joined Martin in sending out the invitations. These men formed a core of the leading symbol against oppression in the South. Acceptances were received from nearly a hundred leaders in cities all over the southern states. Over the next few weeks, in many other conferences at our house, in which I was privileged to share, we planned the agenda for the meeting.

On the night of January 9 we were all in Atlanta, and people were arriving for the meeting. Then, at two o'clock in the morning, Juanita Abernathy telephoned Ralph to tell him about the night of bombings and terror in Montgomery. He and Martin decided that they must rush back immediately to calm our people and comfort them. Martin asked me to represent him in Atlanta.

When the meeting was called to order the next day, in the education building of Ebenezer, I was the first speaker. I explained why Martin could not be present and told the delegates the latest news of white violence in Montgomery. Then I presented our agenda for the meeting. It was unanimously accepted, and the meeting proceeded to follow the day's agenda.

Martin came back to Atlanta the next day exhausted, but determined not to show it. He was soon refreshed and inspired by the enthusiasm of the large number of people gathered in Atlanta. Under his leadership, a temporary organization was formed, called the Southern Conference on Transportation and Nonviolent Integration. Going beyond our agenda, the meeting decided to send a telegram to Herbert Brownell, then the Attorney General of the United States, asking him to take steps to curb violence against African Americans in the South. A telegram was also sent to President Eisenhower, suggesting that he come to the South to learn about the trials of black people and to uphold the mandates of the Court. There was no response from Washington, but the invitation received tremendous coverage in the press.

Much more important was the decision to hold a larger meeting in New Orleans on February 14 to form a permanent organization. At the New Orleans meeting, the purposes of the group were broadened to include a fight against all forms of segregation and a drive for the registration of black voters in the South. Martin wanted to mobilize all classes and people of all levels of education, "the no-D's as well as the Ph.D.'s." Another telegram was sent to President Eisenhower, urging him to call a White House conference on civil rights. It stated, "If some effective remedial steps are not taken, we shall be compelled to initiate a mighty Prayer Pilgrimage to Washington."

The name of the organization was changed to the Southern Christian Leadership Conference, or SCLC. Most of the delegates were activist leaders of their southern black communities, but more important to us, they were also ministers. Our organization was, from the first, church-oriented, both in its leadership and membership and in the ideal of nonviolence—a spiritual concept in deep accord with the American black's Christian beliefs.

The concept of nonviolence which our Movement developed was especially Martin's. He did not call for disobedience to all laws, only for disobedience to unjust laws. These he defined as laws imposed by a majority on a minority which had no voice in formulating them. He believed that such laws were "not duly constituted" and that it was perfectly consistent with personal conscience to disobey them, accepting the penalties. He believed in the supremacy of a higher moral law.

He called for nonviolence, not only because of his dedication to the teachings of Christ, but also because it was the only practical method for changing the condition of the African American. As he once pointed out, violent revolution can succeed only when the rebels are the majority, or at least constitute a large minority, of a population. In the case of American blacks, who constitute twelve percent of the population of the United States and possess a minuscule percentage of available weapons, it is suicidal.

We were not "passive resisters." We were a militant organization which believed that the most powerful weapon available is nonviolence. The nonviolent Movement made a real and permanent contribution to the life of this nation. It was, and still is, powerful and effective. Martin and his colleagues spearheaded the drive for direct confrontations between the just black cause and the white power structure. As long as he lived, Martin also did his best to prevent that confrontation from becoming a bloodbath.

SCLC offices were set up in Atlanta because it was a hub of transportation in the South. Ella Baker was its first executive secretary, and she was succeeded by the Reverend John Tilley. Ella eventually separated herself from Martin, and that was a breach that even he could not heal. But early on she was very involved with Stanley and Bayard. They worked very closely together. Later on she was upset that she did not get the job as executive director of SCLC—Wyatt Walker was chosen instead in 1960. She always felt persecuted as a woman and I cannot say that she was not justified. I am sure there were a lot of slights to her. She was a very intelligent woman. Often she was the only woman in the councils of men. She used to say to me, "Coretta, you need to be among the councils of the men. You have a lot to say."

Following those months of tension in Montgomery, *Time* magazine, on February 18, 1957, ran an excellent cover story on Martin and his leadership of the Montgomery protest, in which they called him "the scholarly Negro Baptist minister who in little more than a year has risen from nowhere to become one of the nation's remarkable leaders of men." The article added, "His leadership extends beyond a single battle . . . [because] of his spiritual force."

One of the most exciting things that happened to us was an invitation from Kwame Nkrumah, head of the government-elect of Ghana, to attend the Independence Day ceremonies in the capital city of Accra. He knew America well and had invited a number of outstanding African Americans to share Ghana's great day.

Martin always saw a close relationship between the black struggle in America and the struggle for independence in Africa. In his early speeches and sermons he had often compared European colonialism with black oppression in America. Now he eagerly anticipated the experience of going to Africa and being a part of the independence celebration of a new black nation.

On March 3, 1957, Martin and I boarded a plane with the other black leaders whom Nkrumah had invited, including Ralph Bunche, Congressman Adam Clayton Powell, A. Philip Randolph, Roy Wilkins, Lester Granger of the Urban League, and Prime Minister Norman Washington Manley of Jamaica.

We flew on to Accra, arriving at night, and were driven directly to Achimota College, where we stayed with an English professor and his wife. Their low stucco bungalow was very different from what equivalent quarters at an American university would be. We slept on cots with thin mattresses and no springs. However—and this was another difference from the United States—there were several servants to bring us breakfast and perform other such duties. Almost everyone we saw in Accra had servants. We were told that they were paid only twenty-eight cents a day, the result of colonialism. Seeing how that system had demoralized them bothered us and marred our trip. Martin was extremely upset by the servile attitude to which their suffering had brought them. They had been trained to bow, almost to cringe; their stature was decreased. It was heartbreaking.

However, when we went into the city we were amazed by the handsome streets and the magnificent government-owned Hotel Ambassador, more modern and luxurious than many hotels in America. We realized that we ourselves had been the victims of the propaganda that all Africa was primitive and dirty.

On the evening of March 6 we went to the last Parliament of the old regime in a fine big building of British colonial style. Representatives of sixty-nine nations, headed by Richard A. (Rab) Butler, Lord Privy Seal of Great Britain, and Vice-President Nixon, were in the galleries.

At one or another of the ceremonies Vice-President Nixon came up to Martin and said, "You're Dr. King. I recognized you from your picture on the cover of *Time*. That was a mighty fine story about you." Then he asked Martin to confer with him in Washington when we got back.

The members of the old Parliament, most of whom were white, were dressed as they might have been in Westminster, in English business suits. The officials wore the traditional white, curled wigs and black robes. There was a series of dramatic speeches about the coming of freedom.

Just before midnight, the last Parliament under British rule adjourned. The members marched out and the spectators followed them. A great crowd of fifty thousand Ghanaians, many of them just in from the bush and wearing their tribal dress, were jammed into the square. From a flagpole on top of Parliament House flew the Union Jack, its triple crosses of red, blue, and white brilliantly illuminated by floodlights. The crowd cheered when Nkrumah, tall and splendid in the bright robe of his Akan people, took his place on a wooden stand. Then they fell silent.

As the bells of Accra began to toll midnight, Nkrumah raised his hand. Very slowly, to the boom of the bells, the Union Jack crawled down the flagpole. Then the red, yellow, and green flag of a new, free nation rose up in its place. As the night wind unfurled it to the light, there was wild cheering.

Again Nkrumah raised his hand and the people listened. He said in English, "At long last the battle has ended. Ghana, our beloved country, is free forever. Let us pause one minute to give thanks to Almighty God." Silent the people were; it was amazing that so great a crowd could be so still. Then, as their leader signaled the long minute's end, there was a mighty roar as fifty thousand voices shouted in unison, "Ghana is free."

It was an immensely thrilling moment for Martin and me. We felt a strong sense of identity and kinship with those African people shouting "Freedom!" in their different tongues. We were so proud of our African heritage, and saw in Ghana a symbol of the hopes and aspirations of all our people. At this moment the Ghanaians were free; free of political bonds, though the shadow of outside economic control and manipulation lingered from their colonial heritage.

Of course, this was in the beginning of Nkrumah's rule. Later he was to be overwhelmed by inexorable economic complications. Financial independence had not been achieved and the new government found itself crippled by the onerous terms of trade with powerful outside interests. Nkrumah was attempting to accomplish a positive goal of uniting African nations, but the means to achieve it eluded him.

There was a great deal of criticism of Nkrumah in America. Martin and I felt that the image of him given by the American press was slanted against him, and though we did not condone all of Nkrumah's actions, at the same time we tried to understand. Martin felt that Nkrumah was embittered and pushed by forces beyond his control.

Though the process has not yet been completed in South Africa, in the thirty-five years since Ghana achieved independence, every other nation in Africa has followed suit. Martin was very aware of the tie between African problems and African-American struggles. He said, "At bottom, both segregation in America and colonialism in Africa were based on the same thing, white supremacy and contempt for life." Just before he was killed he planned to make a pilgrimage to the Holy Land and to go on a goodwill mission to Africa in an attempt to link up with the liberation movements there. He had been invited to serve as a mediator in the Biafran-Nigerian conflict. Though I was concerned about his taking on the added burden of that trip, he planned to leave on April 15, 1968. Of course, he never made it, but people should know that Martin saw the importance of our African heritage long before many of his more "militant" or "nationalist" critics did.

We left Ghana and flew to Lagos, Nigeria, where we lunched at the American Embassy, and then flew on to Kano, in central Nigeria, to spend the night. There, the appalling poverty of the people burst upon us. I think that in Ghana there may have been a certain amount of "dressing up" for the occasion; perhaps we saw not much more than we were meant to see. In Kano we saw people living under conditions of filth and squalor that exceeded even the worst state of blacks in America. Martin talked angrily about the exploitation of Africans by the British, and later, when we got to London, he compared the grandeur of England and the Empire to conditions in Nigeria. But he took comfort from the thought of our people throwing off their oppressors in modern times. He pointed out that there was once a time when the sun never set on the British Empire; now it hardly rises on it.

From Nigeria we went to Rome, Geneva, Paris, and London. We particularly liked Rome—the friendly warmth of the Italian people and the feeling of going back into history and seeing the events we had read about come alive. This was especially true of our visit to the Vatican. Because of our own deep religious beliefs, we had a feeling of identification and even a strong emotional reaction to this center of the Catholic world. This may seem odd for a Baptist to say, but Martin and I never took a narrow sectarian view of religion. I remember well, amid the great beauty of St. Peter's, how we felt emanations of centuries of devotion to our Lord. It was so overpowering that Martin knelt down on the basilica floor and prayed.

Soon after we returned, Martin was awarded the NAACP's Spingarn Medal for the person making the greatest contribution in the field of race relations. At the Morehouse commencement exercises, he received the first of his many honorary degrees. It meant so much to Martin and to me to have his alma mater recognize him in this way. President Mays, his voice resonant with the pride and affection he felt for Martin, told how the leadership in Montgomery had been thrust upon him, and said to my husband, "Your name has become a symbol of courage and hope for suppressed peoples everywhere. Because you did not seek fame, it has come to you. It must have been a person like you that Emerson had in mind when he said, 'See how the masses of men worry themselves into nameless graves when here and there a great, unselfish soul forgets himself into immortality.' You are gentle and loving, Christian and brave, sane and wise, an eloquent preacher, an able interpreter of the Christian Gospel. . . . On this our ninetieth anniversary, your alma mater is happy to be the first college or university to honor you this way. . . ."

This happy time was made complete for us when I found myself pregnant again, as it turned out, with the son Martin had wanted so much.

Martin was, as usual, enormously busy during this period. Because it seemed to us that the Eisenhower Administration was dragging its heels in the matter of black voting rights, Martin moved to put pressure on the Administration. In a series of conferences, it was decided to call for a "Prayer Pilgrimage of Freedom," to be held in Washington in May. Very consciously, it was a meeting planned and managed by an all-black organizing committee. Because of my pregnancy I was unable to go, which I deeply regretted.

At noon on May 17, 1957, thirty-seven thousand marchers, including three thousand white sympathizers, assembled in front of the Lincoln Memorial. They were addressed by almost all the important black leaders of the day. It was about three o'clock when A. Philip Randolph introduced Martin to make the closing address. This was the first of Martin's inspiring political speeches to a national audience. Though I could not be with him in person, I listened proudly to the radio broadcast.

Martin spoke first of the inaction of the federal government and of both political parties in implementing the constitutional rights of African Americans, particularly the right to vote. He called for a strong leadership from the federal government, from white liberals, from the white moderates of the South; and for a strong, courageous, and intelligent leadership from the black community. Then he launched into a rousing appeal which had that great crowd shouting "Amens," as with the full power of his splendid voice he said:

> Give us the ballot and we will no longer plead—we will write the proper laws on the books.
> Give us the ballot and we will fill the legislatures with men of goodwill.

Give us the ballot and we will get the people judges who love mercy.

Give us the ballot and we will quietly, lawfully implement the May 17, 1954, decision of the Supreme Court.

Give us the ballot and we will transform the salient misdeeds of the bloodthirsty mobs into the calculated good deeds of orderly citizens.

For the next year our life was comparatively peaceful, but though there were no big battles or confrontations, Martin was still as busy as ever. As a matter of fact, I hardly saw him as he rushed in and out of our home. According to a *Jet* magazine article called "Man on the Go," Martin delivered 208 speeches and traveled 780,000 miles. It certainly seemed so to me.

Martin's growing national reputation brought him many glittering offers of jobs with salaries that ranged up to seventy-five thousand dollars a year, but these were not even a temptation to my husband. He grew in his certainty that he did not want to own things, that money and material success meant less and less to him. As the years went by, Martin really wished to take a personal vow of poverty. He was forced by his position as a family man to temper this desire, but even so, he did not want those possessions which would separate him from other people. He would say such things as "I don't see why we have to own a house." When he began his ministry, he had felt that clothes were important in representing his congregation. As the years went by, he discarded that view completely and boasted that he could travel around the world without a suitcase, with one suit only and a change of underwear. Martin always tried to eliminate from our own lives all *things* we could do without, and he hoped to influence his followers to do the same.

He understood perfectly that people who come out of great deprivation, who have been oppressed for centuries, are anxious, as they move on, to share in some of the symbols of success and the comforts that society can offer. But Martin would say, "We've got to learn that a man's worth is not measured by his bank account or the size of the wheelbase of his car; it is measured by his commitment." Martin never *was* satisfied that his own life was simple enough and, though it brought him much deep happiness, our own growing family did not make simplicity any easier to achieve.

On October 23, 1957, our son Martin Luther King III was born. We were deeply thankful and happy; Martin of course was ecstatic. I always had reservations about naming our first son for his father, realizing the burdens it can create for the child. But Martin had always said he wanted his son to be named Martin Luther III. He and his father shared this feeling, so I agreed.

During this period, the activities of the SCLC were accelerating, particularly in voter registration. In 1958, the Crusade for Citizenship was our main emphasis. On Lincoln's birthday, February 12, twenty-one simultaneous mass meetings were held in key southern cities. Martin set the keynote for them in what I think was a great speech. He said, "Let us make our intentions crystal clear. We must and will be free. We want freedom—*now*. We do not want freedom fed to us in teaspoons over another hundred and fifty years!"

Those meetings and SCLC's growing pressure for federal enforcement of the right to vote finally led to a meeting with President Eisenhower in the White House conference that SCLC had demanded at its first meeting in New Orleans over a year before. Martin was joined in Washington by A. Philip Randolph, Roy Wilkins, and Lester B. Granger, then executive director of the Urban League. They presented an extremely moderate series of proposals in which they requested President Eisenhower to push for a new civil rights bill to implement African-American rights under the Constitution; to direct the Justice Department to act under existing statutes, to protect blacks seeking to register as voters; and to halt the bombings of churches and homes. The federal officials were very polite, but no action was taken.

Martin had been working extraordinarily hard—in SCLC; on his first book, *Stride Toward Freedom;* as pastor of Dexter; as president of the Montgomery Improvement Association; and as an officer of many other active groups. Then, that summer of 1958, he and I had our first real vacation since our marriage—two weeks in Mexico, without any official business, speeches, or anything else. Our eyes reveled in the beauty of the country, but, as usual, the contrast between the luxurious living of the rich and the wretched condition of the poor made Martin alternately rage and despair.

Hardly were we home again than another unpleasant incident occurred. On September 3 Martin and I went to the courthouse in Montgomery, where Ralph Abernathy was to testify in a private case. We were standing in a group just outside the recorder's courtroom when a policeman ordered us to move on. Martin said, "I am waiting to see my lawyer, Fred Gray."

The policeman said, "If you don't get the hell out of here, you're going to *need* a lawyer."

Martin stood his ground. The officer said, "Boy, you done it now."

He called another policeman, and together they grabbed Martin, twisted his arms behind him, and pushed him down the stairs toward the City Hall. I followed after them, with a feeling of desperation at seeing Martin hurt. The policeman turned around and tried to provoke me, saying, "You want to go to jail too, gal? Just nod your head if you want to."

Martin, looking backward, called, "Don't say anything, darling!"

I ran to get our friends, and when I came back into City Hall Martin had disappeared. He was kicked and roughed up, and then, when they discovered who he was, he was charged with disobeying an officer and released on his own recognizance.

When he got back we had a long talk. Martin knew he would be convicted and fined, but he said to me, "The time has come when I should no longer accept bail. If I commit a crime in the name of civil rights, I will go to jail and serve the time."

He asked what I thought, since I would be affected more than anybody else. I assured him that I agreed with him, that the time had come for someone to take this risk and that he was the best person to do so.

Martin was responding to the influence of Gandhi and his technique of noncooperation. But my husband was becoming firmly convinced that the black leadership must prepare to suffer as Gandhi had. He did not want to go to jail; it was a terrible prospect for a man as sensitive and fastidious as he. We both knew the terrors of southern jails—that over the years many blacks who had been imprisoned even for short sentences had simply disappeared. However, Martin realized that his imprisonment would arouse sympathy for our Movement. He felt that if he asked other people to suffer in the Cause, then he, their leader, should be prepared to do so in still greater measure.

I remember another thing he said during that period, when we were discussing the problem with some friends. In a way, Martin considered our arguments about his going to jail irrelevant. He said, "You don't understand. You see, if anybody had told me a couple of years ago, when I accepted the presidency of the MIA, that I would be in this position, I would have avoided it with all my strength. This is not the life I expected to lead. But gradually you take some responsibility, then a little more, until finally you are not in control anymore. You have to give yourself entirely. Then, once you make up your mind that you *are* giving yourself, then you are prepared to do anything that serves the Cause and advances the Movement. I have reached that point. I have no option anymore about what I will do. I have given myself fully."

As always, I was ready to accept what Martin thought was right, and I agreed with his decision. We talked it over with his colleagues in the MIA and with Daddy King, who was visiting us in Montgomery at the time, and we prayed together. Then Martin waited for the case to come to trial.

As we had foreseen, my husband was found guilty and sentenced to a fine of ten dollars or fourteen days in jail. He immediately asked the judge for permission to make a statement. The permission was granted and this now historic statement was read to Judge Eugene Loe on Friday, September 5, 1958, in Montgomery, Alabama.

Martin's actions caught the judge by surprise. He appeared startled. After he had tried Martin's case, he recessed the court. I left the courtroom with Ralph and Juanita and went to the Dexter Avenue Baptist Church for a mass meeting to enlist support for Martin's unjust conviction. Martin's attorney, Fred Gray, remained with his client. The judge said to Martin, "Dr. King, you know you can get out on bail. Wouldn't you like to get someone to pay your fine?"

"No, your honor," my husband answered, "I do not wish to pay the fine."

When the time came for the prisoners who had been sentenced to be taken to jail, Martin followed at the end of the line. When it came Martin's turn to enter the wagon, the prison officials refused to let him in. He went inside again, and waited for the second load. The same thing happened all over again. By this time, Martin realized that there was a design to keep him out of jail. The authorities seemed baffled as to how to proceed, but Martin was determined to serve his time. Finally, he was told, "Dr. King, you may go now. Someone has paid your fine."

Greatly puzzled, Martin said, "I wonder who it could have been."

"It was probably one of your associates," he was told. Martin insisted that this could not be, because he had informed his associates of his plans and instructed them not to pay his fine. Martin was persistent in trying to find out how his fine got paid and finally he was told that an anonymous person had paid his fine. He had no alternative but to leave.

Police Commissioner Clyde Sellers had a keener sense of public relations than his subordinates. He realized what bad publicity Montgomery and its public officials would get when the nation learned that Martin Luther King, Jr., was in their jail. He paid the fine out of his own pocket and issued a statement that he wanted "to save the taxpayers the expense of feeding King for fourteen days."

9

"Satyagraha"

Stride Toward Freedom, Martin's first book, was published on September 17, 1958. It got excellent reviews, and Martin went on a tour to help with the publicity. Everywhere he went—in Detroit, in Chicago, and especially in Harlem—crowds poured out to see him.

He was in Harlem on the night of September 19, and the next afternoon we were expecting him to return to Atlanta. I was sitting in our bedroom thinking about getting ready to go to the airport to meet him, as I always did, when he returned from out-of-town trips. The telephone rang. It was Dr. O. Clay Maxwell of the Mount Olivet Baptist Church in New York City. Dr. Maxwell, a longtime friend of the King family, said, "How are you, Mrs. King?"

A little mystified, I answered, "Fine, thank you, Dr. Maxwell."

Dr. Maxwell said, "Now, Mrs. King, I want you to prepare yourself. I have some bad news for you."

Of course, I thought instantly of Martin. Was it the word I had always half expected? Was he dead? Was he badly hurt? My heart beat rapidly.

Dr. Maxwell told me that Martin had been stabbed by a black woman while he was autographing books in a department store on 125th Street. The woman, he said, was obviously deranged, and Martin was badly hurt. "He's alive," Dr. Maxwell said, "but it is serious, very serious."

I asked him to keep me informed of every development, while I got ready to fly to New York. My brother had come from Marion to visit me, and when I told him the news, I began to cry. Then I began praying, "Lord, I hope this is not the way Martin has to go, but if it is, help me to accept it."

Ralph Abernathy called and asked if what he had heard on the radio about Martin was true. I tried to give him what details I had, but in the middle of talking to Ralph I broke down again. After a moment or two I pulled myself together and told Ralph I was going to New York. Ralph said he would make the plane reservations and come with me.

By that time people were pouring into the house and the telephone was constantly ringing with calls from people concerned about my husband. I pulled myself together again and calmly began to prepare for the ordeal of what the next several weeks would bring. There were several calls back and forth to New York.

Once the phone rang, with someone reporting that the knife had been removed. A moment later, before I had time to digest the news, someone else called and said, "No, the knife is still in Martin's chest." I decided I was going to believe that the knife had been removed and he was all right—something that was not true at the time.

We left Montgomery about nine o'clock and traveled most of the night because we had to wait for a plane connection in Atlanta, where we were joined by Christine. All those hours while I was en route, I kept thinking about the possibility of Martin's death. At the same time I tried to tell myself that he would survive.

We got to New York about daybreak. At the airport were the Reverend Thomas Kilgore of the Friendship Baptist Church of New York, Bayard Rustin, Stanley Levison, and Ella Baker. I was not aware of what a close call Martin had had until I landed in New York and saw the people at the airport. They were so nervous they were literally shaking. They hadn't slept all night and I could see that they were trying to prepare me for the possibility that he wouldn't make it. We heard the details of how Martin had been autographing books at an improvised table in the shoe department of Blumstein's Department Store when a forty-two-year-old black woman walked up to him and said, "Are you Dr. King?"

He answered, "Yes, I am."

In a low, vindictive voice she said, "Luther King, I've been after you for five years."

There was a flash of steel as the woman pulled a very sharp Japanese letter opener out of her clothing and plunged it into Martin's chest. Immediately a tremendous uproar and confusion broke out. Someone grabbed the woman—Mrs. Izola Curry. Someone else moved to pull out the knife, but Martin stopped him. Martin sat in his chair perfectly calm, with the knife sticking out of his chest. He told me later that he felt no great pain at first, but he realized that this might be fatal. There was little blood in sight, but he knew he might be bleeding internally. Once he accidentally touched the edge of the knife, and it was so sharp it cut his hand.

The police came for Mrs. Curry. There was some talk of her having been used, of a possible conspiracy, but this was not true, nor did we ever really suspect such a thing. She was quite demented and talked wildly about how ministers were responsible for all her troubles. At the police station, where a policewoman searched her, a pistol was found in her bosom. We were grateful that she had not used that.

An ambulance came and took Martin to Harlem Hospital. I was told that while they were waiting for the doctor, Martin lay quietly on an operating table with that knife still sticking in his chest.

Before the doctor arrived and before they could bring to Harlem Hospital special equipment needed for the operation, the police brought Mrs. Curry into the room so Martin could identify her. The moment she saw him she said, "Yah, that's him. I'm going to report him to my lawyers."

Martin said that it struck him as being so funny, he smiled in spite of the terrible pain.

Thousands of people, meanwhile, had gathered in the street

outside Harlem Hospital to sing and pray and to watch quietly. We heard that people all over the nation were praying for Martin.

In the car on the way from the airport, Stanley suggested that we would go to see the chief surgeon, Dr. Aubré D. Maynard, who, with a three-man team, had operated to remove the knife. Dr. Maynard was a Jamaican who was practicing in Harlem. He talked to me first about what a marvelous sense of character my husband had, how calm he was. Dr. Maynard said that Martin's whole attitude throughout the long ordeal was beautiful. "If he had become frightened or emotionally upset," Dr. Maynard said, "it would have affected his chances of survival. Indeed," he went on, "the point of the knife was just touching his aorta. If he had moved suddenly, if he had sneezed, he would have died instantly. Dr. King's wonderful spirit and his cooperation helped to save his life. As you well know, your husband is an extraordinary man."

Then Dr. Maynard told me about the details of the operation and mentioned an aspect of special interest. He said he had made the incision over Martin's heart in the form of a cross. "Since the scar will be there permanently and he is a minister, it seemed somehow appropriate. We had to remove two ribs in order to get the knife free, but we've done everything possible. We feel that his recovery will be complete. Though complications could set in, and we can't be sure for about three days, we think he will be all right."

Then my friends took me to Martin's room in the hospital. He was lying there with a tube in his nose and throat for drainage of his chest, and he was still under heavy sedation. Groggy as he was, however, he recognized me right away. I was told that he had been asking for me all night.

I think it was only then, when I saw Martin lying there, that I realized how seriously he had been wounded. The doctor's words went through my head: "If he had moved suddenly, if he had sneezed . . ." I thanked God for what seemed almost a miracle. Martin and I knew that it was God's grace that had kept him alive and that He would sustain us during this period. Although there was much anxiety and concern for his life by his family, friends, and millions of followers over the world, Martin was calm—and so was I. It was as if both of us knew that this was not the time—that this trial was preparing us for something that was still to come.

While I sat there in the hospital room with my husband, I tried to evaluate what had happened to him. I could not believe it was just a meaningless, senseless act. There was more to this experience. I was sure that it was a message from God. I thought of the crowds that had followed Martin everywhere, of their magnetic reaction to his words as he spoke to them on a street corner in Harlem the night before he was stabbed. It was like Palm Sunday, I thought, when Christ went to Jerusalem and the people glorified him. The experience of the stabbing was like Gethsemane; not a real crucifixion, but a very dark and arduous period in his life when, perhaps, my husband was being tested, as, perhaps, his followers also were. We had spoken of violence and of being able to accept a blow without striking back. Now our words again were being put to the test.

The real test of one's belief is how one reacts in a severe crisis. But Martin said of Mrs. Curry as soon as he was able to speak clearly, "This person needs help. She is not responsible for the violence she has done me. Don't do anything to her; don't prosecute her; get her healed."

Eventually, Mrs. Curry was committed to an institution for the criminally insane, and we hoped that she was well cared for. As for myself, I have no bitterness toward Mrs. Curry, and as near fatal as this attack was, it never produced within me a feeling of trauma. I always felt that it had deep meaning and purpose, as our whole lives had.

Every leader needs a time of quiet contemplation such as Gandhi and Nehru had in their prison cells. The weeks of recuperation were such a time for Martin. The pressures and hurry and strain were in abeyance, and he could rethink his philosophy and his goals, and assess his personal qualifications, his attitudes and beliefs.

My husband was what psychologists might call a guilt-ridden man. He was so conscious of his awesome responsibilities that he literally set himself the task of never making an error in the affairs of the Movement. He would say, "I can't afford to make a mistake," though he knew that as a human being he was bound to.

We had long talks in his quiet hospital room and tried to evaluate what had come from this trial. First was Martin's idea of personal redemption through suffering. We felt that we were being prepared for a much larger work; that, in order to be able to endure the persecution and the suffering ahead, we would have to rededicate ourselves to nonviolence and to the cause of bringing freedom and human dignity to all people. We knew that victory in Montgomery had been only one small step forward. The South was still almost completely segregated; despite the Supreme Court decision, the schools were still almost completely segregated. The attitude of the white southerners had not changed significantly; indeed, to some extent it had hardened. And we knew that despite differences in social patterns, our people in the North also suffered greatly. It would be a long, long struggle to bring full equality to black people.

One thing that this attack so forcefully brought home to us was that even one of our own people might use violence against Martin. We could not help remembering that Gandhi had been assassinated by one of his own people.

Strangely enough, out of the most tragic and evil circumstances often comes good, and crises are filled with opportunities as well as dangers. This tragic crisis did produce some positive results. For one thing, I felt that it helped to bring the black community together in support and concern. Not only did African Americans identify with Martin, but many white persons could also identify with this misfortune. Men and women all over the nation, whether they had previously known much about Martin or not, began to think about him, to know his philosophy, and to pray for him. They began to understand his message. From churches throughout the country, from decent people of all beliefs, came a tremendous outpouring of concern and goodwill. We were smothered in flowers, overwhelmed by hundreds of telegrams and thousands of get-well cards and letters. I had to set up an office in the hospital to try to answer as many as possible.

One of the most touching letters came from a young high school student who wrote: "I read in the paper that the doctor said that if you had even sneezed, you would have lost your life. I am glad you did not sneeze and that God spared you to continue to do good."

Martin turned to me and said, "I too am glad I did not sneeze, because if I had, I wouldn't have been here to see these gains." After that day, Martin used this incident to illustrate ideas in many of his sermons and speeches. In fact, it was used in Memphis on April 3, 1968, his last speech.

On October 3 Martin was released from the hospital. This seemed a good time to fulfill Martin's longtime dream of going to India. For many years he had hoped to visit the land Gandhi had set free, to study his peaceful revolution at first hand, and to talk firsthand with the people who had known and worked with him. We had had visitors from India in August that year who had greatly impressed us both, and whose spiritual qualities, in a sense, had given us part of the accepting peace that had allowed us to survive the stabbing.

Early in March 1959, Martin and I, accompanied by Professor Lawrence D. Reddick, flew to India. Our plane was supposed to land in New Delhi, but due to some difficulty we were diverted to Bombay, where we arrived the night of March 9. Thus, our first sight of India, so eagerly anticipated, was a shock to us. The city was beautiful from the air, with a bright necklace of lights encircling the fine harbor. But as we drove in from the airport through narrow, malodorous streets, we saw thousands of people dressed in rags sleeping on the sidewalks or huddled in doorways, lying wherever they could find space. We were appalled. When we asked why hundreds and thousands of people were stretched out on the dirty pavements, we were told that they had no other place to sleep; they had no homes. They carried everything they owned with them, wrapped up in rags or newspapers. It was very hard for us to understand or accept this. The sight of emaciated human beings wearing only dirty loincloths, picking through garbage cans, both angered and depressed my husband. Colonialism was responsible. Never, even in Africa, had we seen such abject, despairing poverty.

I never thought I would live to see similar homelessness and despair in America. It was quite unusual at the time to see so many people sleeping on the streets. Since the 1980s we have grown accustomed to seeing homelessness and hopelessness in America, but I will never accept it.

As we drove up to the luxurious Taj Mahal Hotel, a man with a child in his arms came up to the airport bus. He couldn't speak English, but he opened his mouth and pointed to it, and then he pointed to the child, making it plain he was starving. Before we had left the United States our sponsor had told us not to give money to beggars because the government was trying to discourage this sort of thing. Martin soon disobeyed these instructions and gave all the money he could to the forlorn humans who beseeched us.

Later, when we returned to America, Martin talked many times about these sad sights. He spoke of our great surplus of grain and the cost of storing it, and he said, "I know where we could store it free of charge—in the wrinkled stomachs of starving people in Asia and Africa."

The next day we flew on to New Delhi. At the airport Martin told the reporters, "To other countries I may go as a tourist, but to India I come as a pilgrim."

That very first evening we were invited to dinner at Prime Minister Jawaharlal Nehru's house. We were thrilled and excited at the prospect of meeting Nehru, the political leader of the Independence Movement. The Prime Minister's residence was a huge classic sandstone house which had been built by the British at the height of the Empire. We drove through high wrought-iron gates guarded by sentries, and around a drive between fine lawns and beds of brilliant flowers.

Nehru, looking very elegant in his long, fitted white coat with a rose pinned on it, greeted us in the spacious hall. He took us up a broad flight of stairs into a formal sitting room, where we met his

501 Auburn Avenue, Atlanta, Georgia. *Copyright Flip Schulke*

June 18, 1953. *Copyright Alexander Adams/Coretta Scott King Collection*

Three generations of the King family: Martin's parents, Daddy and Mother King, Dexter, and his mother, Coretta. *Copyright Jay Leviton/Black Star*

Dr. and Mrs. King in the midst of the Montgomery bus boycott. *Copyright AP/ Wide World*

Dr. King with his son Dexter. *Copyright Flip Schulke*

Arrested on September 3, 1958, in Montgomery, Alabama, Dr. King is hustled into the station while officers dare Mrs. King to protest. *Copyright Charles Moore/Black Star*

Arrested on June 26, 1985, in a protest against apartheid, Mrs. King and two of her children, Bernice and Martin III, continue the civil rights struggle. *Copyright UPI/Bettmann*

While in this cell, Dr. King composed his famous "Letter from a Birmingham Jail." *Schulke Archives*

Dr. King in 1961, the first year of the Freedom Rides. *Copyright Henri Cartier-Bresson/Magnum*

Mrs. King with Yolanda, Martin III, and Bernice in a more peaceful moment. *Copyright Flip Schulke*

Dr. King speaking in church. *Copyright Flip Schulke*

Dr. King addressing a rally in Chicago. *Copyright John Tweedle/The Hartman Group*

Chicago, 1962. *Copyright John Tweedle/The Hartman Group*

Copyright Bob Adelman/Magmum

Washington, August 28, 1963. "I have a dream that . . ."

". . . all of God's children, black men and white men, Jews and Gentiles, Protestants and Catholics, will be able to join hands and sing in the words of the old Negro spiritual,'Free at last! Free at last! Great God A-mighty, we are free at last!'"

Copyright Flip Schulke

The King family moves to a Chicago slum to raise the issues of housing and urban decay, January 1966. *Copyright John Tweedle/ The Hartman Group*

Dr. and Mrs. King renovating a building on Chicago's West Side. *Copyright AP/Wide World*

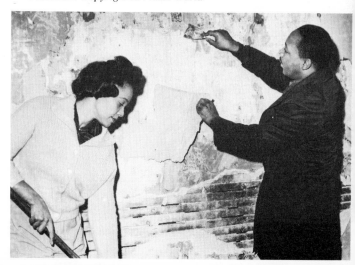

On March 26, 1964, Dr. King and Malcolm X finally meet.
Copyright AP/Wide World

Dr. King stands on the balcony of the Lorraine Motel in Memphis with Hosea Williams, the Reverend Jesse Jackson, and the Reverend Ralph Abernathy on April 3, 1968. On the same balcony the following day, Dr. King was shot. *Copyright AP/Wide World*

At the funeral procession, Mrs. King stands with Bob Williams, Yolanda, Bernice, Martin III, and Dexter. *Copyright Constantine Manos/Magnum*

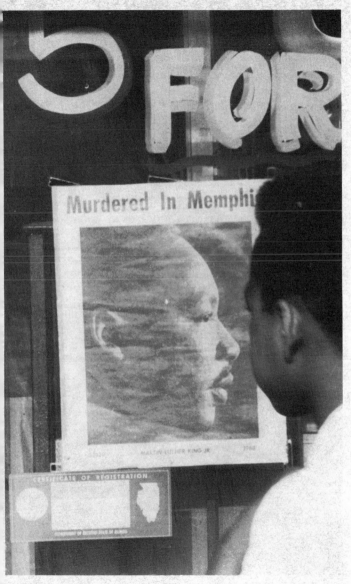

Americans learned of Dr. King's death on walls and windows,
as well as television and radio. Everyone was shocked.
Copyright John Tweedle/The Hartman Group

Bernice King, now an ordained Baptist minister, speaks to a Chicago High School on what would have been her father's fifty-eighth birthday, January 15, 1987. *Copyright AP/Wide World*

Backed up by Yolanda, Martin III, and Dexter, Mrs. King delivers a speech on the twenty-fifth anniversary of the March on Washington. *Copyright UPI/Bettmann*

daughter, Indira Gandhi, who later became the Prime Minister, from 1966 to 1977 and 1980 to 1984. She was quietly charming, a gracious hostess. Of course, Nehru was grace and courtesy itself, and he seemed genuinely glad to meet my husband.

At dinner Nehru talked with Martin, comparing the Indian struggle for freedom with that of American blacks for civil rights. They also discussed the method of nonviolence in our struggle. Nehru stressed the importance of the use of nonviolence. He commended my husband for the leadership he had given in this direction. Martin said to him, "I've read so much about Gandhi and the success of the nonviolent Movement here that I wanted to come and see for myself."

Martin commented on the fact that British-Indian friendship had been possible even though the British had represented a colonial power and the Indians had been its subjects. He felt that this was because the Indians had used nonviolence to achieve their independence instead of bequeathing a legacy of bitterness that violence would have engendered.

As they talked about Gandhi, Nehru said, "You know I did not always agree with him."

We knew this from our reading. Also, our Indian friends who came to Montgomery had told us about the policy battles between Nehru and Gandhi. Gandhi was completely dedicated to nonviolence, while Nehru was inclined to accept it as a useful revolutionary technique. Gandhi did not wish to thrust India into a modern technological society; Nehru felt that India could not survive without becoming industrialized. But their quarrel was not simple. Both men realized the complexities of using nonviolence as a technique of the masses.

Gandhi himself never saw nonviolence as a retreat from confrontation, as an avoidance of risk. He wrote in *An Autobiography:* "I do believe that when there is only a choice between cowardice and violence, I would advise violence. . . . I would rather have India resort to arms in order to defend her honor than that she should in a cowardly manner become or remain a helpless victim to her own dishonor. But I believe that nonviolence is infinitely superior to violence, forgiveness is more manly than punishment."

My husband and the Prime Minister talked about these matters for about four hours. I listened carefully, but I am not sure I would have been so polite still if our meeting had taken place later in the trip. For example, I certainly would have talked about the women of India, had I realized how much progress they had made with the coming of independence. As we traveled through the land, we were greatly impressed by the part women played in the political life of India, far more than in our own country. We knew that Gandhi had involved the women of India in the struggle for independence and that many of them had gone to jail like the men. Gandhi also worked to liberate women from the bondage of Hindu and Muslim traditions.

The next morning my husband and I went to lay a wreath on the shrine of the Raj Ghat, where Gandhi's body had been cremated. Then we met with other officials who had been leaders in the fight for freedom. Among them were the first President of India, Rajendra Prasad, who lived in the two-block-long palace with a golden dome that had been the viceroy's house; and Vice-President Sarvepalli Radhakrishnan, the philosopher-politician. Of all the people we met in New Delhi, we most enjoyed listening to him. He talked about his philosophy of life and, in a way, he reminded me of Mordecai Johnson, who had first inspired Martin's interest in Gandhian ideals. When we left, Martin said that our first twenty-four hours in India had been like meeting George Washington, Thomas Jefferson, and James Madison in a single day.

In the days to come, we met many other Indians who had been disciples of Gandhi. Some of them still dressed as he had, in coarse, handwoven khaki cloth robes. Gandhi had vowed poverty, and he rejected the materialism of Western civilization. One of the things that presented a paradox for us was that certain of these men still dressed in that simple way, while at the same time they lived in the great houses the British had built, and, in their many luxuries, copied their former masters. It was difficult for us to resolve this conflict. We understood that people who have been oppressed often have the need to live luxuriously as a sort of compensation; we hoped that someday they might strike a balance.

However, when we left New Delhi, we did find many people who lived in true Gandhian simplicity.

We loved the Indian people for the warmth and the spiritual quality they possessed. An especially interesting experience was our visit with the saintly Vinoba Bhave, who was walking through India, as Gandhi had, preaching his idealistic doctrine of *sarvodaya*, or a spiritual, decentralized socialism.

We found Bhave and his followers camped in a big meadow dotted with tents. They were cooking on open fires while the children ran about playing. While we were there, they struck camp and started walking up the dusty road. Martin and I walked with Bhave, listening to him talk. He believed that people would be better off if they had no government, because government corrupts, and the more organization people have, the more corrupt they become. I think Martin felt that Bhave's views, while truly idealistic, were too impractical for implementation. However, he was impressed by Bhave's argument that it *was* possible for a nation to totally disarm unilaterally; and if that were done by a country like India, it would have a profound moral effect on the whole world.

In the course of our travels we visited many places that Gandhi had made so memorable by his presence that they had become shrines. Gandhigram (Gandhi Village), in southern India, was a training center, almost like a school, with many young people. We were fortunate enough to attend a religious service conducted as Gandhi had done when he was alive. Before several hundred people sitting cross-legged on the ground in off-white robes, prayers were read from Hindu, Muslim, Christian, Jewish, and Buddhist holy books.

Most of the people we met were dedicated Gandhians, and in our talks with them we gained a deeper insight into the principles of *satyagraha*, or soul force, which was the basic concept of Gandhi's nonviolent movement.

By way of contrast, we went to a cattle show with the Maharaja of Mysore. He was a pleasant, charming, enlightened man who was progressive in his thinking, even if regressive in the opulence of his manner of living. At the fair he was cheered by the crowd and appeared very popular. We could not help feeling that as maharajas go, he was one of the good ones.

Martin made speeches all over India, always emphasizing his debt to Gandhian thinking. Most of the time, I sang on the same program; the Indians loved the black spirituals. And wherever we went we met the officials of the various states. Some of them seemed to us good men and idealists. Others appeared to have been corrupted by power, like politicians all over the world. Though such as these disturbed us, because of our idealistic attitude toward India, we then asked ourselves, "Why should Indians be different from humanity everywhere?"

With all its terrible contrasts of rich and poor, its materialists and idealists, philosophers and self-seekers, the Indian experience had a terrific impact on Martin's mind. One thing he learned was patience. It had taken nearly half a century for the Indian people to gain their independence. Many of their leaders had been imprisoned for ten years or longer, whereas ours had stayed in jail only a few days or weeks. Somehow in America we had felt the gains would come fast, and we were certainly not prepared to wait passively for freedom. The Indians did not have our sense of urgency; but we learned from them that the long struggle for freedom required endurance and even more suffering than we had already known.

Martin returned from India more devoted than ever to Gandhian ideals of nonviolence and simplicity of living. He constantly pondered how to apply them in America. His great problem was the enormous difference between the mechanized complexity of our way of living and theirs. He even considered the idea of changing his style of dress to a simpler one, but he decided that since his main purpose was to attract people to the Cause, unusual dress might even tend to alienate followers. Dress was really a superficial form rather than the spiritual quality he was aiming for.

He was more determined than ever to live as simply as possible. He felt, as in India, that much of the corruption in our society stems from the desire to acquire material things—houses and land and cars. Martin would have preferred to have none of these things. He finally said to me, "You know, a man who dedicates himself to a cause doesn't need a family."

I was not hurt by this statement. I realized that it did not mean he loved me and the children less, but that he was giving his life to the Movement and felt he therefore could not do as much for his family as he might in other circumstances. He saw a conflict between duty and love that prevented his giving himself utterly to the Cause. But I knew that, being the kind of man he was, Martin needed us. He functioned better with a wife and children because he needed the warmth we gave him, and from the standpoint of the Cause, having us gave him a kind of humanness which brought him closer to the mass of the people.

The influence of India was so strong that Martin's conscience continually questioned whether he was being really nonviolent and really ascetic. He realized that in our civilization a man who has to travel a lot will do his job much more efficiently with a car; he could not function without having a place to live, and he would have grave difficulties without a telephone. He finally decided that in the conditions prevailing in America we had to have certain things, and that he must strive to be more like Gandhi spiritually.

Martin never took on the pretentious qualities of the leader of a large movement, nor did he ever feel the need to have people at his beck and call, as happens to so many men who rise in the world. When our staff people tried to make him a person of importance who should have all sorts of attention paid him, he refused to allow it. He would much rather drive a Ford car than a Cadillac. I remember when he was coming back from the Birmingham jail, our staff members were very excited and thought that he should have a real hero's welcome. It was even suggested that we use a motorcade of Cadillacs.

When I told Martin about this, he said, "Now, what would I look like coming back from jail in a Cadillac? You just drive our car to the airport, and I'll drive you home."

But it was very difficult for Martin to keep from being worshiped by the black masses. It was a great temptation to them, because they had never had the opportunity to acclaim a great leader of their own before. They felt that nothing was too good for Dr. King, that he should ride in Cadillacs behind motorcycles and have every sort of pomp and tribute usually paid to the great leaders of mankind.

You see, they thought of him as the outstanding person of their race in the world. He was, to many of them, the President of the African Americans.

10

"Why did Daddy go to jail?"

For three years, since 1956, Martin had been virtually commuting between Montgomery and Atlanta. Toward the end of 1959, my husband had come to the point in his life when he felt that he had to give still more time to the civil rights struggle, and that in order to do this he could no longer perform his duties as full-time pastor of Dexter. The times seemed to dictate the need for a concentrated assault on the system of segregation in the South. Martin felt that if SCLC was to expand and really become the catalyst that would move the South and the nation forward, then he must devote full time to the organization and its development.

Atlanta provided the greatest opportunity for his personal development as well as offering the most favorable climate in which SCLC could grow. He discussed the situation with Daddy King, who pointed out that having Martin with him at Ebenezer would be of enormous help to him, since he was finding it increasingly difficult to manage alone. The matter was taken up with the board of deacons, and they most generously offered Martin the position of co-pastor of the Ebenezer Baptist Church of Atlanta.

On December 1, 1959, Martin served notice on the nation of a great new thrust toward black freedom. He said, "The time has come for a broad, bold advance of the southern campaign for equality. After prayerful consideration I am convinced that the psychological moment has come when a concentrated drive against

injustice can bring great tangible gains. . . . Not only will it include a
stepped-up campaign for voter registration, but a full-scale assault
will be made upon discrimination and segregation in all forms. We
must train our youth and adult leaders in the techniques of social
change through nonviolent resistance. We must employ new
methods of struggle involving the masses of the people."

The unfolding of this intricate offensive was made possible by
our moving to Atlanta, where Martin's direction of the Movement
could be more effective.

On the last Sunday in January, there was a big ceremony in
Martin's honor at Dexter. The deep bond of love which we shared
was movingly expressed by one member of the congregation,
Mother Norman, who said, "I love Dr. King like my own son. His
own mother couldn't possibly love him any more than I do!"

She also referred to me as her daughter. I shall always remember
the time when I gave a benefit concert for the Montgomery Improvement Association. She stood up at intermission clapping
proudly, saying, "That's my daughter!" On that farewell evening
when she came up to say goodbye to us, she handed me an ashtray
which she had made. The base of it was a tin top from a half-gallon
jar, encased by soft-drink-bottle tops strung on wire, with the same
arrangement for the handle. She said, "I know you don't want this
junk in your house, Mrs. King." Deeply touched, I replied, "I will
always keep this ashtray in a special place in my house. I hope you
will come to visit us in Atlanta someday so you can see it." Of the
many gifts we received on leaving Montgomery, this was perhaps
the most meaningful.

The parting was so beautiful, so deeply touching; we felt exalted, yet unworthy of their admiration. We left Montgomery with
the knowledge that our experience there had been so meaningful
that never again would anything quite like it happen to us. We felt
we had grown and developed, as had the Movement.

So much had happened to prepare us personally for the years
ahead, and, at the same time, the Movement had developed to
such a point that its direction had been charted and its growth and
maturation assured by the foundation that had been laid in Montgomery.

* * *

Hardly had we moved into our rented house in Atlanta when Martin was hit by the most serious attack on his reputation he had ever endured. A Montgomery grand jury indicted him on a charge of falsifying his Alabama state income-tax returns for 1956 and 1958. The implication was that Martin had received money from MIA and SCLC that was unaccounted for.

Though the accusation was utterly false, it caused Martin more suffering than any other event of his life up to that point. He said to me, "Many people will think I am guilty. You know my enemies have previously done everything against me but attack my character and integrity. Though I am not perfect, if I have any virtues, the one of which I am most proud is my honesty where money is concerned."

He was, in fact, completely scrupulous and utterly meticulous in his accounting. He felt that this was crucial to his leadership of the Movement; but more importantly, he was the sort of man who was ruthlessly honest with himself in such matters.

His family and friends, among them Ralph Abernathy, Dr. Benjamin Mays, Bayard Rustin, Stanley Levison, Dr. Ralph Bunche, and many others, tried to reassure Martin, but despite all of the bravery he had shown before under personal abuse and character assaults, despite the courage he was to show in the future, this attack on his personal honesty hurt him most.

He told us, when the news first came, "All of you know I don't have the money to fight such a charge in the courts." Besides, we were thoroughly accustomed to southern-style justice. "I won't under any circumstances use any funds from the Movement for such a purpose. And so, for the rest of my life, people will believe that I took money that didn't belong to me."

Our trusted friend, Stanley Levison, answered, "Martin, it isn't your responsibility to defend yourself. You are in this trouble because of who you are and all you have done for the Movement and this country. It is the country's duty to see that you are properly defended."

This was a very difficult time for me because I had never seen Martin affected so deeply. My husband's sense of morality was so offended by being accused of such a crime and attendant national publicity that he agonized to the point of feeling guilty. He realized that he could be vindicated only in the courts or in public debate and he felt that the public would be vulnerable to this attempt to destroy his image and to stop the Movement. I tried desperately to assure him that the vast majority of people believed in him and understood the motivation of the state of Alabama. But I could see that he began to feel that people had lost faith in him and that no one would want to listen to him. To see him in this frame of mind troubled me very much.

Martin finally pulled himself together enough to make a trip to New York, where he talked with our good friend Dr. Ralph Bunche.

Dr. Bunche listened and realized how upset he was. He said, "Look, Martin, it's the word of the state of Alabama against the word of Martin Luther King. There is no question in my mind which the country will accept."

Then he led Martin out of his office quite mysteriously, without explaining, and led him to the office of the Secretary-General. He was most cordial and Martin was deeply moved. Of course, Dr. Bunche had the sensitivity to realize that this would make Martin understand that his reputation had not changed with persons who counted.

After about a week, we began to get some perspective on how people were reacting to this trumped-up charge. It soon became clear that people were outraged. They contributed to Martin's defense and the best lawyers were on hand in Montgomery.

In May we went to Montgomery for the trial with Daddy King, Christine, and Ralph Abernathy. We were in court from Monday to Saturday. I was scheduled to speak in Cleveland on Sunday at three services for the Antioch Baptist Church Women's Day, but I did not see how I could go through with it.

On Saturday, May 28, the case went to the jury. Though the evidence clearly exonerated Martin, we had small hopes of an acquittal in that southern court even though, in an extraordinary admission, the prosecution's star witness said he believed in Martin's honesty. The jury came in, and the judge, with all the pomp and dignity required by such circumstances, asked for their verdict. I could hardly believe it when I heard the foreman say, "Not guilty."

A *southern* jury of twelve white men had acquitted Martin. It was a triumph of justice, a miracle that restored your faith in human good. The words which Martin had so often quoted rang truer than ever before: "Truth crushed to earth will rise again," and "No lie can live forever." The verdict foreshadowed the lesson Martin's enemies were to learn more than once: His integrity was too powerful to be besmirched by direct assault.

Around this time a cross was burned on our lawn in Atlanta. Surprisingly, it did not frighten me. After a point, nothing shocked me that much. I did not think the house would be bombed in Montgomery; I did not think anyone would be that foolish. Once it was bombed, I realized that it could happen; it could happen anywhere. As time went on, the threats against my husband's life kept coming, and he kept saying that he did not expect to live a long life. I tried to be aware of that possibility without being morbid about it. How could I deal with it? How could I handle the children? In the end, I just had to think things through, be realistic, and trust that what we were doing was right.

While Martin and the rest of the family returned to Atlanta, I left the night of the verdict with Ralph Abernathy for Cleveland, arriving at five in the morning, without having finished writing my speech. I could not make up my mind whether I should use the speech I was writing or talk extemporaneously about some of my own experiences. Ralph said to me, "Coretta, I think you ought to speak about your experience this week; just talk about that."

I went to bed in Cleveland, but I didn't really sleep. I lay there meditating until it was time to get dressed for the eleven o'clock service. When I was introduced to the congregation, I spoke without notes for forty minutes—as I spoke, the words came forth, and the audience seemed to listen intently. I felt that I was able to communicate to them the meaning of those long days in court, the terrible anxiety, and the triumphant conclusion.

A dear friend, Mrs. Leola Whitted, who had been one of our most devoted members at Dexter Avenue Baptist Church and was now living in Cleveland, reassured me. She said, "Girl, you held that audience spellbound. I am so proud of you." I was thankful that the spirit had guided me on this occasion.

Nineteen sixty was the year of the student sit-ins to desegregate lunch counters and restaurants. They began in Greensboro, North Carolina, when Joseph McNeil, a freshman at the North Carolina Agricultural and Technical College, was refused service at the bus-terminal lunch counter. His roommate, Ezell Blair, Jr., showed him a book that had been published about Martin and the bus boycott. Inspired by this, Blair, McNeil, and two other freshmen went to Woolworth's five-and-ten on February 1 and sat there, quietly but insistently demanding service. Of course, they were refused, but they also refused to leave. Day after day, they went back and sat, joined by both black and white students coming from the Women's College of the University of North Carolina and Bennett College.

The wire services picked up the story, and the Movement spread like a forest fire. Within two weeks black and white students in college towns south from Virginia to Florida and west to Louisiana organized sit-ins. Some were arrested, but this merely spread the flames.

Martin and the students were very close. At the sit-ins, many of the young people carried signs saying, "Remember the teachings of Gandhi and Martin Luther King." As the protest spread, it was proposed that SCLC sponsor a meeting of student leaders to organize them and set a keynote of nonviolence. Martin was enthusiastic, and money was appropriated by SCLC to finance it.

At that meeting, the Student Nonviolent Coordinating Committee (SNCC or Snick) was formed.

Under Martin's guidance the members pledged themselves absolutely to nonviolence and, of course, to work for complete racial integration through that method. SCLC agreed to help finance the new organization until it could stand on its own feet.

One reason so many young people became involved in the Movement was television. The Movement began in Montgomery just when the electronic era was beginning. Students were educated about social issues through the nightly news. There was always something happening on the screen, and it was very exciting for young people to see those events taking place. Everybody talked about the courageous things that were going on. Students liked that and so they wanted to be a part of it. Today, positive efforts do not make the news; violence builds ratings and so that is what TV looks for. In that sense, television incites, almost promotes, violence by playing it up so much. People think that if they do something violent they will get on the news. They will be noticed. They will be heard. And if they get on television, they think they are important. Television should pay more attention to the quiet efforts which are successful, which build progress. That would attract the attention of more young people.

It was during these student demonstrations that the song which was to become the anthem, or symbol, of the Movement was first sung. It is based on an African-American church hymn which was first sung by black textile workers. During the 1940s, it was brought to Tennessee and later taken up by the students and then by all of us. People sang it at one rally after another, until finally no rally could end without it. "We Shall Overcome," with new verses added all the time, was sung at sit-ins and by marchers; by demonstrators facing police, dogs, and fire hoses; in churches and paddy wagons; and in jail houses throughout the South. It was so spirited and carried so much resolve and emotion that it gave people courage and determination.

The sit-in Movement caught on in Atlanta in the fall of 1960. The buses had already been desegregated by a boycott under the leadership of the Reverend William Holmes Borders, who organized the Love, Law and Liberation Movement. On that occasion, Reverend Borders said, "Thank you, Montgomery! Thank you, Martin Luther King!" But all the restaurants and lunch counters in Atlanta were still completely segregated. There was hardly a place outside our own neighborhoods where an African American could even get a soda except by going to the side door of a drugstore and having it handed out.

It is difficult to describe how inescapably segregation pursued you, even though you instinctively tried to avoid putting yourself into situations where you would be insulted. Martin was once on a trip, flying into Atlanta, well after he had achieved national recognition. He struck up a conversation with the white man sitting beside him on the plane, and they enjoyed their conversation together so much that his fellow passenger invited Martin to have lunch with him at the airport when they landed in Atlanta.

Martin gladly accepted, and the two men went into the restaurant together. They asked for a table for two, and the hostess looked at Martin and said, "I'll have to seat you at a separate table."

She directed Martin to an area behind a curtain and said, "Everything is the same: the food, the table, and the chairs are the same."

My husband answered her kindly but firmly, "Oh, no. It is *not* the same. When you segregate me, you deprive me of fellowship with my brother here, when I want to continue to talk to him."

He pointed to the decorated walls and said, "When I am behind this curtain, you deprive me of the aesthetic pleasure of those paintings. It is not at all the same."

Of course, Martin was not willing to be seated behind a curtain, and he left.

It was against just such discrimination that the students began to organize protest demonstrations. Their main target in Atlanta was Rich's Department Store, one of the largest in the South. They invited Martin to sit in at the lunch counter with them, and of course he accepted with alacrity.

There were about seventy-five students in the group on that particular day and they were all arrested, Martin with them. Among them were people who are still leaders today, including Reverend Fred C. Bennette, Jr.; Marian Wright Edelman; Lonnie King; and John Porter. It had been agreed, in advance, that if they were arrested they would not put up bail, and most of them stayed in jail. Martin said, "I'll stay in jail one year or ten years if it takes that long to desegregate Rich's."

There were other important student movements in Greensboro, North Carolina; in Nashville, Tennessee; and in several other communities. In Birmingham, young and old worked together. Young people today should understand that students were able to organize themselves and build Movements in their own communities. Our disaffected students, and even those not in school, could learn a lot from what young people did in the Civil Rights Movement.

The whole community was aroused when the imprisonments became known. A committee of students and adults was formed to negotiate with the merchants and city officials to try to reach a settlement. Martin stayed in jail for about a week before an agreement was reached. I was pregnant at the time, but I went to see him almost every day. Though the rules of the jail allowed visiting only once a week, Daddy King knew the sheriff, who was a decent man, and he arranged that I could come.

By this time, Yoki and Marty were almost five and three respectively. This was to be the first time they were aware of his going to jail. They had heard the news on the radio as they were being driven home from nursery school. Yoki came home crying and both of them asked me, "Why did Daddy go to jail?"

I had been trying to prepare myself for this day and now I said to them, "Your daddy is a brave and kind man. He went to jail to help people. Some people don't have enough to eat, nor do they have comfortable homes in which to live, or enough clothing to wear. Daddy went to jail to make it possible for all people to have these things. Don't worry, your daddy will be coming back."

Little Marty, who loved airplanes, had said that when he grew up he wanted to be a pilot, so he could fly his daddy around. Now he asked, "Did Daddy go to jail on the airplane?" Because I wanted so much to relieve them of their anxieties, I answered "Yes" to Marty's question. You see, it had been their experience that when Daddy was away, he always went on the airplane. I felt it so important for them not to develop a fear of jail-going, but rather to feel it a badge of honor.

A family friend who happened to be teaching Yoki in the children's literature class at Quaker House overheard a conversation between a white classmate and Yoki. The little white girl, who was Yoki's age, said to her in a derogatory tone, "Oh, your daddy is always going to jail." Yoki replied, calmly and proudly, "Yes, he goes to jail to help people." That was the end of that. You can imagine how it warmed my heart when I was told about this.

Later, he went to jail in Albany in early December of 1961. The children were a year older, six and four, when the news reached us by television. Yoki again cried because she feared her daddy would not be back for Christmas. This time Marty consoled her. It was a deeply touching experience for me. Only four years old then, he sat on the side of the bed with one leg folded under the other, which hung off the side of the bed. He said, "Don't cry, Yoki. Daddy will be back. He has to help the people. He has already helped some people, but he has to help some more, and when he finishes he'll be back, so don't cry, Yoki."

It was gratifying to see the children accept jail-going not as something to be feared, but as something to be admired, even hoped for, for themselves. Yoki said later, "I'd like to go to jail with my daddy."

Though I really wanted to go to jail, Martin never wanted me to do so while the children were so young. I understood the hardships in the Movement from the beginning, but at times felt as if my participation had not been complete because I had not had that experience. I finally had the opportunity to go to jail with Bernice and Martin III in 1985 when we were involved in an anti-apartheid demonstration in Washington. Yolanda had already been arrested as part of that protest. Even before that physical imprisonment, though, I went to jail many times spiritually. I felt so strong an empathy with Martin that when he went to jail, part of me would be imprisoned with him.

Jail-going has been part of freedom struggles throughout the world. You cannot easily invent something to replace it. If there were a movement that was strong enough to challenge mores, folkways, and laws today, it would lead to civil disobedience. Nobody is doing anything radical enough, or creative enough, to be subjected to that kind of test. Given the right cause, though, jail-going can still be a very positive force for change.

One day, news spread through Atlanta that a settlement had been reached and that Martin and the students were going to be released. Jesse Hill, an outstanding business leader in Atlanta, telephoned me at nine o'clock that evening inviting Lonnie King's wife and me to meet the others for a celebration at Paschal's, a fine integrated restaurant owned and operated by blacks. I was very pleased. As I got dressed, I had such a good feeling because I was going to see my husband.

When I got to Paschal's I looked around. Though many of the students who had been in jail were present, Martin was not there. I somehow did not want to ask about him, having a premonition of evil. It was so strange to sit there, amid the celebration, afraid of what I would hear. Then someone told me, "They kept Dr. King in jail."

I could not understand it and I was desperately unhappy. No one had warned me that Martin had not been released. Finally I discovered what had happened. Back in April or May, Martin, who had neglected to exchange his Alabama driving license for one from Georgia, had been arrested for driving with an invalid license.

It had happened one night when we had dinner and spent the evening with Lillian Smith, the eminent writer. Afterward we took her back to Emory University Hospital, where she was undergoing treatment for what she told us was cancer. On the way a policeman stopped Martin simply because he had a white woman in his car. Then, when he saw that he was dealing with that well-known "troublemaker," he issued a summons.

This had happened in nearby De Kalb County, a well-known stronghold of the Klan. The next day, Martin and Daddy King went to answer the summons. Martin had been fined twenty-five dollars, given a suspended sentence, and released on probation. Somehow he was not aware at the time of the suspended sentence. Now, when he was being released on the sit-in charges in Atlanta, De Kalb County officials came and asked for his custody on the grounds that he had violated his probation by the sit-in. This was Saturday night. A hearing was set for Tuesday, and Martin stayed in jail.

On Tuesday morning, the De Kalb County sheriff came to the cell for him. He handcuffed Martin and walked arrogantly out with his prisoner. Naturally, the press photographers were alert. A picture of Martin handcuffed, following behind the sheriff, appeared in newspapers throughout the country.

I went to the hearing at the De Kalb County Courthouse with Daddy King, Christine, and A.D. At the end of the proceedings, Judge Mitchell said, "I find the defendant guilty and sentence him to six months' hard labor in the State Penitentiary at Reidsville."

It was a horrible shock to us all, obviously a viciously unjust sentence for a traffic violation. It was hard to bear. I was five months pregnant and emotionally overwrought.

Christine burst into tears, and seeing her, for the first time since the Movement began in 1955, I cried in public. Daddy King was so upset himself that he scolded me for crying, which seemed to make it worse. I felt so alone and helpless. Martin had already been in jail for eight days, and I was tired out from anxiety and from my daily trips to visit him. Then, such a long sentence meant that our baby would arrive while he was in jail and I would have to have the child alone, without him. I could not help feeling sorry for myself.

Martin was immediately taken back to a jail cell. Daddy King and I were allowed to go in to see him. I was trying not to cry when we went into the cell, but the tears were streaming down my face. When Martin saw me he said, "Corrie, dear, you have to be strong. I've never seen you like this before. You have to be strong for me."

Then I realized that Martin had been weakened by his days in jail, and was greatly depressed by this unexpected shock. He was relying on the deep reservoir of strength which I had always drawn from in crisis situations, but I, too, was totally unprepared for the dreadful decision.

Daddy King said, "You don't see me crying; I am ready to fight. When you see Daddy crying, Coretta, then you can start crying. I'm not taking this lying down."

So he said, but he was emotionally affected. He was thinking, "I have to hold up for Coretta, and I have to hold up for my daughter, and I have to hold up for my wife." This was something I did not want to happen to him. I tried hard, and finally I felt that I had taken myself in hand.

Martin told me, "I think we must prepare ourselves for the fact that I am going to have to serve this time." I said, "Yes, I think we must prepare ourselves for that."

He asked me to see that he got newspapers and magazines and

writing materials and to leave him some money. I went home to take care of these things, and to see my two children, determined to prepare myself for the painful period to come.

Meanwhile, our lawyers had asked the judge not to send Martin to Reidsville immediately, as they were going to prepare a writ of habeas corpus. The judge promised he would not. But at about eight thirty the next morning, A.D. called me and said, "Coretta, they took M.L. to Reidsville last night." This seemed more than I could bear.

Later Martin told me that at four thirty the following morning, several men had come into the jail cell where he was sleeping with the other prisoners. They played a flashlight on his face and called, "King! King! Wake up!"

It was very frightening. Again, he knew only the awful history of such midnight visits, and nothing of where they were taking him. They made him dress and handcuffed him very tightly and put chains around his legs. He rode the three hundred miles to Reidsville in those painful handcuffs and chains, without knowing what his fate would be.

When he got to Reidsville, exhausted and humiliated, he was thrown into a very narrow cell where hardened criminals were kept, and then made to put on a prison uniform. However, the other prisoners managed to send Martin notes saying how much they respected him, and how sorry they were that he was in prison unjustly. Martin said their encouragement made him feel a little better, in spite of the wardens who were very brutal and abusive. Interestingly enough this was the only integrated cell block in the whole prison.

When I got the news from A.D., I felt just terrible, so helpless! I started to think about how Martin must feel. My husband hated being alone. He loved people, and although he was able to discipline himself to get away from people, to do the thinking, writing, and planning that were necessary for the direction he gave the Movement, that was voluntary. He needed and depended upon the support of people he loved. It was always hard for Martin to be in prison, and this would be such a long stay, without Ralph or his other companions in the struggle with him.

I knew that it was three hundred miles to Reidsville, more than a day's journey there and back, and I was so pregnant, I did not know if I could make it. Another thing upset me. I had sent Martin books and magazines but I had forgotten the money. I felt so guilty knowing he had no money to buy anything. So I said to Daddy King, "We must go to Reidsville today. Someone must see Martin today."

But Daddy King was thinking in terms of practical things—of finding lawyers who could get Martin out of jail. He asked me to go with him to see the well-known and respected lawyer Morris Abram, who had become a friend of ours during our struggle and who had been very helpful with civil rights cases.

As I was getting dressed to go see Mr. Abram, the telephone rang. The person at the other end said, "May I speak to Mrs. Martin Luther King, Jr.? Just a minute, Mrs. King, for Senator Kennedy."

Senator John F. Kennedy was in the final days of his campaign for President of the United States. I waited a few seconds, and a voice made familiar by scores of television broadcasts said, "Good morning, Mrs. King. This is Senator Kennedy."

We exchanged greetings, and then Senator Kennedy said, "I want to express to you my concern about your husband. I know this must be very hard for you. I understand you are expecting a baby, and I just wanted you to know that I was thinking about you and Dr. King. If there is anything I can do to help, please feel free to call on me."

"I certainly appreciate your concern," I said. "I would appreciate anything you could do to help."

That was the gist of that famous conversation that has been said to have changed history and elected a President of the United States.

At the time I did not know quite how to react, because I realized that the phone call could be used to political advantage. My husband had a policy of not endorsing presidential candidates, and at this point I did not want to get him or myself identified with either party. I heard later that the Kennedy strategists had discussed having the candidate make a public statement, which, of course, politicians from Georgia opposed, because, I am told, they felt it might cause him to lose the South. I understand that one prominent Georgia politician had said something like "If you leave this to me, I'll get King out of jail." But Senator Kennedy decided that at least he would call me.

Well, things began to happen pretty fast after that. Reporters began calling to know what Senator Kennedy had said. At first, I was reluctant to talk with the press until after I had checked with someone from Senator Kennedy's campaign staff. Soon, I began to hear some encouraging reports about Martin's release. A.D. said, "I'd like to bet you M.L. will be out by tomorrow night."

I said, "I don't want to bet. I don't want to think about it. I don't dare."

A.D. was right. I heard that Senator Kennedy's brother Robert, who was his campaign manager and later became the U.S. Attorney General, called Judge Mitchell to learn why Dr. King couldn't be released on bail pending appeal. That story leaked out to the press, and evidently Judge Mitchell had a change of heart. Now, he said Martin would be released on bail.

I received the news about Martin's release around noon the next day, and I was very, very happy. SCLC chartered a plane to bring Martin home. We all went to the airport to meet him, and so little Marty did get to see his father come home from jail in an airplane.

As we rode back to town together—Martin, Yoki, Marty, Mamma and Daddy King, Christine, and her husband, Isaac—Martin related his experiences and emotional reactions to confinement at Reidsville. Following the usual pattern for these occasions, a mass meeting was held that night at Ebenezer Church. People from all over town came. Martin told about his experiences in jail, but said nothing political. He resolved to continue in the struggle more determined than ever. However, Daddy King, who had been planning to vote for Nixon, had no such inhibitions. He roared out to the crowd, "If I had a suitcase full of votes, I'd take them all and place them at Senator Kennedy's feet."

A few days later, John Kennedy was elected President of the

United States by only about a hundred thousand votes. It is my belief that historians are right when they say that his intervention in Martin's case won the presidency for him. That seemed significant to me because of what happened later in the civil rights struggle and the relationship of the Kennedys to what Martin was trying to accomplish.

11

"We shall overcome"

The sit-ins continued throughout the South with considerable success. Integration was accomplished in hundreds of communities. Then, in March of 1961, the protests were extended into the Freedom Rides, which were designed to desegregate interstate buses and bus terminals in the South. Although the Freedom Rides were primarily a project of the Congress of Racial Equality (CORE), they had the backing of the SCLC and SNCC, and Martin served as chairman of the Freedom Rides Coordinating Committee. On April 28 James Farmer of CORE wrote to President Kennedy telling him the itinerary of the first Freedom Ride. On May 4 pairs of white and black volunteers, with a white observer from CORE, took Greyhound and Trailways buses for a trip through Virginia, the Carolinas, Georgia, Alabama, and Mississippi to New Orleans.

This well-advertised project seemed to infuriate southern reactionaries beyond all reason. Bands of raging whites attacked the buses in cities in the deep southern states. The riders were hauled off, beaten up, and thrown into jails. In Anniston, Alabama, a roaring crowd attacked a Greyhound bus, smashed its windows with iron bars, punctured the tires, and threw an incendiary bomb into it. The bus was destroyed.

This was the largest violent attack that the people of the Movement had experienced thus far. I remember seeing television pictures of the bus burning, and it was a gruesome, frightening thing.

Martin was terribly concerned for the safety of our people. He also knew that the senseless violence of the whites could provoke our people to retaliation.

The Freedom Rides continued and the attacks grew in intensity. Martin joined in appeals to the federal government for protection for the freedom riders. The Kennedy Administration assured us that it would stay in close touch with those developments.

Meanwhile, another group of freedom riders was due to arrive in Montgomery on May 20. Martin went there to meet them. He told me how a mob of three hundred people surrounded the bus as it stopped. The first rider off was a white exchange student from Fisk University named James Zwerg. Women screamed, "Kill the nigger-loving son of a bitch." Men rushed in to knock him down and beat him unconscious. However, true to our non-violent principles, James Zwerg made no attempt to defend himself. He lay unconscious in the street for an hour before an ambulance came.

Others getting off the bus, including John Seigenthaler of the Justice Department, who later became the publisher of the Nashville *Tennessean*, were beaten. Some were spirited safely away in cars driven by members of the Montgomery Improvement Association. For twenty horrible minutes the police did nothing to stop the terrible attacks on the people. Throughout the day there were eruptions of violence. Then, as darkness fell, the federal government sent six hundred United States marshals into the city to restore order. Governor John Patterson of Alabama contended that there was no need for federal intervention and threatened to arrest the marshals. "We can handle the situation ourselves," he said. Of course, the Governor's idea of how to handle the situation seemed to be to let the mob take over.

Meanwhile, the radio announced that Martin Luther King, Jr., would hold a mass rally for the freedom riders at Ralph Abernathy's First Baptist Church. Twelve hundred whites and blacks were jammed into the church as carloads of angry white racists poured into Montgomery from the countryside. A crowd of several thousand surrounded the church. Martin said rocks began crashing through the stained-glass windows, showering the close-packed crowd with splintered glass. Maddened elements in the mob began shouting that the church should be burned. My husband rushed to the telephone and called Attorney General Robert Kennedy in Washington to send more marshals to help those already present, who seemed barely able to keep the crowd from breaking into the church.

Martin stood before that brave and beleaguered assembly, and, while rocks continued to crash into the sanctuary, the people prayed and sang hymns, freedom songs, and "We Shall Overcome."

After they had been besieged for several hours, things seemed quieter, and Martin decided to see if he could talk the crowd outside into letting them leave the church. He and Ralph Abernathy stepped through the front door. As Martin came out, a gas bomb whizzed by, within a few inches of his head. One of his aides who was very close to him, Reverend Fred C. Bennette, picked up the bomb and threw it out over Martin's shoulder. Someone pulled him back inside the church, and there he stayed, with all the people, through most of the night. This action was typical of the kind of devotion to Martin displayed by many of the people closely associated with him in the Movement. Often, when there was the possibility that he would be injured, they would place themselves in the path of danger in an effort to protect him. Always unarmed, they were willing to give their own lives, if need be, in order to spare his. Martin's selfless devotion to the Cause inspired this response from them. Eventually the reinforced marshals were able to disperse the mob, and by daylight the people were able to go home. But it was a night of horror and it was very discouraging because it revealed the irrationality and cruelty of racism.

That whole summer the Freedom Rides continued, and they accomplished a good deal. The Freedom Rides took the Movement from the college campuses, which were primarily located in cities, to the rural hamlets of the Southland. The idealistic youth who went to Mississippi, Alabama, Louisiana, and southwest Georgia were to give the Movement its broad rural base as they moved from campus to community. Thus, the Movement of southern ministers who followed my husband's pattern of bus protests gained a welcome ally in southern college students who committed themselves to nonviolent action.

At about this time the Field Foundation gave a grant of forty-five thousand dollars for a voter-education program under the auspices of the United Church of Christ, and a young black minister, Andrew J. Young, was chosen to administer it in close association with Martin. Andy Young later joined the staff of SCLC and became one of Martin's closest friends and colleagues. He served first as administrative assistant to Martin, then as executive director of SCLC, and finally as executive vice-president, the position he held at the time of Martin's death; he is now a member of SCLC's board of directors. He has served as a Congressman, U.S. Ambassador to the United Nations, and Mayor of Atlanta.

The Reverend James Bevel came to us from the Nashville Student Movement. Later his wife, the former Diane Nash, also joined our staff. James Orange is still very active and is one of the finest organizers who has kept in touch with young people. Down south, anybody having a march calls James Orange to coordinate it because he is about the only one left who is doing that sort of thing. Willie Bolden, Lester Hankerson, and Ben Clark came by way of the Savannah Movement, which was led by the dynamic Hosea Williams. Martin and Hosea had conflicts, but my husband said Hosea had more raw courage than anybody he ever met. Hosea was one of those people who could get out and relate to the street folks, which was a great help to Martin. He was also a master at organizing marches. Bernard Lafayette, the senior scholar in residence at the King Center, has probably done more nonviolent training than anyone else since my husband's death. He is the present program director, and a product of the Student Movement. Walter Fauntroy became the first nonvoting delegate in Congress from Washington, D.C. Septima Clark brought to the SCLC's Citizenship Education Program valuable insights gained from her experiences teaching adult education in her native Charleston, South Carolina. Dorothy Cotton was the only woman on the executive staff of the SCLC. She paid a lot of dues too—she was beaten, went to jails, and so on.

It is difficult to name everyone who contributed in some way to the success of SCLC. Yet, these people, and others whose names do not appear in our story, are certainly among the most valuable persons who worked with my husband during his twelve and one-half years of struggle in the Movement. The combination of youth, intellect, and dedication, as well as wisdom, in the SCLC organization created for the conference an enviable place among organizations working for social change.

SCLC's next campaign led Martin to Albany, Georgia. Albany has about fifty-odd thousand inhabitants, and is approximately 270 miles southwest of Atlanta, in the heart of the hard-core white racist country. It was then totally segregated. The Albany Movement, as it was generally called, was headed by a respected African-American physician, William G. Anderson, and it was inspired by two very young SNCC field workers, Charles Sherrod and Cordell Reagon, who had established a voter-registration center there. Its sponsors were the Ministerial Alliance of Albany, the Federation of Colored Women's Clubs, SNCC, the local NAACP branch, and the Negro Voters League. The organization set out to copy the program of the Montgomery Improvement Association.

On November 25, 1961, the Movement began when three black young people and two adults sat down in the bus terminal dining room and asked to be served. They were arrested. On December 10 a group of freedom riders, including SCLC's youth director, Bernard Lee, arrived. Bernard, who died in 1991, traveled with my husband constantly and could handle crowds better than anyone I have ever seen. The riders came to help a group who were trying to integrate the railroad station. They were jailed. Then, on December 15, a unit of the Georgia National Guard was mobilized at the request of Mayor Asa Kelley of Albany. Dr. Anderson telephoned Martin for help.

The Albany Movement began before Martin became involved. Martin, who was then concentrating on the unification of a national Movement, did not feel that it was the time for our strength to be diffused in local confrontations which might better be settled by national action. Nevertheless, his conscience and his sense of the obligations of leadership made him go at once to try to help.

Martin and Ralph Abernathy arrived in Albany that very evening after Dr. Anderson's call. The next morning they marched at the head of a procession of two hundred and fifty people to the City Hall. Every one of the marchers was arrested.

Negotiations followed this mass arrest. The city commissioners agreed to desegregate the bus terminal and railroad station, and in return the protesters agreed to halt mass demonstrations. The prisoners were released. At the end of December the bus company agreed to desegregate the buses, though the commissioners refused to make it official. Martin later thought that it would have been better strategy to have temporarily accepted these gains and held back for a while until the community could peacefully adjust to the changes. But the leaders of the Albany Movement had tasted victory, and they wanted to continue, and Martin himself encouraged them to do so. He suggested a boycott of selected stores, but because he did not have the time to supervise the organization, it was largely ineffective.

On February 27, 1962, Martin, Ralph, and several others were tried and convicted for leading the December march in Albany. They were not sentenced until July 10, when the judge gave Martin and Ralph the choice of a fine of $178 or forty-five days at hard labor. In accordance with their principles, both men refused to pay the fine, but, taking the example of Commissioner Clyde Sellers in Montgomery, someone was smart enough to pay their fines for them, and they were "ejected" from jail.

Throughout that summer of 1962 the struggle continued in Albany, but the city commissioners were adamant against any further concessions. Rather than integrate the city parks, they closed them. They also closed the public library.

One redeeming aspect of that period was that Police Chief Laurie Pritchett was not at all typical of southern policemen. He was not brutal, though some of his officers engaged in brutality. He tried to be decent, and as a person he displayed kindness. He would allow the protesters to demonstrate up to a point. Then he would say, "Now we're going to break this up. If you don't disperse, you'll be arrested."

Our people were given fair warning. Often they would refuse to disperse, and would drop on their knees and pray. Chief Pritchett would bow his head with them while they prayed. Then, of course, he would arrest them and the people would go to jail singing.

Many people came from other states to help the Albany Movement. Seventy-five ministers, priests, and rabbis, black and white, Protestant, Catholic, and Jewish, came to pray and were arrested. In July there was a violent outburst when two thousand young people threw rocks and pop bottles at the police. Martin called for a "Day of Penitence" for this disorder. He also insisted that for the rest of the week direct action would be confined to prayer vigils.

On July 27, Martin, Ralph, and Dr. Anderson led the first of these vigils. They were arrested and jailed. Their trial was set for August 10, which meant that they would be in prison for nearly two weeks.

I was in Atlanta with our three children—our second son, Dexter, named for our beloved church in Montgomery, had been born in January 1961, and was still an infant. I drove over from Atlanta to see Martin frequently. Chief Pritchett was very decent to the prisoners—though we knew of many instances of brutality inside the jail from bigoted white prison guards. He allowed food to be brought to them and he let Martin have books and a radio in his cell. The jail was very dirty, but they cleaned up the part he was in; I could smell the disinfectant every time I went there.

One day, I took the two oldest children with me. It was the first time Yoki and Marty saw their father in jail. However, he was allowed out in the corridor to talk to them, so they did not see him behind bars. It did not seem to bother them at all. They played happily up and down the corridors.

We all expected that the men would get a jail sentence at their trial. So when the idea was conceived that the wives of the leaders should lead a demonstration after the hearing, we were terribly excited.

Juanita Abernathy; Andy Young's wife, Jean; Dr. Anderson's wife, Norma; Wyatt Walker's wife, Ann; Slater King's wife, Marion; C. B. King's wife, Carol (Slater and C. B. King were lawyers for the Albany Movement); James Bevel's wife, Diane; and I were going to lead the march. We thought that if we could get a number of women in jail it would be a dramatic way of getting our case before the American public, which might then put pressure on the local authorities. So strong was the support of the female contingent of the Albany Movement that one member, Diane Nash Bevel, who was nine months pregnant, refused to go home and had her baby in Albany during this period.

But at the trial Martin and Ralph Abernathy were given suspended sentences and released. I must confess that I was very disappointed, because I had looked forward to going to jail the next day.

Martin and Ralph were freed on a weekend, and they immediately began to organize a huge, massive demonstration for Monday. Somehow the word got out; I imagine our strategy meetings were bugged, and there were always lots of police around outside. This time the city officials succeeded in getting a *federal* injunction against the demonstration.

This was the first time local officials had ever succeeded in getting the federal courts to enjoin one of our demonstrations. I remember that my husband was much disturbed. He spent hours trying to decide whether to disobey the injunction or not. His argument had always been that we were breaking local laws in order to obey the federal law; this time, it was the federal law that was in question. The federal courts in the South had demonstrated their intention to be fair, but now we were confronted with a situation in which these very courts were enjoining us. Martin had to think the problem through very, very carefully and assess all the implications.

Many of the leaders, especially the student leaders, felt Martin should disobey the injunction. Martin called Attorney General Robert Kennedy and also Burke Marshall of the Justice Department, and I remember he was quite annoyed because they did not seem to understand our plight. They suggested it might be wise to "close up" in Albany. Martin said, "You know, they just don't understand what we're up against." He was terribly disappointed.

I remember quite vividly how he agonized that night after the mass meeting. The possibility of calling off the demonstration had already affected the morale of the staff and people involved in the Movement. Most of the staff came to sleep at Dr. Anderson's house, headquarters for the Albany Movement, where we always stayed while there. Martin needed desperately to have a strategy session with his staff and workers. When he looked around, the key people had fallen asleep. The occasion reminded me of Christ and the experience with His disciples in the garden of Gethsemane. I felt deeply for Martin. We finally went to bed, and his was indeed a restless night.

Out of his agony and prayerful deliberation he decided not to march. Later he felt that this was the factor that broke the backbone of the Albany Movement. When they could not demonstrate, the Movement lost its momentum.

Martin was to regret this decision. He later said, "Now that they're successful in getting a federal injunction, they're going to do it over and over again; and that means we will be stymied."

My husband was severely criticized by some people for obeying this federal ruling. Yet, since the federal government had always supported us on constitutional questions, it was difficult for Martin to go against it. It had been the only friend we had had in the South.

Though we had many problems with the Albany Movement, it gave the people of Albany a new sense of dignity and respect, and an awareness of their plight that they did not have before. The success was not as dramatic as it was in Montgomery, and did not have the national impact of Montgomery, but each community has to be involved in its own struggle for freedom. The Movement in

Albany did lay the groundwork for many later reforms in south west Georgia.

The freedom spirit spread rapidly to surrounding counties. Also, the SCLC staff learned many valuable lessons in community mobilization which were soon to bear fruit in Birmingham.

12

"Turn on the hoses damnit!"

In order to tell a consecutive story about the Movement in the South, I have concentrated on that, but all the time those things were happening—the sit-ins, the protests, the jailings—our lives were going forward on several other levels. Martin was rushing about the country making speeches to gain moral and financial support for the Movement. I was giving concerts and also making speeches to help our Cause.

In late March of 1962, while the Albany Movement was in full swing, I was invited by the Women's Strike for Peace to go as a delegate to Geneva, Switzerland, for an international effort to influence the atomic-test-ban talks going on there. Even in my college days I had taken an active interest in promoting world peace through the Quaker peace groups at Antioch. Later when we moved to Atlanta I joined the Women's International League for Peace and Freedom. I was, and still am, convinced that the women of the world, united without any regard for national or racial divisions, can become a most powerful force for international peace and brotherhood.

Of course, my husband had always been concerned about the entire question of world peace, but he had become so completely involved in the civil rights struggle that he had less time for the peace movement than I.

With Martin's encouragement I arranged to join the fifty American women who went to Geneva. There were professional women, mothers who had never before been active politically, and other women who had been very actively engaged in the peace movement. There were four black women in the group. When I met the delegation on the plane, I realized they were a very stable, intelligent, and levelheaded group of women. In Geneva we were joined by women from other countries—Scandinavians, Englishwomen, Australians, and Russians. Of course, the American women formed a majority.

We were all deeply concerned with stopping war and, in particular, with getting a test-ban treaty. We felt that this would be the first step and one that was enormously important for the welfare of our children.

We Americans met with the United States representative, Arthur Dean. Unfortunately, we did not get a very warm reception. Mr. Dean's attitude was hard and unsympathetic. He seemed to regard us as "hysterical females," and he acted as if he was determined not to be influenced by any emotionalism we might display. In truth, we *were* upset, but the issue of radioactive fallout from atmospheric tests as it affected our children's milk, their bone structure, their life itself, was a serious and disturbing matter.

Mr. Dean acted as though he felt that what we were asking was so impossible that he did not even bother to consider it. We were deeply hurt, but this feeling was intensified because our own representative, the *American* spokesman, did not seem to realize that he held his appointment in order to serve the wishes of the people, and that we represented a large segment of our country who wanted a no-test agreement.

Finally, just before he stormed out of our meeting, he said angrily, "You go talk to the Russians. We've tried. Why don't you talk to them."

We did just that; all of us met with the Russian delegation, and I must confess that that meeting was much more congenial. They held a reception in our honor and then we talked, and the dialogue seemed very encouraging. The contrast between our treatment by the Russians and by our own delegation was striking.

Of course, we were not so naive that we were not aware that the Russians were masters of the art of propaganda and knew just how to treat us so we would react positively—regardless of their actual motives. Nevertheless, we felt it was unfortunate that our own representative had not been more interested or even attempted a meaningful discussion with us. Yet, we represented many women who had strong influence and a deep concern for the welfare of this nation and the world.

During this period, of course, Martin and I, like any other young couple, were vitally absorbed with raising our children. However, we shared with our black brothers and sisters the especially demanding and often agonizing job of bringing our children up without fear or bitterness in their hearts. That is difficult enough in a segregated city, as Atlanta was, but our activities in the Movement made it doubly difficult.

Yoki would sometimes come home and say, "Mommy, I'm so tired of having people ask me, 'Are you Martin Luther King's daughter?' "

I would try to explain to her on a level she could understand that this would happen, not because her father was notorious, but because of the good he was doing for all people. I would say, "Yoki, people ask you that because they think well of your father."

Still, it was difficult to strike a balance for my children between the many aspects of our position that pulled upon them. One of the difficult aspects of growing up is the manner in which children can unwittingly inflict cruelties upon each other. As a young child, Yolanda displayed unusual perception of her situation, and a unique ability to handle her own problems.

One day she came home from school with a look of satisfaction on her face. She told me that she had just "got tired of the whole thing" and that when, during the day, her teacher stepped out of the classroom, Yoki had turned to the other children and said, "Look, all I want is just to be treated like a normal child."

Watching that sensible and proud little seven-year-old, I laughed to myself and said, "Good for you." She had articulated, in her childish wisdom, exactly what Martin and I had in mind for our children.

His name has been a special problem for our son Marty. First, he has had to learn to be his own person, though he carries his daddy's well-known name. Then, since we lived in the South, he had to cope with the hostility his name evoked in some of the whites around us.

Once, when Marty had been in an integrated school for about a year, I drove down, with Dexter, to pick him up after a Saturday-morning football game. As boys will do, the two of them wandered off, and I had to call them away from two bigger white boys to whom they were talking.

They got into the car, and Marty blurted out, "Mommy, do you see those big boys over there? They asked me what my father's name was, and, Mommy, what I did was, I told them I had forgotten."

My heart bled for him and I said gently, "Marty, you know what your father's name is. Why did you tell them that?"

Marty dropped his head onto his shoulders. He replied, "Well, Mommy, you see, I was afraid they'd beat me up."

I was painfully aware at that moment that it must sometimes have been a terrible thing for our little son to know that if he let his identity be known, he would meet with hostility.

How I prayed that he would not be harmed by this! I resolved to be alert as I could and to help him with this special and so poignant problem.

Marty was in the third grade when he and Yoki first attended an integrated school, and on the second day of school a boy in his class came up to him and said, "Say, what's your father's name?" He answered proudly, "Dr. Martin Luther King, Jr.," and the little boy said, "Oh! Your father's that famous nigger." Marty said, "The word is 'Negro,' " and that seemed to be the end of it.

More than anything, he seemed to have been embarrassed at the use of the word "nigger," which Martin and I had tried to explain to our children in a way that would keep them from the traditional hateful response—"And you're a Georgia cracker"— and yet would help them retain their own pride in themselves and their race.

At one point we had a funny echo of this after our children

and the Abernathy children had been called "niggers" at the downtown Atlanta YWCA, where they were attending a summer program—it was shortly after the YWCA had been integrated.

The children were telling me about the incident, and I guess I was groping a bit to find the right words to say to them.

Dexter, who was four at the time, broke in and said, "Mommy, you know why some people say 'nigger'? Some people say 'nigger' because they don't know *how* to say 'Negro.' " "You are exactly right, Dexter," I answered.

How hard it is, and how crucially important, for black children to be taught a sense of their own worth that is strong enough to withstand the pressure of a white society which every day tries to show them that they are inferior.

Of course, I think our children were helped in this regard by the knowledge that their parents were fighting hard for racial justice. Even so, we had to think about what we were doing so as to protect our children from the humiliation of being excluded. For example, I might be driving through a white neighborhood with Yoki in the car when she was three or four years old, and we would pass a playground. Yoki would call out, "Mommy, please stop the car. Look at the swings. I want to stop and swing."

I would never stop. The playgrounds we passed were for white children only. I would say something like "We have to get home and have lunch, dear," to try to spare her a little, to give her time to develop her own inner strength before confronting the terrible problem of being black in America.

Martin sometimes mentioned in his speeches one of the incidents with our children that hurt us most. A new amusement park had been built in Atlanta, called Funtown, and it was advertised extensively. My children would watch television and see so many commercials for Funtown that they even learned to sing the lyrics of the song.

They would plead with us to take them, and we would keep making excuses, not wanting to tell them that the television invitations were not meant for black children. Martin would say, "Not this week, children. I have to go on a trip," or some such thing, week after week, until finally Yoki, who was about six at the time, said, "You just don't want to take me to Funtown."

I hated the hurt look in her eyes, and I told her, "Yolanda, Funtown was built by people who decided that they did not want colored people to come there. They were not good Christians. You see, we are colored."

My daughter started crying, then I heard myself echoing those old words: "Yoki dear, this doesn't mean you are not as good as those people. You know, God made all of us and we are all His children. He made some white, some brown, some black, some red, and some yellow. He must have thought a lot of his colored children because he made so many. Don't cry because it won't be long before you can go to Funtown. This is really what your daddy is doing in all his work; he is trying to make it possible for you to go to Funtown and for you to go any other place you want to go." This was her first emotional realization and understanding of being black in a white world.

This was the first time Yoki realized that as a black child there were places she could not go. She cried because it hurt her, yet it helped her to understand that her father was working to do something about these conditions—that things could be changed. Even his absences became more meaningful to her.

Much after this episode, we heard, in the spring of 1963, that Funtown had been quietly desegregated, and Martin and I decided to take Yoki, Marty, and Dexter, who was now old enough to join us. The children were just bursting with excitement and anticipation. They—*and* Martin—had a glorious time. They went on all the rides, and Martin was just as boyishly happy as he had been at Revere Beach, near Boston, many years ago during our first year of marriage.

While we were at Funtown, a white woman came up to me and asked, "Are you Mrs. King?"

I told her I was, and she said, "Oh, I'm so glad you are here. Is your daughter with you?"

"This is my daughter, Yolanda," I answered.

The woman looked at her and said again, "I'm so glad you're here," and walked away.

When we left, I kept thinking how wonderful it was that the children had been able to see that what their daddy was doing had brought concrete results in their own lives.

In many other areas, black parents face much more subtle problems. The whole concept of beauty based on white standards is a particularly destructive difficulty. In our society—commercials, movies—everything emphasizes the desirability of Caucasian features, fair skin, straight hair, keen nose, thin lips. All this is beautiful; and if you do not fit the type, you are not beautiful. During and since the days of slavery, a fair skin has made a difference. Mulatto children were better treated by their masters—and sometimes even by their own victimized parents—than those who were dark skinned.

The emergence and gradual acceptance of the "black is beautiful" concept is the most emotionally and psychologically constructive weapon with which the black child can be armed. I have always been very much aware of how important it is for our children to develop a healthy and proper attitude toward the color of their skin. I thought I had succeeded in this regard until one day when Yolanda was seven she said, "Mommy, why is it that white people are pretty and Negroes are ugly?"

I gasped in dismay, "But, Yolanda, that's not true. There are pretty people in all races." "No," she said, vehemently. "White people are pretty and Negroes are ugly."

I picked up a copy of *Ebony* magazine that happened to be on a table. I sat down with her, and we looked through the pages. I would say, "See her, see how beautiful she is!" Or, "Oh, isn't he handsome?" Yoki kept murmuring, "Mmm-mmm." When we finished the magazine, she said, "You know, colored people are pretty, and white people are ugly."

I almost shouted, "Oh no! That's not right either." I had to start all over again.

Yet "getting it right" was what our fight was all about, wasn't it? This is why we can't wait, as our white fellow citizens sometimes urge us to. For my children, like any other children in the world, have only one life to live, one education to get, one chance at dignity and peace. That is why we need *freedom now*, not ten years from now.

To ask us to "be patient," to ask that of any parents, black or white, is to ask that we deprive our children of their birthright.

In spite of Martin's being away so much, he was wonderful with his children, and they adored him. When Daddy was home it was something special. Occasionally when I had to go to a church meeting, or do some shopping, Martin would baby-sit, and how they loved that! They had a wild time together. They often played on the bed. The children would roughhouse and jump on top of him. I might come into my bedroom and find all our family sitting on top of him. I must admit that I occasionally got cross about things being thrown helter-skelter in the room and the house almost being dismantled, but Martin would appear to be so surprised at my annoyance, which always completely disarmed me.

When Yoki was very young, Martin invented a game in which he would put her on top of the refrigerator and tell her to jump, and then he would catch her in his arms. She loved it! She would say, "Let's go up," which meant being put on top of the refrigerator. It frightened me so because I thought someday he might miss his catch. But he never did—even as Marty, Dexter, and Bernice came along and they all had their turn at the game.

One of the games which gave me the greatest pleasure to watch was a kissing game between Bernice and Martin. Whenever Martin came home, as soon as he entered the doorway Bernice would run and swing into his arms. He would stoop to lift her up and say, "Give me some good old sugar!" With her arms around his neck, she would smack him on the mouth. He had previously taught her where the sugar spot was for each person in the family. He would then say, "I bet you don't know where Yoki's sugar is!" She would then smack him on the right side of his mouth. "Where is Dexter's sugar?" Then she kissed him on the right cheek. Next he would say, "I know you don't know where Marty's sugar is!" She would quickly kiss him on the forehead. "I just know you've forgotten where Mommy's sugar is!" She would kiss him in the center of his mouth. Finally, he would say, "And Bunny doesn't have any sugar." "Yes, I do!" And with a loud smack, she would kiss him on the right cheek.

When she found all the designated sugar spots, which she always did quickly, the game ended.

There were a few quiet evenings, too, when Martin would read to the children from their favorite books. Whatever he did, they were happy just being with him.

Martin was also very much involved in his duties as co-pastor at Ebenezer during this period, and of course his work in the Movement continued.

The lessons we had learned in Albany made for our eventual success in Birmingham. In May 1962, at a board meeting of SCLC in Nashville, Reverend Fred Shuttlesworth proposed that our organization join his Alabama Christian Movement for Human Rights in a massive campaign against segregation in Birmingham. The board of SCLC agreed to his proposal, but delayed action until early in 1963.

It was a daring decision. Birmingham was a great manufacturing center, the richest city in Alabama. Most of its white people and the city officials were adamantly opposed to integration of any sort. Mayor Arthur Hanes was an arch-segregationist, and Commissioner of Public Safety Eugene (Bull) Connor was a virulent racist whose nickname aptly characterized his brutality. To make things worse, George Wallace was elected Governor of Alabama in November 1962. His campaign slogan was "Segregation Forever." Although forty percent of Birmingham's population was black, there were only ten thousand registered voters out of eighty thousand. In the preceding five years (1957–62) there had been seventeen unsolved bombings of black churches and homes. Local racists intimidated, mobbed, and even killed African Americans with impunity. Martin had said, "It is the most thoroughly segregated city in America. All the evils and injustices the Negro can be subjected to are right there in Birmingham."

On the other hand, Fred Shuttlesworth, who was a fearless man, had dared to send his children to public schools and tried to desegregate them. He had been beaten and his home and his church had been bombed. His wife had been jailed and beaten;

his whole family had suffered terribly. By this time he was a genuine symbol of the struggle for social justice.

Reverend Shuttlesworth's organization was one of SCLC's strongest affiliates in the South. In January 1962, the students of Miles College joined with the organization to begin a boycott of segregated stores in Birmingham. They had made significant progress. Martin believed that although "the campaign in Birmingham would surely be the toughest fight of our civil rights career, it could, if successful, break the back of segregation all over the nation."

After a three-day planning session of SCLC's high command, in which "Project C" was outlined, Martin carried the campaign to Birmingham. Field staff from SCLC began working in Birmingham in January of 1963. Since Albany had proved that the scatter-gun attack on segregation was impractical, they decided to concentrate on more specific objectives—the desegregation of lunch counters, dressing rooms, and rest rooms, and the reform of hiring practices of Birmingham's big downtown stores. The protest demonstrations were set to start on March 12, 1963, to disrupt Easter shopping. Actually, we also delayed because an election was to take place on March 5, in which Bull Connor would oppose two comparatively moderate candidates, Albert Boutwell and Tom King, for Mayor of Birmingham. Martin did not want to do anything that might help Connor.

Meanwhile the work of organization went forward meticulously. Our staff had already begun to prepare the community through mass meetings and workshops on nonviolence.

People who would be willing to go to jail were asked to sign a commitment card that read:

I hereby pledge myself—my person and my body—to the nonviolent movement. Therefore, I will keep the following ten commandments:

1. Meditate daily on the teachings and life of Jesus.
2. Remember always that the nonviolent movement in Birmingham seeks justice and reconciliation—not victory.
3. Walk and talk in the manner of love; for God is love.

4. Pray daily to be used by God in order that all men might be free.
5. Sacrifice personal wishes that all men might be free.
6. Observe with both friend and foe the ordinary rules of courtesy.
7. Seek to perform regular service for others and for the world.
8. Refrain from the violence of fist, tongue, and heart.
9. Strive to be in good spiritual and bodily health.
10. Follow the directions of the movement and of the captains on a demonstration.

Meanwhile, Harry Belafonte called a meeting of seventy-five prominent people in his New York apartment. Martin and Fred Shuttlesworth spoke to them of the difficulties and dangers of the Birmingham protest. Fred, wearing the scars of other battles, told them, "You have to be prepared to die before you can begin to live."

In January 1963, my husband, Ralph Abernathy, and Fred Shuttlesworth had a conference with President Kennedy and Attorney General Robert Kennedy at the White House to urge the federal government to initiate civil rights legislation in 1963. The Kennedys were, as always, sympathetic, but they said they had no plans for proposing any civil rights legislation in 1963. The President said he was going to propose some important domestic legislation, and he feared that anything in the civil rights area would divide the Congress and imperil these bills.

Naturally, Martin was very disappointed. He felt he had no choice but to go ahead with his plans to force a confrontation in Birmingham so that the federal government would have to act. He frankly told the President his intentions, because if white violence erupted we would need the support and help of the federal government. He wanted the President to be informed in advance.

In the election in Birmingham on March 5, 1963, Boutwell led, with Connor second, and Tom King third. Since no candidate had a majority, there had to be a runoff between Boutwell and Connor.

On April 2, Martin again delayed the start of the protest until after the runoff.

This time Boutwell won a clear majority, but Connor claimed some legal technicality whereby the new city government could not take office until 1964. While all this was being decided in the courts, the old officials remained in office, with Connor as commissioner for public safety. Martin felt he could delay the demonstrations no longer. The Birmingham Movement began.

We were expecting the arrival of our fourth child at any moment. My husband was constantly out of town making speeches all over the country, and the time was fast approaching when he would have to move into Birmingham. I had been afraid he would have to go before my baby came, but Bernice Albertine was born on March 28. Martin was there to take me to the hospital, but the next day, after the baby was born, he left for Birmingham. Then he dashed back to Atlanta in time to bring me home from the hospital, but left the same evening for his headquarters.

Though it was difficult for me at the time, I had tried to prepare myself for Martin being away most of the time during my recuperation. I suppose that with each new baby a wife wants her husband to be there to share the experience, even though, in my own case, I had gone through the experience three times before. However, I recognized that what Martin was doing could not be delayed and that it was so important that he be in Birmingham. As a matter of fact, I deeply regretted that circumstances had prevented me from being there with him. I knew that he had anticipated the possibility of going to jail and I was deeply concerned that I would not be there to comfort him. Of course, that is exactly what happened.

In Birmingham, Martin found some resistance to SCLC's program in the black community itself. Under the system of complete segregation, this attitude was not uncommon. There were several reasons. One was that the black masses had been brainwashed into accepting the idea that it was impossible to fight the system. The second was that a few of the Birmingham black leaders felt the timing was poor—that the new Boutwell government should be given a chance. Also, there was slight resentment among local leaders of "outsiders" running the show.

The protest started on April 3, 1963, with lunch counter sit-ins. In the first three days alone, thirty-five people were arrested. On Saturday, April 6, an orderly march of carefully selected demonstrators moved toward City Hall. They were stopped three blocks from their goal. Forty-two people were arrested for parading without a permit. They were politely escorted to the paddy wagon and driven to jail. They were singing freedom songs while thousands of blacks cheered them from the sidewalks.

After that, demonstrations were staged every day with increasing strength. Thus far, Bull Connor's police had behaved very well while making the arrests. Between four and five hundred black people were arrested, and though some got out on bail, about three hundred remained in jail.

During this time Martin was trying to get the merchants and the Birmingham city officials to negotiate our very moderate demands—desegregation of store facilities, upgrading and hiring of African Americans on a nondiscriminatory basis, dropping of charges against the imprisoned protesters, and creation of a biracial committee to work out a timetable for further desegregation in Birmingham. The businessmen were willing to negotiate at this point. The city officials were not.

On Wednesday these city officials obtained an injunction against the demonstrators, but it was issued by an Alabama state court, not a federal court. Martin promptly announced that the injunction would be disobeyed. He pointed out that the African Americans were not "anarchists advocating lawlessness," but that the courts of Alabama had misused the judicial process. He said that "we could not in good conscience obey their mandate." As a countermove, the courts announced that bail bonds would no longer be accepted; it would be necessary to post cash. As it happened, our organization was fresh out of cash.

Martin had set Good Friday, April 12, for the day that he and some of the other leaders would provoke arrest by breaking the injunction. He had deliberately chosen that day because of its symbolic and religious significance. Early that morning a tempestuous meeting of the leaders took place in the Gaston Motel. Several of the ministers felt that they should obey the injunction. Ralph Abernathy pointed out that he was the only pastor of his church and would be unable to perform his duties at this holy season of the year. Martin, on the other hand, was co-pastor of Ebenezer, and his father could carry on.

Martin recognized the validity of this argument. At the same time, he remembered that obeying the federal injunction had wrecked the Albany Movement. After a long discussion he said, "I want to meditate about this decision."

For half an hour the others waited while Martin thought and prayed alone in his room. When he came out he was wearing work clothes—blue jeans and a shirt—and his face was set in the stern lines of his resolve. "I've decided to take a leap of faith. I've decided to go to jail. I don't know what's going to happen; I don't know whether this Movement will continue to build up or whether it will collapse. If enough people are willing to go to jail, I believe it will force the city officials to act or force the federal government to act. So I'm going today."

Then Martin turned to Ralph Abernathy and said, "I know you want to be in your pulpit on Easter Sunday, Ralph, but I am asking you to go with me."

Ralph said, "Well, you know, I have always been in jail with you, Martin, and I can't leave you at this point."

The twenty-five men in Room 30 all linked hands and sang "We Shall Overcome." Then Martin embraced his father and they all drove to the Zion Hill Church, where the march was scheduled to start. As they came into the church, the people were singing and praying. Martin went directly to the pulpit to tell them of his decision.

There is no exact record of his words, but people told me afterward that he made a very dramatic and moving address. He said that things were so bad in Birmingham that he had decided they could be changed only by the redemptive influence of suffering. Then Martin spoke of wanting to be a good servant of his

Lord and Master, who was crucified on Good Friday. He told the brothers and sisters that he had decided to go to jail.

As he left the pulpit and walked down the aisle, women and men were calling their response. Someone shouted, "There he goes, just like Jesus." And people poured out into the aisle and followed him. It was tremendously moving.

Martin wrote of this experience:

> It seemed that every Birmingham police officer had been sent into the area. Leaving the church . . . we started down the forbidden streets that lead to the downtown sector. It was a beautiful march. We were allowed to walk farther than the police had ever permitted before. . . . All along the way Negroes lined the streets. We were singing, and they were joining in. Occasionally the singing from the sidewalks was interspersed with applause.
>
> As we neared the downtown area, Bull Connor ordered his men to arrest us. Ralph and I were hauled off by two muscular policemen, clutching the backs of our shirts in handfuls. All the others were promptly arrested.

For the first time in going to jail, Ralph and Martin were separated. Each of them was held in solitary confinement. Not even the lawyers were permitted to see them. "Those hours were," he said, "the longest and most frustrating and bewildering of my life." He was besieged with worry about his friends, about the fate of the Movement, and about me and our brand-new baby, and the other children at home.

Back in Atlanta, I waited anxiously to hear from Martin. When I got the news that Martin had been arrested that Friday afternoon, I just knew he would telephone me from jail, which was always the first thing he did after he was arrested. No call came. All the next day I waited. Then it was Easter Sunday morning. In Birmingham Martin's brother, A.D., held Easter service in his church. Then, wearing his ministerial robes and carrying the Bible, he led a group of worshipers toward the city jail, where they intended to pray for Martin and his fellow prisoners. They were arrested after marching only a few blocks.

Still I had heard nothing. In desperation I telephoned Wyatt Walker in Birmingham. He said, "Coretta, I haven't been able to get a phone message through to Martin. I've tried all day. They are not even allowing his lawyers to see him now. They're holding him incommunicado."

I asked, "Wyatt, do you think if I made a statement to the press about this situation it would help?"

Wyatt answered, "Do you know what I think you should do? I think you ought to call the President."

I thought about it and said, "I will try if you think I should, but first I wish you would try to check with Martin to see if it's all right with him, because I wouldn't want to do it if he didn't approve."

That was the first Easter Sunday in my adult life that I was not able to go to church; but Easter had more meaning for me than ever before because of this particular experience. I was terribly anxious about Martin's safety and wondered what was happening to him. I waited and waited for Wyatt to call back. Finally he did. He said, "It's no use, Coretta. I can't get through to Martin. You have no alternative but to call the President."

I called the White House several times to see if I could get a number in West Palm Beach, where the President was reportedly staying, but each time the operator would say, "I have no number for the President or members of his family at West Palm Beach."

I thought, "Now whom should I call?"

I told the operator to try Vice-President Lyndon Johnson, but he too was out of the city. Quite frantically I said, "There must be someone I could call who would be able to help me get to the President."

Since she was a kind and sympathetic woman, the operator said, "What about Pierre Salinger?"

Immediately I reached Pierre Salinger, the President's press secretary, who told me that he would make every effort to get in touch with the President and get him to call me. While I was waiting, Harry Belafonte called and said, "I was just thinking about you and the children. I don't want you to worry about Martin."

I said, "I haven't heard from him, and I *am* deeply concerned. As a matter of fact, I have just tried to reach the President."

Harry was a little alarmed at that. But I explained that all I had wanted to do was to tell the President how anxious I was about Martin's safety. I explained to Harry that I had thought the matter through carefully and had decided it was right to seek some intercession so that my husband could talk to me. I reassured Harry that I would in no way give the impression that I was trying to get Martin out of jail. We both knew that he would certainly not want that.

I was awfully depressed, and I told Harry the problems I was having—the telephone ringing all the time, with people concerned about Martin as well as about me, and at the same time I was trying to take care of my children and the new baby, and wanting desperately to go to Birmingham to be near my husband. Harry listened and took charge. He, good friend that he is, told me to hire a secretary and a nurse, at his expense, and he added that he wanted to go to Birmingham with me.

While we were talking my other telephone rang, and when I answered, a familiar voice said, "Mrs. King, this is Attorney General Robert Kennedy. I am returning your call to my brother. The President wasn't able to talk to you because he's with my father, who is quite ill. He wanted me to call you to find out what we can do for you."

I poured out a rush of words: "I was calling because I am concerned about my husband. As you probably know, he is in jail in Birmingham, and he's been there since Friday. At this point, no one is able to see him. Usually they let him telephone me, but I have heard nothing from him directly. I understand that he and Reverend Abernathy are being held incommunicado, and I am awfully worried. I wondered if the President could check into the situation and see if he's all right."

I tried to make it clear that I was concerned about Martin's safety and was not asking for his release. I explained that, at first, they had allowed his lawyer to talk with him and that it was my understanding that Martin was sleeping on bare steel springs, without blankets or a pillow.

Attorney General Kennedy said, "Well, I'm sorry you have not been able to talk to your husband, but I'll tell you, Mrs. King, we have a difficult problem with the local officials. Bull Connor is very hard to deal with. Maybe after the new city government takes over we can get something done in Birmingham. But I promise you I will look into the situation and let you know something."

The Attorney General seemed deeply concerned and I felt better after I hung up, because there seemed some chance that something might be done.

But it was not until the next day, Monday, that I heard anything more. At about five o'clock in the afternoon the telephone rang, and as I picked up the receiver, I heard little two-year-old Dexter babbling away on the extension. The operator said, "Will you get your child off the phone, please?" I had someone get him off the phone, and waited until a voice came on saying, "Hello, Mrs. King. I'm sorry I wasn't able to talk to you yesterday. I understand my brother called you. I just wanted you to know that I was with my father, who is ill, and couldn't leave him."

By that time I realized it was President Kennedy. In the confusion about Dexter I had not heard the operator announce him. I told him I was sorry that his father was ill, and the President asked how I was and explained that he knew I'd just had a baby.

I answered, "I am all right, but I'm terribly concerned about my husband."

President Kennedy said, "I know you'll be interested in knowing that we sent the FBI into Birmingham last night. We checked on your husband, and he's all right." And the President said, "Of course, Birmingham is a very difficult place."

He talked a little while about the situation there and the city officials. Then he added, "I want you to know we are doing everything we can. I have just talked to Birmingham, and your husband will be calling you shortly. If you have any further worries about your husband or about Birmingham in the next few days, I want you to feel free to call me. You can get me or my brother or Mr. Salinger. You know how to get me now."

I could hardly thank him enough. What relief he had brought to my heart. I could hardly wait for the telephone to ring. Within fifteen minutes Martin called. It was almost like a new miracle.

"Are you all right, my dear?" I asked.

Martin told me he was all right, but he sounded so tired—he usually fasted when he was in jail. There was no energy in his voice.

We talked a little before I told Martin about my phone conversation with the President.

There was a sort of smile in Martin's voice as he said, "So that's why everybody is suddenly being so polite. This is good to know."

I learned later that Martin had suddenly been taken from his cell for exercise and allowed to take a shower, and he had been given a mattress and a pillow.

Over the telephone Martin told me—indirectly, without mentioning names, because jail officials were standing around him—to get word to Wyatt Walker about my conversation with the President so that a statement could be released to the press.

I believe that President Kennedy's intervention gave real momentum to the Birmingham Movement. The fact that he was concerned and wanted justice done heartened our people. It also helped the city officials to realize that they could not commit such inhuman practices and not be exposed. As for me, even though I understood that there were political overtones, I believed President Kennedy sincerely cared about what happened to us. There was an amazing warmth about him. Of course, his action in the Atlanta sit-in case had already endeared him and the Kennedy family to the black community.

Martin was in jail for eight days. While in prison he wrote his famous open letter, "Letter from a Birmingham Jail," to a group of eight white Alabama clergymen who had issued a statement calling the protest "unwise and untimely" and had characterized Martin as an "outside agitator" who had come to Birmingham seeking publicity. Martin wrote the letter on the margins of newspapers and scraps of toilet paper. He said, "I am in Birmingham because injustice is here." Then he delved deeply into his whole philosophy of the Movement, and what he believed the attitude of the Christian churches should be toward it. He wrote that in the same way that one should obey just laws, one has a moral responsibility to disobey unjust laws, and he quoted St. Augustine, saying, "An unjust law is no law at all." Martin castigated the white moderates who put order above justice. In answer to the ministers' statement that he was an extremist, he replied, "Was not Jesus an extremist for love?" And he told them of his disappointment that so many white Christian ministers had not seen fit to follow the words of Jesus. He pointed out that the Apostles were "outside agitators" in the countries to which they carried Christ's message.

In closing, Martin said, "One day the South will know that when these disinherited children of God sat down at lunch counters, they were in reality standing up for what is best in the American dream and for the most sacred values of our Judaeo-Christian heritage. . . ." And he expressed the hope "that circumstances will soon make it possible for me to meet each of you, not as an integrationist or a civil-rights leader, but as a fellow clergyman and a Christian brother."

It was clear in his letter and in his life that Martin felt no bitterness against these men of God who had attacked him. His feeling was one of brotherhood and compassion always.

Juanita Abernathy and I flew to Birmingham on Thursday to visit our husbands. On Saturday, April 20, they were released from jail. That very evening, at the Gaston Motel, a leadership conference hit upon the brilliant scheme of enlisting the black schoolchildren of Birmingham in the crusade for freedom. Martin realized that he would be severely criticized for using our children in this fashion, but he thought that the time had come to give the Movement "a dramatic new dimension." In addition, he felt that it was the children who would benefit most from desegregation, that it was the children for whom we were fighting, and that taking part in the Movement would give them a sense of worth and dignity and increase their spiritual values. At the same time, everything possible would be done to protect them from physical danger.

Andy Young, Bernard Lee, Jim Bevel, and others went recruiting to all the high schools of Birmingham (as well as the black colleges), and the children responded by the thousands. They attended mass meetings and training sessions in the philosophy and techniques of nonviolence. Of them Martin said, "We found them eager to belong, hungry for participation in a significant social effort." Even children too young to march asked for a place in our ranks. Andy Young told them, "You are too young to go to jail. Go to the library. You'll learn something there."

Six small children shyly followed his advice and, all by themselves, desegregated the library, because no one dared touch them.

On "D Day," May 2, Martin addressed a group of eager youngsters at the Sixteenth Street Baptist Church. Then they marched downtown, singing "We Shall Overcome" as they came. They were all arrested. Wave after wave of children marched off singing, to suffer the same treatment; 959 young people were arrested that day.

The next morning Martin announced, "Yesterday was D Day in Birmingham. Today will be Double D Day."

With the spotlight of the nation on him, Bull Connor was becoming desperate. He massed police in the streets around the Sixteenth Street Church. As a thousand children and teenagers marched toward them, he ordered the fire hoses opened. Jets of water under a hundred pounds of pressure knocked the children flat, ripping the clothes off some of them. Then Connor unleashed the police dogs—they ran wild, biting the children. The youngsters maintained nonviolence, but it was too much for some of our people who watched in agony from the rooftops. They began to throw rocks.

Late Sunday afternoon the Reverend Charles Billups led a group of adults from the New Pilgrim Baptist Church to the police barricade. They knelt in the street and prayed. Then they walked forward. Bull Connor himself arrived and ordered Reverend Billups to turn back. Billups refused, and his people shouted, "Turn on the water! Loose the dogs! We ain't going back. Forgive them, O Lord."

In a fury, Bull Connor shouted, "Turn on the hoses damnit!"

But a miraculous thing happened. As the black people rose from their knees and moved forward, Connor's men, with the hoses sagging in their hands, fell back to each side. The moral pressure of a watching world and the spiritual force of that little band of blacks broke their discipline—disarmed them. Between their ranks, past the leashed dogs, Billups led his people. They held a prayer meeting in a nearby park and marched back to their church singing freedom songs. It was the first crack in the morale of the racist forces.

All the next week the Children's Crusade continued. Birmingham's jails were full. The arrested young people were held in stockades or halls. Finally there were too many to cope with. As five hundred youngsters marched on Tuesday, the police broke up the demonstration but arrested no one. Three thousand people, mostly youngsters, infiltrated past the police by different routes and marched around the downtown streets, in and out of the stores, singing, "Ain't Gonna Let Nobody Turn Me Around" and "I'm on My Way to Freedom Land." Governor Wallace called out the National Guard.

Meanwhile tremendous moral pressure was building up in the nation. The newspaper and television pictures of the young people prostrated by fire hoses, beaten up, and bitten by dogs brought a storm of telegrams to the White House. To people everywhere, Bull Connor came to represent the force of evil. Martin had said, "I hope to subpoena the conscience of the nation to the judgment seat of morality." And that is exactly what happened.

On May 4 President Kennedy sent Burke Marshall to Birmingham to try to negotiate a settlement. All that week, while the protests and arrests were going on, he conferred with the white businessmen and with Martin and the other black leaders. Through his influence the white leaders were also holding secret talks with Martin and his colleagues. At first the whites were so intransigent that Marshall despaired of bringing them to reason. After the meeting on Tuesday, May 7, one hundred and twenty-five white leaders adjourned for lunch. When they left the building they found thousands of blacks had marched into town. According to Martin, "There were square blocks of Negroes, a veritable sea of black faces. They were committing no violence; they were just present and singing. Downtown Birmingham echoed to the strains of the freedom songs."

After this sight of such large numbers of militantly nonviolent blacks, the white leaders returned in a much more reasonable mood. Martin and the others negotiated with them all night Wednesday, practically all day Thursday, and all Thursday night. On Friday, May 10, an agreement was announced. It was almost word for word an acceptance of the original demands of the Movement. The stores were to be desegregated, hiring of African Americans upgraded, charges dropped, and the Senior Citizens Committee or the Chamber of Commerce would meet regularly with black leaders to reconcile their differences.

Martin, Ralph Abernathy, and Fred Shuttlesworth immediately issued a conciliatory statement: "The acceptance of responsibility by local white and Negro leadership offers an example of a free people uniting to meet and solve their problems. Birmingham may well offer twentieth-century America an example of progressive racial relations; and for all mankind a dawn of a new day, a promise for all men, a day of opportunity and a new sense of freedom for all America."

Of course, that was not the end of it, but Martin came home to me that night and we rejoiced together. There was an awful eruption of violence in Birmingham the next night, just as there had been in Montgomery after the bus settlement there.

A.D.'s home was "double-bombed." When the first bomb exploded, he grabbed his wife, Naomi, and pulled her with him into the back room, just as a second bomb blew the whole front of the house off. Still another bomb aimed at Room 30 blew up the office of the Gaston Motel where Martin had been staying. In Birmingham thousands of enraged black people went onto the streets, and violent rioting broke out. Whoever planted the bombs *wanted* African Americans to riot.

A.D. did his best to stop it. Standing in the ruins of his own home, he exhorted the people to keep to nonviolence. Though he could not fully control them, it was felt that his plea and presence restrained them. Governor Wallace's National Guard moved in to seal off the black ghetto. Martin rushed back to Birmingham on Sunday and went through the town, speaking wherever our people were gathered. He, Ralph Abernathy, Fred Shuttlesworth, Wyatt

Walker, and A. D. King went to all the black shops and restaurants. They even went into the poolrooms, preaching nonviolence. What a marvelous display of the spirit of nonviolence as the people gave them the knives and guns and other weapons with which they had armed themselves. They returned with a load of weapons and Birmingham gradually calmed down to implementing the agreements.

Birmingham represented a real victory for the Movement because the officials of the city and the white merchants sat down with the black leadership and negotiated a settlement. Peace finally came because *militant nonviolence* had forced negotiation and agreement. Though it cost much struggle and turmoil and pain, real progress was achieved.

The victory had broad implications. Martin's long-range strategy in going into Birmingham was to focus national attention on the grave injustices endured by African Americans, and to bring about federal legislation. To this end he deliberately chose a very tough city, because in that setting the evil of the system was highlighted and the world could see it for what it is.

My husband had written that Birmingham was the colossus of segregation; a victory there would radiate across the South, cracking the whole edifice of discrimination. And it happened as he had predicted. Within a few months, nearly one thousand cities were engulfed in the turmoil of change. Except for the Civil War and the Reconstruction, black people had never acted along such a broad front, in a direct-action drive to alter the conditions of their lives. Nearly a million African Americans, with their white allies, had marched or otherwise demonstrated in the streets of hundreds of cities in that historic summer. By its end, thousands of public accommodations were wedged open and a new chapter in race relations was begun. Objectively, exclusion was narrowed; subjectively, the confidence of African Americans was widened and deepened. This confidence was later to become the foundation for black pride and slogans of black power. The fall of Birmingham was a turning point almost too significant to be grasped at the time of its happening.

Politically, as a result of the struggles there, President Kennedy reassessed the position of his Administration and decided to propose a civil rights bill in 1963. It was eventually passed by Congress in 1964.

At a conference on the proposed bill at the White House, President Kennedy said to Martin with a wry grin, "Bull Connor has done as much for civil rights as Abraham Lincoln."

13

"I have a dream"

Nineteen sixty-three was a year of fulfillment and of tragedy for us. First, there was Birmingham, with the sense of hope and accomplishment we derived from it. Then, hardly a month later, on June 12, the young Mississippi NAACP leader Medgar Evers was shot dead in the very door of his home in Jackson. His wife, Myrlie, heard the shot, and she and her children ran outside to find her husband lying on the ground, covered with blood. Medgar looked up, saw his young boy, and called, "Help me, my son, help me."

There was no help for Medgar. He died about an hour later, the victim of a powerful and vengeful hatred.

Medgar had been a good friend of Martin's, and we were deeply grieved. Then, how could I not feel that it might have been Martin?

That June, Martin went off on a speaking tour, and bigger crowds than ever before turned out to hear him. Twenty-five thousand came in Los Angeles, and nearly two hundred thousand people took part in a parade that he led with Walter Reuther, the president of the United Automobile Workers, in Detroit.

I remember saying to Martin, "People all over the nation have been so aroused by the impact of Birmingham that you should call a massive March on Washington to further dramatize the need for legislation to completely integrate the black man into American society. I believe a hundred thousand people would come to the nation's capital at your invitation."

There were others who felt that the momentum Birmingham had generated should not be allowed to die out. A conference was held with the heads of other organizations—A. Philip Randolph, head of the Negro American Labor Council; Roy Wilkins of the NAACP; John Lewis of SNCC; Dorothy Height of the National Council of Negro Women; James Farmer of CORE; and Whitney Young of the Urban League. It was Mr. Randolph who proposed a massive March on Washington for Jobs and Freedom.

We all enthusiastically accepted the idea. Because of the tremendous turnout in the cities Martin had visited, we hoped that a hundred thousand people would join the Washington march. Then, since Martin was greatly troubled by sporadic outbreaks of rioting in some cities, he felt that a great peaceful demonstration in Washington would provide the black masses with a chance for nonviolent protest and at the same time put pressure on Congress to pass President Kennedy's Civil Rights Bill.

The Washington march was set for August 28, 1963. It was to be a short march down the Mall from the Washington Monument to the Lincoln Memorial, where the speeches would be made. We were very hopeful for the success of the demonstration. Everything looked right. Our own leaders were united, and working together very effectively; we were getting enthusiastic support from the people, black and white, and encouragement from the federal and local governments in Washington.

On August 27, Martin and I went to Washington from Atlanta with members of the SCLC staff. In our hotel suite Martin began revising his speech, trying to condense it to the eight minutes that had been allotted to him. He worked on it all night, not sleeping a wink. It was about three o'clock in the morning when I fell asleep. I must say that I felt guilty at being able to sleep while Martin anxiously pored over his speech. In Detroit he had spoken about his dream of a free united land, but in view of the shortness of the time given him, he decided against using that theme. Instead he planned to speak from the theme of America issuing blacks a bad check, and what this meant in terms of the Emancipation Proclamation, since 1963 was its centenary. He intended to echo some of the Lincolnian language.

As Martin worked, he would call on those of us who were in the room for some word that better expressed his thought, but as often as not it was he who would supply it. He was to be the final speaker, and his words would be carried on television and radio to millions of people in America and throughout the world, so it was vitally important that his speech be both inspiring and wise. When Martin finished it, bone weary, almost in collapse from exhaustion, he had written a good speech. But he delivered a better one that next day.

The sound of typewriters and voices in the next room awakened me early. I found my husband watching the crowds from the window of our hotel suite. As it approached the time that the march was to begin, we became anxious about how large the turnout would be. The reports on television were very discouraging. "A very small number of people have assembled," they said. Before we left the hotel they were saying, "About twenty-five thousand." We were subdued and saddened because that was a far cry from the hundred thousand we had hoped for.

Then, when we reached the Mall, our spirits soared. The reporters had grossly underestimated the crowd—there were ninety thousand assembled by ten o'clock, and, by the time we arrived, that whole vast, green concourse was alive with two hundred and fifty thousand people. They had come by plane, train, bus, automobile, some by bicycle, and a few by foot, from all parts of the nation. Almost a fourth of that enormous crowd was white. It was a beautiful sight.

At the Mall I was separated from Martin. It had been my great wish to march beside him, not from any desire to share the spotlight, but because I wanted the joy of being with him on this special day. However, it had been decided by the planning council that the march would be led by the top leadership, and of course I had to accede to their wishes. I must confess, though, that I felt that the involvement in the Movement of some of the wives had been so extensive that they should have been granted the privilege of marching with their husbands and of completely sharing this experience together, as they had shared the dangers and hardships.

Although no seat had been provided for me on the platform, Ralph helped me get a seat almost directly behind Martin. As I sat there and looked out over the great colorful assemblage, I realized it was the biggest crowd I had ever seen, or anybody else had seen in the same place, at one time. The tremendous gathering of people seemed to stretch along the wide Mall all the way back to the high stone needle of the Washington Monument. If you have never seen two hundred and fifty thousand people in one place before, it is an awesome but inspiring sight!

We knew that, in addition, there were millions watching on television, including President Kennedy in the White House.

About one o'clock the ceremony started with Camilla Williams, lovely in the strong, hot sunlight, singing "The Star-Spangled Banner." Marian Anderson had been scheduled to sing "The Star-Spangled Banner," but her plane was delayed. She arrived later, obviously flustered and disappointed. A. Philip Randolph, the chairman of the ceremonies, introduced the Reverend Fred Shuttlesworth, who said, "We came here because we love our country; because our country needs us and we need our country." One after another, the leaders were introduced and spoke. They were all powerful speakers who had strong feelings to express. It was such a long program, I remember thinking how Martin must have been growing tired and how awfully hard it might be for him as the last speaker to arouse the audience. The speeches were interspersed with freedom songs sung by some of America's greatest artists. Mr. Randolph introduced Roy Wilkins, who, as always, spoke convincingly and effectively. When Mr. Wilkins finished, it was past three o'clock, and the heat was intense. You could see that the crowd was growing restless as people drifted away. But when Mahalia Jackson was introduced, they came back and the restlessness ceased. We all listened to her wonderful voice with so much "soul," which Martin dearly loved, as she sang "I've Been 'Buked and I've Been Scorned." Then A. Philip Randolph rose to introduce Martin. He called my husband "the *moral* leader of the nation." Two hundred and fifty thousand people applauded thunderously, and voiced in a sort of chant, *Martin Luther King.*

Martin was tremendously moved. I could tell by the line of his back and the sound of his voice—a little husky at first, then going out in a strong and beautifully resonant tone that came when he was inspired to his best. He started out with the written speech, delivering it with great eloquence. His main contention was that "instead of honoring her sacred obligations, America has given the Negro a bad check. We are here today to redeem that check, and we will not accept the idea that there is no money in the Bank of Justice." When he got to the rhythmic part of demanding freedom *now,* and wanting jobs *now,* the crowd caught the timing and shouted *now* in a cadence. Their response lifted Martin in a surge of emotion to new heights of inspiration. Abandoning his written speech, forgetting time, he spoke from his heart, his voice soaring magnificently out over that great crowd and over to all the world. It seemed to all of us there that day that his words flowed from some higher place, through Martin, to the weary people before him. Yea—Heaven itself opened up and we all seemed transformed.

He said,

> I say to you today even though we face the difficulties of today and tomorrow, I still have a dream. It is a dream that is deeply rooted in the American dream. I have a dream that one day this nation will rise up, live out the true meaning of its creed: We hold these truths to be self-evident, that all men are created equal.
>
> I have a dream that one day on the red hills of Georgia the sons of former slaves and the sons of former slave-owners will be able to sit down together at the table of brotherhood. I have a dream that one day even the state of Mississippi, a state sweltering with the heat of oppression, will be transformed into an oasis of freedom and justice.
>
> I have a dream that my four little children one day will live in a nation where they will not be judged by the color of their skin, but by the content of their character.
>
> I have a dream that one day every valley shall be exalted, every hill and mountain shall be made low. The rough places will be made plain and the crooked places

will be made straight. This is the faith that I go back to the South with. With this faith we will be able to hew out of the mountains of despair the stone of hope. With this faith we will be able to work together, to pray together, to struggle together, to go to jail together, to stand up for freedom together, knowing we will be free one day.

This will be the day when all of God's children will be able to sing with new meaning, "Let freedom ring." So let freedom ring from the prodigious hilltops of New Hampshire; let freedom ring from the mighty mountains of New York. But not only that. Let freedom ring from Stone Mountain of Georgia. Let freedom ring from every hill and molehill of Mississippi, from every mountainside.

When we allow freedom to ring from every town and every hamlet, from every state and every city, we will be able to speed up that day when all of God's children, black men and white men, Jews and Gentiles, Protestants and Catholics, will be able to join hands and sing in the words of the old Negro spiritual, "Free at last! Free at last! Great God A-mighty, we are free at last!"

As Martin ended, there was the awed silence that is the greatest tribute an orator can be paid. And then a tremendous crash of sound as two hundred and fifty thousand people shouted in ecstatic accord with his words. The feeling that they had of oneness and unity was complete. They kept on shouting in one thunderous voice, and for that brief moment the Kingdom of God seemed to have come on earth.

When Martin's speech was over, the marshals made an attempt to get him away, because the people would have mobbed him. They formed a circle around him. I remembered that just before the march started, Mrs. Roy Wilkins, who had been marching with the social workers and was hot and tired and had difficulty getting to the platform, had said, "If I ever get my hands on Roy, I'm not going to turn him loose." And I said to myself, "If I ever get *my* hands on Martin, I'm not going to turn *him* loose." I got up immediately and put my arm through his so I wouldn't be left behind. As we left the platform, I clung to Martin. At one point I felt a marshal pulling at me and heard another one say, "Watch it, man, that's Mrs. King."

We finally made it to where cars were waiting to take the ten top leaders to the White House to confer with President Kennedy. Though I rode with Martin, when we arrived at the White House gate, Mrs. Wilkins and I slipped out and got a taxi back to the hotel.

This was perhaps the closest I came to meeting our beloved President John F. Kennedy, and it was not very close. When I asked Martin if I might sit in on the conference, he informed me that I could not because it would be against protocol to have me come unless I had been previously invited. Just the same, I was hurt, and even more so when the horrible event at Dallas took place only three months later.

The Abernathys and other friends went out to dinner and to celebrate that night, but I stayed right in the hotel because I was so anxious to see Martin and to share with him the experiences of that great day. Martin had had to go from the White House to a television appearance to be transmitted to Europe, and when he finally came it was ten o'clock.

Of course, we talked for hours about how wonderful it all had been. I told Martin of my pride and joy in him, and we discussed the effects the march would have on the American people. Imagine, with all those people, black and white, from all walks of life, from all parts of the country, there had not been one unpleasant incident—that was the wonderful part of the demonstration. Though some commentators had predicted violence, there had been none. The enormous crowd had come quietly and with great dignity, and when it was over they dispersed peacefully to their homes. Martin and I knew how important this would be for the Cause and the nation.

I also felt that the tremendous response to his great speech—perhaps his greatest—had completely restored the people's faith in the principle of nonviolence, and that it had established Martin beyond doubt as what A. Philip Randolph had named him, the moral leader of the nation.

We were so exalted when we left Washington, as was everyone who had participated. So many people have told me of their feelings in the days following the march, and they were mine also. We all had felt that a great human milestone, a great spiritual communion, had taken place on August 28, 1963. One of the most important things to be remembered in terms of the impact of Martin's speech at the March on Washington is that many white people who were not involved or sympathetic to the demands of African Americans, for the first time, got the message of what we had been trying to say in Montgomery, Albany, and Birmingham. They had surely gained a new respect for him and his Cause. Yet, when we went home, we returned to another kind of reality. Though the march had great symbolic and logistic effect in expressing the will of so many people, the world was still unjust. Segregation still existed, as did poverty and unequal opportunity.

Then, tragedy came snapping at the heels of triumph. Less than three weeks later, on September 15, someone put a bomb in the Sixteenth Street Baptist Church in Birmingham. It exploded while Sunday school was being held. Four beautiful and innocent little girls were killed.

It was a devastating shock to Martin and me that anyone could have such hate in his heart as to kill innocent children. It made us sadly reassess the whole situation. We had won a victory in Birmingham, and though we knew that there was still much to be done, we had underestimated the virulent depth of white hatred. Now we again confronted the evil fact that the guardians of the status quo would do any cowardly and brutal thing to preserve it. The sober prospect faced us that it would take much more time and a far more concentrated effort to change the hearts of many of the people in white America.

After preaching that morning at Ebenezer, Martin went straight to Birmingham to talk to the families who had lost their children and to try to help them find and accept the meaning of their sacrifice. Martin and I knew full well that it is easier for those in a position of leadership to live with brutality and even death, because they know the danger beforehand and have accepted it along with that leadership. But people who are not directly involved never think of themselves as vulnerable. As parents ourselves, Martin and I realized how painfully horrible must be the suffering of those families, how bitter their cup must be. Martin desperately desired to give them what spiritual guidance and comfort he could.

A joint funeral service was held for three of the little girls. Despite his sincere efforts, one of the families was so embittered it would not take part. Martin was to pronounce the eulogy, but before he spoke, novelist John Killens made a statement to the effect that this tragedy marked the end of nonviolence in the Black Freedom Movement. "Negroes must be prepared to protect themselves with guns," he said.

Christopher McNair, the father of one of the dead children, said, "I'm not for that. What good would Denise have done with a machine gun in her hand?"

In his eulogy Martin called the children "heroines of a holy crusade for freedom and human dignity." And he said, "Their death says to us that we must work passionately and unceasingly to make the American dream a reality." Then voicing his enduring faith, he said, "They did not die in vain. God still has a way of wringing good out of evil. History has proved again and again that unmerited suffering is redemptive. The innocent blood of these little girls may well serve as the redemptive force that will bring new light to this dark city."

The next tragedy we shared with all the people of the world. On November 22, 1963, Martin was upstairs, attending to some things, with the television set on in the background. I was downstairs talking on the telephone to a dear friend, Esther Turner. Esther was one of those rare friends who was always there when she was needed most. She had been the first white person to integrate Ebenezer Church in 1961, inspired by both Martin and Daddy King.

Now, Martin called to me, "Corrie, I just heard that President Kennedy has been shot—maybe killed."

Of course, I rushed up to be with Martin, and we sat there hoping and praying that John Kennedy would not die. We thought of the great national tragedy, and, additionally, of the particular effect his death might have on the Black Movement. We felt that President Kennedy had been a friend of the Cause and that with him as President we could continue to move forward. We watched and prayed for him.

Then it was announced that the President was dead. Martin had been very quiet during this period. Finally he said, "This is what is going to happen to me also. I keep telling you, this is a sick society."

I was not able to say anything. I had no word to comfort my husband. I could not say, "It won't happen to you." I felt he was right. It was a painfully agonizing silence. I moved closer to him and gripped his hand in mine.

Nothing had ever affected me as deeply as President Kennedy's death, not even the news that Martin had been stabbed in Harlem. Because John Kennedy had been so kind and thoughtful to us, we felt that he was a friend to be relied upon, as well as our President. Our family shared that feeling, and when the children came home from school that afternoon, Yoki came flying up the stairs, wailing, "Mommy! Mommy!" Daddy King was going downstairs, and as he passed her, he asked, in a troubled tone, "What's the matter, Yoki?"

She did not stop to answer, but kept on running to me. She said, "Mommy, they've killed President Kennedy, and he didn't do one single thing to anybody." And then Yoki added, "Oh, Mommy, we're never going to get our freedom now."

I took her in my arms and moved into the guest bedroom with Marty and two-year-old Dexter following. They sat down, and I said, "Yolanda, I know how you feel. We all feel this way. This is a terrible tragedy, but we are going to get our freedom. God is still above, and He's going to take care of us. So don't you worry, we're going to get our freedom."

That is, in truth, what I also kept saying to myself. I had always believed—and I still believe—that what we are doing has a purpose, and that our work is helping to fulfill a plan God has for this universe. I realized that John Kennedy, too, was an instrument of this Divine plan to bring about a just society and brotherhood to all men. Even so, I was deeply troubled that God had allowed him to be cut down. Finally I said to myself, "Though I don't understand why this happened, I believe in the passage from Scripture, 'All things work together for the good of them that love the Lord.' " I saw the President's death as part of God's permissive will, and I believed that John Kennedy's unearned sacrifice would be redemptive for all of us.

Months later when Martin and I assessed the situation, we realized that President Kennedy had faced a great deal of opposition in Congress to his Civil Rights Bill. But his death moved the nation in such a way that the people felt that the legislation must be passed as a tribute to his memory. This should have been done because it was right, but also it was for the sake of the entire nation, which had continued to backslide on its promise of democracy for black people.

Watching Jacqueline Kennedy, who was so courageous in her tragedy, and watching her small children, I could not help thinking about my husband, especially because so many people considered Martin's work more dangerous even than the President's. It was as if, watching the funeral, I was steeling myself for our own fate.

Martin and I, for all our philosophical explanations and our deep faith in God, were still personally in a dark abyss of sorrow for this gallant, compassionate, and wise young man—a true statesman. On that somber day, little Marty, who was six, said to his father, "Daddy, President Kennedy was your best friend, wasn't he, Daddy?"

In a way, he was.

14

"No lie can live forever"

The Nobel Prize, of course, was for us the major event of 1964, but other incidents occurred in which we had vital interest. The most important of these was the Civil Rights Bill, sent to Congress by John Kennedy in 1963, seen through to passage by Hubert Humphrey in the Senate and Lyndon Johnson in the White House. President Johnson invited my husband to come to the White House for the signing, and this was the first of their several meetings. After this visit, Martin was much reassured about the new President, and we both began to feel he was on the side of racial justice.

We had a great shock when, on Sunday, June 21, 1964, three civil rights workers—black Mississippian James Chaney, CORE staff member Michael Schwerner, and volunteer Andrew Goodman, both white New Yorkers—were reported to have been arrested on speeding charges in Mississippi. The young men disappeared and local authorities claimed that they had been released from prison about six hours after their arrest. However, shortly after this time, the burned station wagon in which they had been riding was found, though the men were missing until August 4, when the FBI found their bodies buried in a local dam. As we have seen, we were in Paris following the Nobel ceremony by the time the murderers were finally identified. It was a terrible example of the Mississippi climate, and Martin later said of the incident that when he delivered the memorial service for these three slain civil rights workers he knew what it was like to stand in the valley of the shadow of death after standing in front of Sheriff Rainey's courthouse in Mississippi.

The Democratic Convention met while we were in New York that summer, and Martin appeared before the Platform Committee. He fought untiringly to get the delegation of the Mississippi Freedom Democratic Party seated. When Martin got as much as he could from the committee he stopped. He brought his results back to the group and many people were upset at how few seats they had. They called him an Uncle Tom and went to the press. Reporters questioned Martin about why he accepted only token representation. He answered that he felt a victory had been achieved and that sometimes we have to accept what seems to be a minor gain and project it as an important breakthrough. Feeling a sense of achievement inspires people to continue to work for a final victory. That is exactly what took place four years later in 1968 when all of the Freedom delegates were seated. Martin was right: In a difficult struggle, people have to have victories, even if they are not major.

I began to give my Freedom Concerts that year, in a format similar to the final section of the 1956 New York concert, which I called "Portrait of the Montgomery Bus Protest."

I feel that the Freedom Concert was an inspired concept seeking to combine, in dramatic form, art and experience in a practical, relevant, meaningful way. My background as a performer in music, coupled with my years of experience as a public speaker, gave me a unique means of communicating these experiences in the freedom struggle which I felt was more powerful and effective than either speaking or singing alone could be. The Freedom Concert was "The Story of the Struggle from 1955 to 1965" told in narrative and song. There were eight parts to the concert in which I alternated between narrating and singing.

The following is a copy of the Freedom Concert program:

The American Dream

"The House I Live In" .Earl Robinson

The Dream Blighted

"Come by Here, My Lord" . . . . .Angolan Folk Song

A New Hope: Portrait of the
Nonviolent Integration Movement in Montgomery

"Walk Together, Children" . . . . .Traditional
"My Feet Are Tired" . . . . .Frances Thomas
"Lord, I Can't Turn Back" . . . . .Robert Williams
"Hold On" . . . . .Hall Johnson
"Honor, Honor" . . . . .Hall Johnson

National Movement Developed

"We Shall Overcome" . . . . .Traditional

One World—One Brotherhood

*"He's Got the Whole World
in His Hand"* .Hamilton Forrest

Supreme Sacrifices

"Witness" . . . . .Hall Johnson

The March on Washington

"Seeking for a City" . . . . .Hall Johnson

Montgomery: The Long Road Back

"No Crystal Stair" .Frances Thomas
"We Shall Overcome" . . . . .Traditional

My first official Freedom Concert was given November 14, 1964, at New York City's Town Hall.

The place was filled and the proceeds, amounting to six thousand dollars, were divided between SCLC and the Goodman-Chaney-Schwerner Fund.

At first Martin did not think the concerts would succeed as a fund-raising effort, but when they brought in more than fifty thousand dollars for SCLC and its affiliates, he had to admit he had miscalculated.

I sang regularly with the Church Choir of Ebenezer. Sometimes on the Sundays that he preached, Martin would ask me to do the Meditation Hymn. "Sweet Little Jesus Boy" was one of his favorites. He used to ask me to sing it at Christmastime, and sometimes at Easter. While I shared this with Martin as one of my favorite spirituals, I now seem to find a new meaning and interpretation of the words of this song. They are so reminiscent of Martin's own life experiences:

Sweet little Jesus boy, they made you be born in a manger.
Sweet little Holy Child, didn't know who you was.
Our eyes was blind, we couldn't see—we didn't know who you was.
The world treat you mean, Lawd, treat me mean, too.
But that's how things is down here,
We didn't know who you was. . . .

Martin had a high baritone voice, and he loved to sing. We and the children used to sing together whenever we could, but especially at Christmastime. When they were together, Martin, Ralph, Andy, Bernard Lee, and Wyatt Walker would sometimes sing freedom songs as a quintet. Once, his willingness to sing in public caused Martin a very embarrassing time. He was speaking at a large meeting, and when he finished, he had wanted the audience to join in singing "His Eye Is on the Sparrow." But the people had not understood what he meant, and Martin was left standing there, only *his* voice sounding in the large auditorium. He told me how emotionally the people responded when he came to the part that said:

I sing because I'm happy,
I sing because I'm free. . . .

It was as if the emotional pull on the audience had lifted them from their seats. Martin continued singing:

> His eye is on the sparrow,
> And I know He's watching me.

He told me that he had real stage fright, but had no choice but to sing through to the end. The audience responded with great emotion, shouting and applauding. When Martin got home, he told me proudly, "I really did well. You think I can't sing, but the people say I *can*."

The children turned out to be, I think, normal rambunctious youngsters, but I sometimes look at them in amazement that they have survived so bravely some of their experiences. For example, it was in the summer of 1965 that the Atlanta elementary schools were integrated, and we were of course anxious that our own children transfer to an integrated school. Although we believe that this process should work both ways—white families sharing the burden of "pioneering" with black students by going to all-black schools—we knew that that was not a likely prospect anywhere in this country, and especially not in the South.

Martin said, "Coretta, you will have the job of finding a good school and getting our children registered in this integrated school by September." We had tried to register our two older children in private schools when they were each in the first grade in an effort to have them receive an integrated education. Yolanda had been denied admission by one church school, and Marty had been denied admission by another. They were rejected solely because they were black.

Martin's heavy responsibilities to the Movement prevented him from giving any time to this concern and I agreed to do the job, though the summer was already half spent and, I must admit, I was caught off guard.

At times like this, when I had to take care of the children by myself, I generally did not mind. Only occasionally would I think about the fact that I was there by myself. I did not think that

Martin should be there, but sometimes I did feel a little sorry for myself because things were so overwhelming. Being a parent can be very frustrating. Later that same year, 1965, there was a point when the two boys had to have their tonsils out at the same time. Martin was so busy I went ahead and made the plans without telling him. It worked out that he was not in town when they both woke up and needed attention at the same time. That went on for a good long time, and all of a sudden I had the television on and I saw Martin at the signing of the Voting Rights Bill. I felt very supportive of his being there, but I just had this feeling of being here again, by myself. In the end I just had to get used to the fact that he would not be there.

When I discussed the matter of changing schools with the children, they said they did not want to be the only two black children at an otherwise all-white school. I called Juanita Abernathy and we discussed the feasibility of having our children transfer to the same previously all-white school. Her children felt the same apprehension as mine did. We finally selected what we were told was one of Atlanta's best public elementary schools, the Spring Street School.

The night before school was to start, we were notified that all five children—the Abernathys' three, Juandalyn, Donzaleigh, and Ralph III, and Yolanda and Marty—had been accepted by the superintendent of the school district, and they started school together on the very next day—Monday morning.

Though the children were naturally excited, I don't think they were afraid, because they had each other—the Kings had the Abernathys, the Abernathys had the Kings, and it made the initial strangeness, the stares, and the occasional remarks easier to take.

That first morning, as Juanita Abernathy and I walked through the school cafeteria, where registration was taking place, we were stopped by a reporter. Almost before we could speak, the school's principal came up to us and said, "Don't talk to him. We don't talk to the press in this school." She then turned to the newspaperman and ordered him to leave.

The principal recommended separating the children into five different classes, so that they could make friends more easily. At first, we and the children were a little apprehensive about that, but we were willing to try it. It worked out very well and we all, even by the end of that first day, had a very good feeling about the experiences.

Still I did not agree with the school administration that the enrollment of our children should be kept secret, and after I got home that first morning, when a reporter questioned me, I told him at what time we would be picking up the children in the afternoon.

This was not a matter of seeking publicity. In fact, we always tried to protect the children from that kind of public focus. However, I felt that it was extremely important that the nation see that integration could be accomplished peacefully. I also hoped that, seeing our experience, other black families would be encouraged to send their children to previously lily-white schools.

I am afraid that the principal of the school did think that we were publicity-seeking. We, on the other hand, had learned to accept the loss of privacy as part of the price we had to pay in the work we were trying to do.

It was during this same period that the SCLC had launched its offensive for voter registration in the deep South. In our home state of Georgia, the registration of black voters was proceeding fairly satisfactorily. In 1963, thirty thousand African Americans had been added to the rolls, and forty thousand more were added in 1964. However, in George Wallace's Alabama there had been very little progress, almost none in the country districts. For example, not one black voter was registered in Lowndes County or Wilcox County, and there were almost no African Americans registered in the other black-belt counties of Alabama.

My husband had chosen Selma, the county seat of Dallas County, the heart of the black belt of Alabama and, therefore, the symbol of black oppression, as the target for our demonstrations around voting rights. It was a medium-sized town situated between Montgomery and Birmingham. I was pleased by the choice because Selma was quite near my home town of Marion, and, also, because I realized that this meant that the Movement was spreading out from the urban centers to the smaller communities.

Right after New Year's Day 1965, shortly after he returned from Oslo, Martin went to Selma with some of our staff. He did indeed "go back to the valley" to try to alleviate the suffering there. Their first step was to test public accommodations. Black people went to all the hotels and restaurants in Selma to ask for service. Martin had been warned that there was likely to be trouble and that he might not get out alive. SCLC's efficient Operation Dialogue Department had surveyed the attitude of the white community in Selma and had predicted that there would be violence. But there were no incidents on this day, and our people were served.

A week or so later, Martin returned to Selma. All during the first day he was there, a white man followed Martin around the streets, waiting to speak to him. No one seemed too alarmed, because he looked and talked like a reasonable person. At one point, he followed Martin into the Hotel Albert, and as Martin was registering, the man came up behind him and said something. Martin turned around to answer, and the white man hit him as hard as he could in the head. Martin staggered and almost fell, but members of his staff supported him and others grabbed and held his attacker until the police arrived to arrest him. Though Martin was not seriously injured, he did have a terrible headache for some days after, and we were all made very aware of how easy it was for an assailant to get close enough to injure my husband.

As always, we sent our staff ahead into Selma to prepare the people for the voter-registration drive. SNCC had already begun working in the area the previous fall trying to get black people registered. All through January and February, we held mass meetings in Selma and in Marion; and people were escorted to the voter-registration offices in an attempt to have them registered. My own parents, on whose home territory the struggle now took place, attended the mass meetings and contributed money to the Cause.

As a matter of fact, the first casualty of the campaign occurred in Marion. Several people had been arrested, and one night a protest march moved from the church to the Marion jail. In the middle of the march, the streetlights were suddenly turned out. The police and their white racist comrades charged the demonstrators, clubbing and beating them. While trying to protect his mother, a young man named Jimmy Lee Jackson was shot on February 18 and died eight days later on February 26.

Jimmy Lee was from Marion; his aunt, Juanita Lee, a former classmate, had been one of my best friends in high school. He was just out of high school and was the main support of his family. He was not engaged in any violent activity. He was a victim of senseless white rage.

We received a call in Atlanta that night to tell us the terrible news, and we were informed that the police had sealed off the area and that not even an ambulance could get in to take the wounded to the hospital.

Jimmy was given a martyr's funeral, buried in blue denim. An overflow crowd of people came to pay final respects to him at this time when the tension of the Movement was very high.

Martin pronounced the eulogy and afterward, in a steady downpour of rain, marched with the mourners to the cemetery where Jimmy was laid to rest. My father, who was then sixty-five, marched beside Martin. He felt that he had to walk with his children in the struggle for freedom. My brother, Obie, was there; he also has been active in the Movement. A minister in the A.M.E. Zion Church, he ran for tax collector of Perry County in 1966 and almost won. In 1969, he integrated a post office in a small town near our parents' home by becoming a mail carrier. To my knowledge, until that time, there had been no black postal employees in the small towns and rural areas in the South since Reconstruction.

Though Martin had predicted that there would be strong resistance and possibly retaliation by death when we made an all-out assault against the system of oppression in the black belt, we were deeply saddened by the news from Marion. Somehow, we felt that this was the foreshadowing of what was yet to come. Yet, despite this awareness, freedom's time clock had been set and no one could stop it.

Around the first of February, Martin and Ralph Abernathy led a march of two hundred and fifty blacks and fifteen whites from Brown's Chapel A.M.E. Church to the Selma Courthouse to protest the difficulty of registering African-American voters. They were all arrested. Most of them were released on bail, but Martin and Ralph refused to put up bail. They were put into the same cell—an improvement, at least, over the last Alabama jail experience of solitary confinement Martin faced so bravely but dreaded so much.

During the five days they were in prison, Juanita and I went to Selma to see them and to participate in the struggle. The day we arrived at Brown's Chapel for a noonday mass meeting, Andy Young came up to me and said, "You're going to have to come inside and greet the people, because Malcolm X is here and he's really roused them. They want to hear from you."

I said, "Andy, I'm just not in a speaking mood."

He said urgently, "You must do it. By the time you get inside, you'll feel like it."

Juanita and I went into the church and were enthusiastically received. Juanita spoke first. Then I gave a short inspirational speech, emphasizing the nonviolent approach and urging them to continue. After I spoke, I was introduced to Malcolm X for the first time. I was impressed by his obvious intelligence, and he seemed quite gentle as he said to me, "Mrs. King, will you tell Dr. King that I had planned to visit with him in jail? I won't get a chance now because I've got to leave to get to New York in time to catch a plane for London, where I'm to address the African Students' Conference. I want Dr. King to know that I didn't come to Selma to make his job difficult. I really did come thinking that I could make it easier. If the white people realize what the alternative is, perhaps they will be more willing to hear Dr. King." I thanked him, and said I would give Martin his message.

I was impressed with Malcolm's sincerity, but found it difficult to reconcile myself to some of the Muslim principles which were so different from our thinking. They advocated separation of the races and condoned violence, so they were open to the charges of teaching hate and violence. Martin insisted that violence was the derivative of despair; both Elijah Muhammad, the leader of the Black Muslims, and Malcolm had suffered terribly at the hands of white racism and their bitterness was a derivative of the suffering.

One of the first documentaries on the Black Muslims was appropriately named "The Hate That Hate Produced."

Yet Martin firmly agreed with certain aspects of the program that Malcolm X advocated. For example, he shared with Malcolm the fierce desire that the black American reclaim his racial pride, his joy in himself and his race—in a physical, a cultural, and a spiritual rebirth. He shared with the nationalists the sure knowledge that "black is beautiful" and that, in so many respects, the quality of the black people's scale of values was far superior to that of the white culture which attempted to enslave us. Martin too had a close attachment to our African brothers and to our common heritage.

And, on the other side, Martin too believed that *white* Christianity had failed to act in accordance with its teachings. However, my husband felt not that the Christian ethic must be rejected, but that those who failed Christianity must be brought—through love—to brotherhood, for their own redemption as well as ours. He believed that there was a great opportunity for black people to redeem Christianity in America.

Martin also believed in nonviolent Black Power. He believed that we must have our share of the economy, of education, of jobs, of free choice. We must have the same quality and quantity of power that other ethnic groups possess, so that blacks, as a group, can hold their own in a society where, instead of a melting pot, separate peoples function beside each other, exchanging the power they control for the power the other fellow has. Blacks have not predominated in local politics, the way many Irish have, or in finance, the way many white Protestants have, or in the professions, the way many Jews have. Black Power is necessary before black equality is possible. Yet, we are not asking for anything the rest of society does not have, merely for our rightful share.

Martin believed that we must have *freedom now*. He believed that freedom must be militantly grasped from those who hold it from us. But he believed that the only effective way to accomplish that goal is through nonviolence—nonviolence to those we confronted, nonviolence to our own souls, which could be destroyed by hatred.

Freedom now is what Martin fought for, with his spirit *and his body*, on the front line. Who could doubt that? I remember him on the platform, exhorting his people to keep their courage up, to gird their loins for the hard battle ahead. He had the children with him that day, and he turned from the crowd and shouted to our son, who sat behind him, "Marty . . . Marty! What do we want?" And Marty called back to his daddy, "Free—dom!" And Martin called out, "Marty, when do we want it?" And the boy shouted, "We want *freedom now!*"

With that spirit as a shield and as a program, Martin moved mountains. And he did it without destroying his own soul and without leading his own people to self-destruction.

I told Martin about my conversation with Malcolm that day, but our time together in the Selma jail was so limited that we didn't spend much of it discussing Malcolm X. A few days later the British refused to allow Malcolm to enter England, and he came back to America, where, eighteen days later, he was assassinated at a public rally in Harlem.

The death of Malcolm X affected me profoundly. Perhaps that was because I had just met him, and perhaps it was because I had begun to understand him better. Martin and I had reassessed our feelings toward him. We realized that since he had been to Mecca and had broken with Elijah Muhammad, he was moving away from hatred toward internationalism and against exploitation. In a strange way, the same racist attitude which killed others who were working for peaceful change also killed Malcolm X.

I said to Martin, "What a waste! What a pity that this man who was so talented and such an articulate spokesman for black people should have to die just as he was reaching for something of real value."

Martin believed that Malcolm X was a brilliant young man who had been misdirected. They had talked together on occasion and had discussed their philosophies in a friendly way. At the same time, I know that, though he never said so publicly, Malcolm X had deep respect for Martin. He recognized that Martin was unique, not alone in talent or eloquence, but in fearlessness and courage.

Malcolm admired manhood and he knew how supremely Martin exemplified it.

While the Movement was getting started in Selma, Martin went back and forth constantly, unable to stay continuously because of his many speaking commitments. The SCLC continued to try to register voters, but there were many problems. The authorities would have blacks stand in line for hours. Then the office would close, and they would say, "You come back another day." Sometimes they would let a very few at the head of the line register and then close up abruptly.

As in Birmingham, the city officials of Selma were rabid segregationists. Mayor Joe T. Smitherman was a friend of Governor Wallace, and, in a way, Sheriff Jim Clark of Selma was Bull Connor all over again. We were prepared for violence against us, and we tried to teach the people to resist it—in militant non-violence.

There is a constant undercurrent of violence against the black man. This is the political and emotional violence which denies rights to men, education to children, and respect and medical care to the family. My husband saw that it was better to accept physical violence in public for a short time than to suffer spiritual and emotional violence for generations. The public reaction to physical violence could be mobilized to bring the kinds of political and economic changes which would remove the more subtle and deadly psychological and spiritual violence against black people.

On Friday, March 5, Martin flew to Washington and spent two and a half hours with President Johnson describing conditions in Alabama and urging the President to expedite the new Voting Rights Bill and make sure that it provided for *federal* registrars of voting applicants. On his return, he announced that on Sunday, March 7, demonstrators would march fifty-four miles from Selma to Montgomery. Governor Wallace promptly issued an order prohibiting the march. Martin told the people of Selma, "I can't promise that you won't get beaten; I can't promise you won't get your house bombed; I can't promise that you won't get scarred up a bit, but we must stand up for what is right."

At the last moment, Martin was persuaded not to lead the march himself. It was SCLC strategy for the leaders to avoid arrest in the opening phases of a campaign, because that would leave an army without generals. Martin did not really foresee any violent conflict that day. He thought Governor Wallace would have all the demonstrators arrested, so he asked Hosea Williams and John Lewis to lead the marchers.

In Selma that sunny, bloody Sunday afternoon over five hundred black men and women and a few white people walked out of town, up the four-lane Highway 80; Sheriff Clark and Colonel Al Lingo of the Alabama Highway Patrol, with sixty state troopers and some cavalry, confronted them just beyond the Edmund Pettus Bridge, which was to become almost as famous as the bridge at Concord, Massachusetts.

The marchers were ordered to halt and given two minutes to turn back. At the end of less than a minute of dead silence, during which the troopers put on gas masks, Major John Cloud shouted, "Troopers, forward!" His sixty men charged into the defenseless column of demonstrators, clubs swinging. Twenty people were knocked flat; others knelt to pray. The troopers charged again, throwing tear-gas grenades. Then Sheriff Clark shouted to his mounted posse, "Get those goddam niggers! Get those goddam white niggers!" The horsemen charged with shrill, wild rebel yells.

The whole nation was sickened by the pictures of that wild melee. Tear gas, clubs, horsemen slashing with bullwhips like the Russian czar's infamous cossacks, and deputies, using electric cattle prods, chasing fleeing men, women, and children all the way back to Brown's Chapel. Sixteen people were hospitalized; fifty others were hurt.

All during that brutal attack, the whites, watching the show from the sidelines, their faces distorted with hatred, called out, "Get those niggers! Kill them! Get the S.O.B.'s!" And worse.

A white nurse told later how she watched a trooper swinging a bullwhip at a young boy, screaming hysterically, "March, nigger. You wanted to march and now I'm gonna help you!"

The tear gas was so bad that elderly people lay helplessly vomiting while the troopers charged right over them.

If the country was horrified, Martin was aghast. "If I had known it was going to be like that I'd have gone myself," he said. He announced that on Tuesday he and Ralph Abernathy would lead another march. Alabama officials got a temporary *federal* injunction against it.

I was now in San Francisco, having finished the third in a series of five Freedom Concerts on the West Coast which I was doing as a fund-raising effort for SCLC. The news of the confrontation at the Edmund Pettus Bridge in Selma reached me just before my concert that late Sunday afternoon. I waited anxiously to hear from Martin. He telephoned me Sunday night—Monday morning, really—at three o'clock. Rumors had been flying that he would be assassinated if he led the march on Sunday. He told me of his plans to go to Selma on Monday, to march on Tuesday, in spite of the problems with Wallace and the injunction.

I told him, "If you get enough people, you can write your own decisions." Martin said that people were already arriving in Selma to support the Movement.

Then Xernona Clayton, wife of Ed Clayton, the SCLC public relations director, who was traveling with me on this tour, spoke with Martin and he told her he was going to Selma, but he implied that he felt he would not get out alive.

When she hung up the telephone after talking with Martin, she said, "Coretta, I've never heard Martin talk like that. Have you thought of the possibility that something might happen to him?"

"Actually, I have thought about it a great deal," I answered hesitatingly. "But I have to resist worry. We know what we are doing is right. If we stop now, people will feel we've been intimidated, and will lose faith in us."

Still I was terribly worried. Despite the fact that there were two concerts left on this tour, there was no doubt that if anything happened to Martin I would cancel everything and return home.

I was also concerned about the children's reaction to all the tension produced by Selma. Somehow, I felt that my presence there could offer the security they may have needed at that time.

I telephoned them the next day, and although they were aware of what was happening, they seemed relaxed and in good spirits. I asked Marty how he felt about his father leading another march. He said, "All right."

"Do you think anything will happen to your daddy, Marty?"

"No!" He answered quickly. Then he added, "Of course, if Granddaddy King was there he could straighten the whole thing out, but he has to stay here to take care of the church."

The next days were spent in much anxiety and I kept close to the telephone and listened for news reports from Selma. Martin went to Selma on Monday. Attorney General Nicholas Katzenbach telephoned him several times begging him not to break a federal injunction. Then former Florida Governor LeRoy Collins, who was head of the federal Community Relations Service, flew to Selma to plead with Martin and talk to the officials.

Martin agonized because it was against his principles to flout federal law. He made a nationwide appeal to clergymen and laypeople to join him on Tuesday for the march from Selma to Montgomery. Black and white people began pouring into Selma from all over the nation to support the march, including clergymen of all denominations—ministers, priests, rabbis—and nuns. Martin remembered what had happened in Albany. He knew that if he called the march off, they would feel let down. They would say, "King chickened out." He told Collins he would have to march. "It's better to die on the highway than make a butchery of my conscience," he said.

That Tuesday fifteen hundred people marched out of Selma, more than half of them white. There were four hundred and fifty clergymen and a contingent of Catholic nuns. The procession crossed the famous bridge and came to the rank of troopers. The order to halt was given. Fifteen hundred men and women knelt in the roadway and prayed. Realizing the imminent possibility of a violent confrontation resulting in needless death, Martin told the marchers to turn back. He was criticized for this action, but to have gone on would have produced a confrontation before we had assembled our maximum strength.

Martin always believed it wrong to pursue action with small numbers. He constantly emphasized that the presence of masses is both proof of support and a discouragement to violence. We had

ar more behind us than the hundreds there that day; indeed, we
ad the sympathy and support of the majority of America, as later
vents demonstrated.

The inconclusive ending of the march might well have produced a
stalemate in Selma. But, as usual, the white extremists acted so
brutally that they themselves highlighted, for the nation's con-
cience, the evil system they stood for. That night, James Reeb,
father of five children, a white Unitarian minister from Boston, had
dinner at a black-operated restaurant in Selma with two other
clergymen. As they came out, four Klansmen in sports jackets at-
acked them, shouting, "White niggers! Where's your hammer and
sickle?" Reeb's skull was crushed with a wooden plank and he died
two days later in Birmingham without regaining consciousness.

The police chief and "Director of Public Safety" Wilson Baker of
Selma quickly arrested three of the murderers. It made no difference. The whole nation was aroused by a second atrocity. Demonstrations were held in cities from coast to coast. Four thousand
religious leaders assembled in Washington to push the Voting
Rights Bill, and picketed the White House.

On Monday, March 15, two thousand people joined in a memorial service for James Reeb at the courthouse in Selma, in what was
perhaps the greatest and most inspiring ecumenical service ever
held. Archbishop Iakovos, primate of the Greek Orthodox
Church in North and South America, conducted the memorial
service from the courthouse steps. Martin spoke the eulogy, in
which he asked, "Why must good men die for good?" and answered, "James Reeb's death may cause the white South to come to
terms with its conscience." Then Martin laid a wreath in James
Reeb's memory at the courthouse door.

That very evening President Johnson at last spoke out before a
joint congressional session which was broadcast on all television
networks. He said:

> At times, history and fate meet at a single time in a single
> place to shape a turning point in man's unending search
> for freedom.

So it was at Lexington and Concord. So it was a century ago at Appomattox. So it was last week in Selma, Alabama.

There, long-suffering men and women peacefully protested the denial of their rights as Americans.

What happened in Selma is part of a far larger movement which reaches into every section and state of America. It is the effort of American Negroes to secure for themselves the full blessings of American life.

Our mission is at once the oldest and the most basic of this country—to right wrong, to do justice, to serve man.

Their cause must be our cause, too. Because it is not just Negroes, but really all of us, who must overcome the crippling legacy of bigotry and injustice.

And we shall overcome!

Later in his speech, Johnson assigned the Voting Rights Bill first priority among his proposed legislation.

I remember saying to myself as I listened in my bedroom in our home in Atlanta to what has now become Johnson's famous We Shall Overcome speech, "Thank goodness, they've finally got the message of what my husband has been saying for years."

Despite the speeches, the marches, the singing, and all the brave words, the Selma Movement dragged on. People continued to march and to be arrested. After *two murders* and nearly thirty-eight hundred arrests, only about fifty African Americans had been registered to vote.

But suddenly everything changed. The injunction against a march from Selma to Montgomery was lifted. Martin called for a massive march. Since Governor Wallace still forbade it, President Johnson federalized the Alabama National Guard and committed four thousand regular Army troops to Alabama. Now we would march under the protection of the United States government.

On Sunday, March 21, only two weeks after the brutality at the bridge, Martin marched out of Selma on Highway 80 at the head of about five thousand people of both races. They crossed the Edmund Pettus Bridge and continued for eight miles. There, by agreement between Martin and federal officials, all but three hundred left the column. The rest continued on to Montgomery.

I had a commitment to speak at Bennett College at Greensboro, North Carolina, that day, but I said to Martin, "I would so much rather march in Selma."

He answered, "You are making a contribution by going to Greensboro. You can join us on Monday." And so I did.

There were medical units to take care of anyone who fell ill, a commissary to feed people, arrangements for camping in the fields at night, and a shuttle service to the towns for those who were not up to camping out. There were guardsmen or federal troops all along the roadside. I remember Monday night Martin was very tired and his feet were in poor condition. He was treated by a doctor. One of the marshals said to Andy Young, "Where is Dr. King going to be tonight?"

Andy said, "We're going back to Selma." Then the man whispered that there was a plot to assassinate Martin by a man disguised as a minister. We did not change our plans. While we maintained unarmed guards, we understood the FBI was on hand guarding Martin all the time.

Famous artists, including Harry Belafonte, Leonard Bernstein, Billy Eckstine, Nina Simone, Sammy Davis, Jr., and dozens more, put on a spectacular show for the marchers. I remember how dark it was, except for the lighted platform, how we struggled through the crowd to reach it, and how I had to be lifted up onto the high platform. When we arrived, Harry Belafonte asked me to speak, and though I begged off, he and Martin insisted.

I told our companions on the march that this was in the area where I had grown up and spoke of how returning to Montgomery ten years after we first went there had a very special meaning for me. Then I spoke directly to the women about what all this meant for the future of our children, and left them with the challenge of Langston Hughes' poem "Mother to Son":

> Well, son, I'll tell you:
> Life for me ain't been no crystal stair.
> It's had tacks in it,

And splinters,
And boards torn up,
And places with no carpet on the floor—
Bare.
But all the time
I'se been a-climbin' on,
And reachin' landin's,
And turnin' corners,
And sometimes goin' in the dark
Where there ain't been no light.
So boy, don't you turn back.
Don't you set down on the steps
'Cause you finds it's kinder hard.
Don't you fall now—
For I'se still goin', honey,
I'se still climbin',
And life for me ain't been no crystal stair.

The next day was to be the climax of the Selma drive. All night long busloads, trainloads, and planeloads of people were coming into the city to join us—I can't even guess how many. We were fifty thousand people in all, by the time everyone got there. They came from almost every state! They represented every race, religion, and class. They knew there were risks, but a genuine love of justice drove them on and a human torrent of brotherhood engulfed the "Cradle of the Confederacy."

We assembled at St. Jude's and marched about two miles into the heart of the city. We went up Oak Street to Jefferson Davis Street, through the black section, up Mobile Street to Dexter Avenue, all those old familiar streets we knew so well. Oh, it was good, very good! The people on the sidewalks seemed to be very happy to see us, and when they recognized Martin they would cheer and wave. There was maximum security all the way—federal troops along the line and on rooftops, and helicopters circling overhead. We also had our own security. Our own unarmed marshals marched in front and behind Martin—more cautious than usual because of the repeated threats against him.

Then, we marched past Dexter Avenue Baptist Church—a special thrill for Martin and me—and through the square to the beautiful old State Capitol, with its classic columns and great dome. Just before we got there, I noticed my father and mother standing in the crowd. They didn't seem to see me, but I asked Reverend Fred Bennette of our staff to get them so they could join us. Daddy King was with us too by that time—he could not march all the way, but to march into Montgomery with our family that way was a unique experience. Of course, Juanita and Ralph Abernathy and their children (I've always regretted that we didn't bring our children) and Christine and A.D. all marched with us. Ralph Bunche, Mrs. Rosa Parks, Julie and Harry Belafonte, and many other old friends were there. A place was found for my parents on the platform, which pleased me greatly, for I wanted them to share this experience with us.

As the speeches began, I looked at Rosa Parks. I sat there and began to think back over the years of struggle from 1955 to 1965. I realized we had really come a long way from our start in the bus protest, when only a handful of people, relatively speaking, were involved—all black people who were fighting for their dignity and the right to sit down in a bus. Now ten years had passed. We had desegregated the buses; we had desegregated public transportation, interstate as well as intrastate. Our right to use public accommodations had been guaranteed. We had progressed toward school integration.

Most important of all, there was more national awareness of our problems than there ever had been in the whole history of the black struggle. When I looked out over the big crowd, I saw many white people and church people. There were more church people involved than in any demonstration we had ever had, and I said to Martin later that it was perhaps the greatest witness by the church since the days of the early Christians. I still believe that.

I felt that this whole experience was another unique moment in American history, a great moment of truth. People like Jim Clark had said, "If you march, you do so over my dead body"; and Wallace had said, "They shall not pass." But here we were. Ten years ago we had talked about dignity, but we really felt it now.

When I asked my father how he felt about it, he said, "This is the greatest day for Negroes in the history of America." He certainly spoke for all of us and for himself!

Martin made a superb speech in which he said, "I stand before you this afternoon with the conviction that segregation in Alabama is on its deathbed. . . . We are on the move now, and no wave of racism can stop us. Let us march on to the realization of the American dream. The road ahead is not altogether a smooth one . . . we are still in for a season of suffering. How long? Not long, because no lie can live forever. Our God is marching on."

That night, as we started for our plane, the airport was jammed with thousands of people waiting for their planes. They were sitting in all the seats and on the stairs, even on the floor. Despite the delay, they were all in a cheerful mood, laughing and talking, munching sandwiches and drinking colas—strangers when they came, friends now; black and white together sharing a moment of happiness. Martin said that the scene gave him even more hope than the rally at the Capitol. He said it was a microcosm of a society of real brotherhood.

Then, when we reached Atlanta, Martin was being paged for the telephone. He received the terrible news that Mrs. Viola Liuzzo, a white woman who was the wife of a Detroit official of the Teamsters union, had been shot to death on Highway 80 while she was driving some demonstrators back to Selma. Whatever elation we had felt was gone in the sadness of the death of that lovely and brave woman. As a mother, I felt my heart go out to her now motherless children, and to her devoted husband who had been widowed and now had the sole responsibility for the children. Of course, what had obviously inflamed the racists who killed her had been the sight of a white woman in a car with black men, on a dark Alabama road.

Though we had our suspicions as early as 1956, and had our first confirmation directly from President Kennedy in June 1963, by 1965 we were sure that the FBI was tapping lines and was treating the Movement as if it were an alien enemy. We accepted that as part of the evil and injustice that come with leadership which challenges the status quo. This is one of those things that you have to rationalize. We knew we did not deserve that treatment from our government but we believed that suffering was redemptive and that it was part of what we had to go through in order to achieve our goals. We believed in our vows; we never became embittered or disillusioned; we held on to our faith. At times we were discouraged, but never permanently. That was how we were able to continue. It was difficult to prove what the FBI was doing, and the bureau was so powerful even Presidents were intimidated by it. We were not intimidated; we just realized that it was too much to try to take on an organization like that while also maintaining our struggle for civil rights. How much further we still had to go!

15

"We will take the nonviolent movement all over the United States"

The Voting Rights Bill was signed on August 6, 1965. Although further federal legislation would be needed, this bill and the Civil Rights Act of 1964 represented a major advance in the legal protection of African-American rights. However, the new laws did little to help the plight of millions of blacks in the ghettos of the great northern cities. They were held down, not by segregation laws or voting restrictions, but by a more subtle yet powerful *de facto* segregation and by economic discrimination. For that reason their situation was in some respects worse than that of blacks in the South. They were without hope. With astute insight into the problem, Martin soon realized that the significant long-term political gains and the victories for human dignity, fundamental though they were, did not adequately relieve current intolerable distress. The agony of poverty required direct, immediate remedies, and he turned the direction of the Movement more fully to bread-and-butter issues.

Immediately after the Selma campaign, at a meeting of the SCLC board in Baltimore on April 2, in spite of strong opposition on the board, Martin proposed that SCLC expand its activities into the North and West. "You can expect us in Baltimore, Philadelphia, Detroit, Los Angeles, and Chicago," he said. "I tell you, we will take the nonviolent movement all over the United States."

Martin's determination to move north was reinforced by the outbreak of rioting in the great urban centers. There had been a bad riot in Harlem, in the summer of 1964. Two weeks after the President signed the Voting Rights Bill, there was a devastating eruption of rioting in the Watts district of Los Angeles. Martin was then at the world convention of the Disciples of Christ in San Juan, Puerto Rico. He flew to Los Angeles immediately to confer with city officials, Governor Pat Brown of California, and the black leaders in an attempt to calm the turbulence. Beyond this, and more important, he sought to impress upon the Establishment the fact that the people had legitimate complaints and that the solution was not to quell riots and return to business as usual, but to ensure economic and political equality.

Some "commentators" have said that Martin Luther King appealed only to middle-aged southern church people and had no rapport with young people or blacks in the North. His close comradeship with the student protests and later with the black people in Chicago and New York, of course, belies the charge. And Martin told us, after his trip to Watts, that as he walked the streets those terrible nights, the people, young and old, would gather and listen to him, thoughtfully and sympathetically. Martin almost felt that on that night the response had been so strong a new movement might have been founded, so ready were the people to follow him.

Of course, the problem was that it was physically impossible to get to see most of the people, and that once a riot starts, the violence multiplies upon itself and tragedy is almost inevitable. An additional problem was the insensitivity of the power structure; its concern was almost entirely for damaged property. The damaged human lives resulting from years of segregation and discrimination only remotely touched those in power.

Martin was always saddened by the outbreaks of violence, not only because of the death and destruction that resulted but also because he felt that such events set back the cause of black freedom. He was intensely sympathetic to the despairing blacks who rioted, and he understood their reasons. As he said, "Rioting is the language of the unheard."

He also realized that palliative measures were not enough and that the roots of black discontent lay in the appalling poverty in which they existed—"lived" is too fine a word. This must somehow be corrected. At the same time, he felt that the burning and killing and looting terrified people, black as well as white, and intensified white backlash without accomplishing any but the most token reforms.

Many whites felt guilty about the deprivations of African Americans, and these outbreaks eased their consciences and gave them an excuse to say, "If blacks are going to behave in this irresponsible way, they don't deserve the rights they are demanding." Rioting gave the white Establishment an easy way out.

Some ultra-militants criticized Martin and tried to identify him as an Uncle Tom. They sought to depict his compassion and humanity as weakness and cowardice. They had little effect because the native wisdom of black people told them that a leader who goes down again and again into the streets at the head of his followers and faces guns and clubs is a valiant of legendary proportions.

However, Martin was never embittered by criticism, nor would he withdraw from the dialogue to dissuade black people from the path of violence. He divided the ultra-militants and black nationalists into two basic groups. A few were convinced terrorists, and these he sought to isolate. The larger number were often honestly confused on tactics, and with them he had many long discussions. He understood their terrible conflicts, and when he had the opportunity to reach them he usually convinced them that there were effective *and* manly alternatives to blind violence. In Chicago, Cleveland, and elsewhere, Martin drew to his side men who had accepted violence as the way until they came under his influence. Many of them became his unarmed bodyguards, others suppressed violent tendencies in the ranks, and more than a few converted so completely to nonviolence that they joined the SCLC staff.

Some black conservative leaders could not walk the streets of some ghettos because the hostility against them was too threatening, but Martin could walk alone anywhere. Even when there were reservations about his tactics, the respect people had for his personal bravery and honesty was a shield. In all his years of activity in close proximity to millions, no black person ever laid a hand on

Martin. The sole exception was the clinically insane woman who stabbed him in Harlem.

Martin did not have a one-dimensional, negative view of black nationalism. He saw it, partially, as black self-respect trying to surface. He realized that it was not necessarily anti-white, but that it is extremely difficult to be proudly black and to feel equal in so repressive a white society. Above all, he kept in mind that the whites who reproached militants in self-righteous indignation conveniently forgot that the evil was caused by white racism in the first place. Yet Martin would not compromise with hate or violence, and the careful balance he maintained earned him respect from both whites and blacks who could not yet understand each other.

After Martin's death we went through a period of nationalism and separatism. Unfortunately, there was no voice like his to speak forthrightly about nonviolence as a method of social change. That is one reason today's young people do not know enough about the nonviolent Movement. While they were growing up, all they saw on television was violence, and they came to believe it was the only thing which would work.

Of course, Martin never merely dismissed disagreement or criticism. He constantly reevaluated his position and himself in the light of each new circumstance. He was quick to say, if he felt he had erred, "I was wrong that time." As I have explained, he criticized himself more severely than anyone else ever did.

As Martin pushed the Movement out from the South to the national scene, he did even more traveling than before. Sometimes he would take the children on these trips. I remember his taking Marty and Yoki on a tour of the black-belt counties of Alabama in connection with a "get-out-the-vote" drive for the 1966 primaries. Later on, Marty went to a rally in Baltimore with Martin. He had a great sense of pride in being with his daddy, and especially did he love to ride in a motorcade from the airport with Martin, with motorcycle police clearing the way and sirens screaming. We had to be careful not to let him get puffed up with pride over this special treatment.

One strange effect of such experiences is that they gave Marty a very positive attitude toward policemen. Unlike most black children, who, because of the brutality they can see for themselves, think of the police as enemies, Marty found policemen fascinating. I would feel somewhat ironic about this with my own recollection of certain police in our experiences. When, at about five or six years old, Marty went with me to the airport to meet his father, he would go up to the airport policeman on duty and start a conversation with him, ask him questions about himself and his God. One day I saw him reach over and put his hand on the policeman's revolver. I almost shouted out, but the man seemed perfectly relaxed, and I told myself, "Well, I guess it's all right. If Marty has no fear of the gun, and the policeman isn't worried, this is very good."

My children were able to avoid a lot of stereotypes that many people grow up with because I taught them to see each situation for what it was. Because I told them that going to jail was a badge of honor and that their father was helping people by doing it, they never thought of police people as bad people. It helps when you do not teach your children to hate; it helps them to be more positive people, and they do not have to get rid of that bitterness later on. We protected and sheltered the children to some extent, but you can always find something positive to say rather than emphasizing the negatives all of the time. I felt that once they were older and could make decisions on their own, then they could know the truth.

Martin was pretty impetuous about his trips. In the summer of 1967 we had no time to take a vacation, so we moved with the children to a motel on the outskirts of Atlanta to get away from the pressure at home for a few days. As we were unpacking and getting settled into our room, Martin said, "I have to go to Chicago this afternoon."

Terribly disappointed, I said, "I thought you were going to be able to spend a week here with us."

"Well, I'll be back tomorrow," he said. "I was just thinking I'd like to take Marty and Dexter with me."

"That's a good idea, but we haven't got the right clothes for them here," I said.

That kind of sudden trip was the story of his life. On this occasion we were all settled in a hotel and had to send home to get clothes for the boys. Martin was trying to find a way to spend more time with the children. But every time we started to have a break, something happened. We never got together. That was the story of our lives too. At least he managed to take the boys on that trip. I was delighted knowing how good the experience was for them.

After Martin decided that we should launch a campaign in the North, he and the staff would discuss possible cities; Chicago, Philadelphia, Washington, New York, Cleveland, and Detroit were considered. Earlier in Chicago, there had been a drive for better school integration by Albert Raby's Coordinating Council of Community Organizations. There were no segregation laws, of course, but the ghetto schools were all black and completely inadequate. On his trips to Chicago, my husband had talked to many of the people on the streets, and he understood their despair and the terrible conditions under which they lived. He also realized that it was, in a sense, harder for northern blacks to pinpoint their grievances than for those of us in the South who had as obvious villains the Wallaces, the Jim Clarks, the Bull Connors. Martin felt the tensions and the problems in Chicago were so serious, and the crisis so urgent, that he must address himself to them to avoid the worst kind of chaos.

It was decided that Chicago would be the target city for the SCLC drive—a pilot project designed to dramatize the issues and focus the attention of the nation on the despair, hopelessness, and desperation of ghetto existence.

In the summer of 1965 Martin made several trips to Chicago, and at one point he led a parade of twenty thousand people to City Hall. In January 1966, the SCLC staff moved in to lay the groundwork for the Chicago Movement. This time Martin decided not to stay at a hotel, but to rent a slum apartment for us in order to share with the people of the ghetto the kind of life that was imposed upon them daily by the system. I went with him when he formally took up his residence there, and rarely in all my life had I seen anything like it. Our apartment was on the third floor of a dingy building which had no lights in the hall, only one dim bulb at the head of the stairs. There was no lock on the front door of this house; it always stood open. As we walked in, I realized that the floor was not concrete, but bare dirt. The smell of urine was overpowering. We were told that this was because the door was always open, and drunks came in off the street to use the hallway as a toilet.

We walked up three rickety flights of stairs, in gloom you could hardly see through, and into our new quarters. When the owner heard Martin was to be his tenant, he had cleaned the apartment up and painted it—people laughed about that. It was a railroad flat, with a sitting room in front and the rest of the rooms going straight back—two bedrooms, a kitchen, and a bath of sorts. You had to go through the bedrooms to get to the kitchen. There was an old refrigerator which, once it was filled with food, would not keep the food cold or make ice. There was also a dilapidated gas stove. The temperature outside was about fifteen degrees, and the heat in the apartment was hardly noticeable. Rickety wooden fire escapes led down to a narrow court. For this magnificent abode Martin had to pay ninety dollars a month, unfurnished. At the same time, nice, larger apartments in white sections were going for eighty dollars a month. How the poor are exploited! Martin and I lived in and out of this apartment until the summer, when we brought the children to be with us.

However, before our family settled in Chicago, on Monday, June 6, 1966, Martin was presiding over a meeting of the SCLC staff at our headquarters in Atlanta. Word came in: "James Meredith has been shot."

Meredith was the young man who had personally integrated the University of Mississippi in 1962. On June 6, 1966, he and four friends had started on a march through Mississippi to test civil rights progress there. First reports said Meredith was killed; but Martin soon learned that he was only wounded and had been taken to a hospital in Memphis, Tennessee.

Martin flew to Memphis immediately, where he was joined by Floyd McKissick of CORE; Stokely Carmichael, who had just been elected chairman of SNCC; and Jim Lawson, who headed SCLC's affiliate in Memphis. They went to see Meredith in his hospital room. Knowing that Meredith was a "loner," Martin asked if it was all right with him if Martin and the others continued the march in Meredith's place. Meredith said, "Yes. This thing is bigger than me."

The leaders set up headquarters in Jim Lawson's Centenary Methodist Church. The next morning they drove out to the place where Meredith had been shot and started walking Highway 51 toward Jackson, Mississippi, with a couple of Mississippi Highway Patrol cars following. There was some unexpected criticism of Martin for doing this from conservative black leaders. Martin saw the gunning down of Meredith as an effort not just to stop one man, but to intimidate the whole Movement for equality in Mississippi. His own sense of responsibility and deep commitment to racial justice impelled him to take up this crusade.

Some of the most agonizing experiences Martin had in the whole struggle of the nonviolent Movement came during the Mississippi March. For the first time there appeared persons among his ranks who questioned the effectiveness of the nonviolent approach. In other words, nonviolence was to be severely tested, but it would survive the test.

Stokely Carmichael had proposed that it should be an all-black march—with no whites invited or even tolerated. Martin defeated that idea by threatening to withdraw. Later on, at Grenada, Mississippi, Stokely started shouting the then new slogan "Black Power." In a heated meeting of the leaders, Martin objected and proposed "Black Equality." That was unacceptable to the young radicals. But by using the full leverage of his name, Martin forced them to abandon the "Black Power" chant during that demonstration. Martin did not object to the concept of Black Power at all. He merely was protesting the violent context into which the slogan was being placed, and the deliberately provocative way in which it was being shouted.

As they marched along together the next day, Carmichael said, "Martin, I deliberately started the Black Power thing to get you committed to it."

"That's all right," Martin answered smiling. "I've been used before. One more time won't hurt."

James Meredith recovered enough to join the group for the final day's march from Tougaloo College to the State Capitol in Jackson. There Martin addressed the largest turnout of black people that had ever gathered in Mississippi. At the end of his speech he prophesied, "One day, right here in Mississippi, justice will become a reality for all."

In Mississippi, for the first time, Marty and Yoki had marched with us. Then, in Chicago, "Freedom Sunday" was set for July 10, 1966. Right after the Mississippi march ended, Martin and I took the children to our slum apartment there. It was pretty difficult living there with four children. In summer, with the windows open, it was extremely noisy—the roar of traffic off the main avenue just beyond us, the shouts and yells of young people playing in the streets, and, of course, noises of everything from radios to conversation from the other apartments crowded together.

By that time we had some furniture that had been bought at a secondhand store and some that had been donated. Though the landlord had freshly painted our apartment, "because it was for Dr. King," he had put the paint on without scraping off the old paint, so that it looked smeared and uneven. The living room floors and hallway had been tiled, but the bedroom and kitchen floors were bare. I had put some curtains up and tried to do some decorating to make the apartment a little more livable. In spite of all this, it was grim.

However, I think the experience was very meaningful for my children, who had never before known such poverty. Although we lived as simply as we could at home, our mode of life was totally different from that of our comrades in the slums. There was nothing for the children to do except go outside the apartment building and play in the black dirt. There was nothing green in sight; even the playground was black dirt. The moment they were dressed and went outdoors, their clothes became soiled. I realized that this was everyday life for the children who lived there. My children were there by choice.

Even at that, we were living on a far higher scale than many of our neighbors. I remember going through the ghetto with my husband. On the third floor of one building, a family of ten was xisting in one small apartment. There were two young babies mong them, and the apartment had no running water and no eat in the winter. I have never seen such depressing conditions. The people were glad to see us, but at the same time they were mbarrassed about their state. There was just nothing they could do about their multitude of problems, and they seemed to have given up trying. I wondered how they managed to get enough to at.

Martin told them how concerned he was and that he wanted to help them to try to get the water turned on—there was plumbing—as well as the heat. Eventually we went to work on this building ourselves. With the help of some of our SCLC staff and supporters we swept down the stairs and halls and took several days' collection of garbage out. We encouraged the people not to pay rent but to take the money and fix up the apartment themselves. Later the landlord sued the SCLC!

The reactions to Martin among the people of the ghetto were extremely favorable. He was almost like a Messiah to them. Some of them came to greet us and welcome us to the neighborhood. They came to our apartment and talked to Martin about their problems and needs—heat, light, water, and food—and sometimes asked his help in paying their rent. Certain younger people seemed at first to resent our presence in the neighborhood. One day a teenage gang came by. Martin was taking a nap, so I met with them. They started by complaining that they did not want white people around—of course, some of our staff were white. At that moment, luckily, three SCLC colleagues, Bernard Lee, Andy Young, and Al Sampson, came in. Al told them that there were a lot of white people who were helping our Cause and that some had even died for us.

I could feel the tension rising, and I was somewhat frightened. My fear had grown out of my knowledge of the violence which such groups had customarily practiced. Bernard Lee tried to make these youngsters believe that we could understand their feelings. Eventually some of them left, but Andy, who is so gifted at working with young people, encouraged the leaders to stay. I had gone to the kitchen, and Andy came out and asked me to fix some sandwiches for them. Dora McDonald, Martin's secretary, helped me prepare and serve the food.

When Martin woke up and came out, one of the teenagers said, "Is that really you? Is that really Martin Luther King?"

My husband said, "This is me. I'm Martin Luther King."

The boy said, "You don't mean to tell me I'm sitting here with this cat who's been up there talking to Presidents! He's been up there eating filet mignon steaks, and now he's sitting here eating barbecue just like me." We could see that our presence in their neighborhood did help to create a feeling of identity which was to become especially meaningful as we escalated our Chicago program.

Martin continued to hold meetings and to work with the gangs, and they became very protective toward him. They said, "You don't need any police around to guard you. We'll take care of you." We never encouraged their protection, though we understood they were always around.

And, in the matter of working with white people, they finally said, "Well, Dr. King, we'll accept the ones which you recommend."

As he preached nonviolence to them, many of them still said, "We believe in violence," though gradually we won some of them over to our point of view. As one man said, "You know, I've been in the basement all my life. I have a daughter, and I want her to go to college, but I'm still in the basement."

They were decent young men with aspirations, but the system had forced them in the direction of hate and violence. It meant a great deal to them and to us that they came to our apartment and felt free to talk. We tried to show them how they could use their energy constructively—how they could go out and get people registered, and elect the right men to office to represent them. They claimed they had no faith in anyone anymore, but they finally said, "The only person we have faith in is Dr. King."

We held workshops with the gang leaders, trying to communicate the discipline of nonviolence. In the end, many members of the gangs pledged themselves to nonviolence and demonstrated with us in accordance with our beliefs. The effectiveness of our work with the Chicago teenage gangs is one of the greatest tributes to the nonviolent method, and to my husband's leadership.

The big rally and demonstration toward which we had been working since October 1965 took place at Soldier Field on Sunday, July 10, 1966. Fifty thousand people came, an unprecedented number in Chicago. We took all four children with us on the platform, even though Bernice was only three.

Back in June, Martin had announced a massive, detailed program to bring about racial justice in Chicago. At Soldier Field, after the speeches and the music—Mahalia Jackson sang—Martin read his demands to all those people while they cheered him. When the rally was over, he led them to City Hall to present the demands to Mayor Richard Daley.

We had planned to let the three older children march, even though we were afraid it would be tiring for Dexter. Bernice had heard her sister and brothers talking about it, and all that day she kept asking, "When are we going to march?" After the speeches were over, she said, "But we haven't marched yet."

Martin never could resist Bernice's wishes. As a child she was the greatest charmer of them all, full of affection and joyful spirit and an extra-large dose of her father's ability to persuade people.

Martin used to say, "Sometimes I wish we could freeze Bunny just the way she is—so cute, so full of innocence and sweetness."

It was strange. I used to watch the two of them together, playing their games, loving each other, and I would pray that nothing would happen to Martin. More than with the other children, perhaps because she was so young, I would have the most painful consciousness of how much Bernice needed her daddy.

In Chicago that day, seeing that Bernice wanted so badly to come with us, I finally asked Martin, "What are we going to do about Bunny?"

He answered, "Let her march with us."

So we all started out together at the head of that enormous crowd of people. It was, I believe, the hottest day of the year. It was not a long march—fifteen or twenty blocks—but after the first three or four, Bernice got tired. She was carried the rest of the distance on the shoulders of Bernard Lee and Andy Young. Soon she was fast asleep with all of her tired innocence. She never did see City Hall.

Of course Mayor Daley was not there. In fact, City Hall was closed up tight. Martin was prepared, and in a magnificent symbolic gesture that rang down the centuries from his namesake, he nailed his demands to the closed door of the City Hall, as Martin Luther had nailed his Ninety-Five Theses to the door at Wittenberg. Yoki, Marty, and Dexter stood beside their father as he performed this ritualistic act.

The march had been a beautiful nonviolent demonstration, with singing and apparent goodwill from bystanders and participants alike. We were not facing anyone like Jim Clark or Bull Connor, then. In 1968, of course, Mayor Daley's police were brutal to *white* demonstrators for Senator Eugene McCarthy and peace in Vietnam, but in our case they handled the crowds efficiently and politely. The peaceful conditions at our march encouraged us immensely. As a follow-up, the next morning, Martin and a cross section of the leadership of the Chicago community met with Mayor Daley to discuss their demands. Mayor Daley rejected them flatly. This news spread rapidly over Chicago. Then, the very same night, as suddenly as a summer thunderstorm, violence erupted.

A mass meeting had been scheduled for Monday night, and that evening, Martin and I had dinner at Mahalia Jackson's house. As we were leaving, she said, "I used to sing at all the churches around here, so I know where your meeting is being held. I'll come along and show you the way."

Driving toward the church, we saw a crowd of people running up the street. Martin said, "I wonder if there's a riot starting."

As we went on, we saw gangs of young men milling around and heard the sharp sound of guns. Police were detouring traffic, and we asked them what was going on. They told us that some kids had turned the fire hydrants on to cool themselves. Since there were no swimming pools provided for children in the ghetto during the hot summer, this was common practice. When the police turned them off, the fighting started. We heard later that some of our staff people had tried to intervene, but the police would not let them handle the situation.

The youngsters started by throwing rocks and breaking windows, and then the gangs got involved. There did not seem to be any plan at all. It was a spontaneous outbreak. Yet, even a small thing can lead to bloody rioting, where so desperate conditions exist and with improper handling by police officials. All too often, it is the police who provoke the riots.

When we got to the meeting, everyone was upset and angry. Several black youths had been badly beaten, and others had been arrested. Two groups, the Cobras and the Vice Lords, had gathered across the street from the church, and they sent a delegation to the church saying that if the prisoners were not released immediately, they were going to tear up the city.

Martin, Bernard, Andy Young, Al Raby, Mahalia, and I went to the police station to see what we could do. The place was crowded with angry people, including the parents of some of those arrested. The police, while not exactly hostile, were not too receptive to our coming.

Martin persuaded the authorities to allow us to post bail for the prisoners. We took these young men back to the church with us and asked what they wanted. They talked about a swimming pool and other recreational facilities. Then an unwise member of the audience got up and said he had lived in the area all his life and he just did not understand why people wanted to tear down the neighborhood and break windows.

Naturally this was not what the young men wanted to hear. They walked out, and the rest of the audience began to melt away.

Outside the church, crowds had gathered, and cars with white people in them were being stopped. The police arrived, and you could see there might be shooting. Martin was greatly concerned and was trying to stop the trouble. Members of his staff kept saying to him, "We'll stay here and take care of things. Dr. King, please get into the car and leave."

When the crowds came surging back toward us, we finally got Martin into the car and drove away. We became separated from

Mahalia, and we were terribly worried. We had several offices in the various neighborhoods of Chicago and we went from one to the other to receive reports.

Many of the SCLC staff were in the streets all night. Among them were James Orange, who worked very effectively in organizing the gangs, Reverend Charles Billups, Stony Cooks, James Bevel, and Al Sampson. They kept coming in to report. Finally someone found Mahalia and brought her to us. We talked to people in the streets, and when things seemed to have calmed down, we went to spend the night at Mahalia's home.

Our good friends John and Ruth Thurston had taken the children just that day to visit with their six children for a few days in order to give me a rest; they were safe on another side of town. It was a lucky coincidence, since it enabled me to be on the streets with Martin for most of the night.

The next day SCLC held meetings all day to try to determine the deeper causes of the riot and what could be done to stop it. SCLC staffers did meet with some of the gang leaders. But Chicago is such a big city, and we were so few, that our effectiveness was diminished. Once violence starts, it is contagious. The problem was that we had to deal, not with one neighborhood, but with pockets of people scattered over an enormous area.

I had to address a women's meeting at the YWCA on the North Side the next day at noon. I had been up nearly all night and was depressed, depleted, and completely exhausted. I was supposed to talk about unity, but that was hardly the day for it. Everyone was preoccupied and disturbed about what had happened the night before, and many of the women had been out on the streets trying to help. They had seen for themselves just how desperate the conditions of these young black people were.

It was proposed that one hundred women sign a telegram to Mayor Daley supporting Martin's proposals. Some of the women seemed to be afraid to sign. Perhaps it was because their husbands held jobs with the city, and the wives did not want to jeopardize them. Because these were my husband's proposals, at first I was a little reluctant to push for the telegram; but at one point I felt I had to say something. I asked, "What are you afraid of? The time comes when we have to make a decision and we have to make a choice."

After that they decided to send the telegram. They also decided, as I had suggested, to form an organization of women to support the work we were doing in Chicago. Then the director of the Y—a white woman—came along and said it so much better than I. She proposed an organization which was later called Women Mobilized for Change. It was integrated—white and black. It grew to over one thousand members, according to its director, Joan Brown, and continued doing good work.

That night we again stayed with Mahalia, and brought the children to join us. The following day the children and I went back to the apartment. I had to speak to a group that night on the North Side of town and my husband was addressing a mass meeting on the West Side. Without a baby-sitter, I had to take the children with me.

While I was getting dressed, we heard glass shatter in the street. My children, who were looking out of the window, saw some boys go up and break a plate-glass shop window, shout "Black Power," and run away. Then we realized the riot had moved to our neighborhood.

The people came to take us to the meeting, and I sat the children on the platform with me. When it came time for me to speak, I introduced all the children. It was long past Bernice's bedtime, and she was very tired and restless. I picked her up in my arms when I introduced her, but she slid out of my arms and made a grab for the water pitcher down below. I apologized to the audience and explained how tired she was. I was very much aware that Bernice was on display, and I was afraid people would think she was spoiled—not just tired. I got Yolanda to take her out while I was speaking.

Before I finished my talk, an usher interrupted me to say, "Mrs. King, you have an emergency call from Dr. King."

I spoke for two or three minutes more, explaining to the audience the problem, and then went to the telephone. Martin was very worried. "What happened?" he asked. "I called the apartment and didn't get an answer. I hear they're rioting on that side of town. I thought it had gotten so bad you had to get the children out."

"No," I said. "They're right here with me."

Martin told me that he could not leave the neighborhood he was in because there was still trouble there. I told him that I would take the children back to the apartment but I hoped he would keep in touch with me.

What followed was a nightmare. When we were driven back to the apartment, the riot was going full swing. There was a lot of broken glass on the streets, and as we drove down Fifteenth Street we could hear shooting, though I didn't know whether it was the police or the rioters.

I went upstairs and found a British reporter and an AP reporter waiting. I asked them to be seated while I started getting the children ready for bed. The first thing the children did was to run to the window to see where the shots were coming from. I really shouted at them: "Get away from that window or you'll get your heads shot off!"

Of course, that is exactly the kind of thing headlines are made of. It sounded as though I was terrified, though I really wasn't. I just wanted the children to move fast to a safer place, and perhaps because of my anxiety, I spoke in an overly dramatic way.

After that the reporters sat and talked for a while. They were pretty nervous, and I tried to reassure them, though I could understand that because they were white and in that neighborhood that night, anything could happen. The British newsman was really appalled. He couldn't seem to understand what was going on, or why.

After a while the reporters left, but the next day, unfortunately, the headlines screamed, "Mrs. King fears for her children's lives."

The rioting went on almost all that night. I remember after getting the three younger children to bed, Yolanda and I were looking out the back window at a grocery store a few yards away. Young rioters were looting the store. I heard them when they smashed the glass, and I could see them getting the groceries, piling them into shopping carts, and wheeling them away. It was very distressing to me to watch.

At last I got Yoki to bed, and lay down myself, listening to the shooting. It sounded horrible.

In the meantime my husband had called several times. The last time he said, "I'm here in a restaurant in the neighborhood with some of the fellows who are involved in this."

He told me that he was being treated to barbecue sandwiches and that he felt that it was important for him to stay out there with them and try to keep things under control. I finally went to sleep about four o'clock. Martin must have come in sometime after that, but I didn't hear him.

Soon after the rioting ended, I took the children back to Atlanta. Martin kept going back to Chicago for three or four days a week. It had been decided to concentrate the Chicago Movement on open housing first. There was tremendous resistance to this in some white suburbs where Martin led one or two protest marches. He told me that never, even in the South, had he seen such hatred in the eyes of white people. On one occasion, when there was an open-housing demonstration in Gage Park, someone hit Martin in the head with a rock. It knocked him down, but he got up again quickly and went on. He was not seriously injured, but he did get another bad headache.

This aspect of the Chicago Movement ended when, to avoid what seemed an inevitable bloody confrontation, a conference was held, over which Martin and Mayor Daley presided. Archbishop John Cody came, and there were representatives of the Chicago Real Estate Board and the Chicago Housing Authority, as well as business and industrial leaders and, of course, people from SCLC and black leaders from Chicago. An agreement on open housing was reached and announced on August 26.

We felt that we had achieved a victory after a long struggle against recalcitrant forces. The opposition knew that change was inevitable, but change does not come without pressure and without sacrifice and real determination. Unfortunately the agreement was never properly implemented. The city officials failed to keep their promises. I believe that Chicago could have avoided much tension, strife, and bloodshed later had this agreement been lived up to.

In order to grapple with Chicago's problem of poverty and

unemployment, SCLC next organized an Operation Breadbasket in Chicago. We realized how much money was taken out of the ghetto and how little put into it; most of the businesses, stores, houses, and apartments have white absentee ownership. The people who live there pay rent and buy food; yet all the profits go to outsiders, and blacks don't even have an equal chance at a job. We were concerned not only with obtaining or upgrading more jobs for the blacks, but with getting more positions of management and ownership in the chain stores, the franchised businesses, and other such establishments.

Operation Breadbasket had already been successful in Atlanta and was operative in seven other southern states. The technique had been to first make a survey of how much blacks spent in the various business establishments; then we would send a committee, preferably of ministers, to call on the owners or managers of the businesses and ask them to make a proportionate effort to employ African Americans. If they did not comply voluntarily, their businesses would be boycotted. Daddy King was one of the most effective workers in this cause. He would tackle a business street by himself—"without a committee," as he'd say—and very soon after Daddy King announced to the shopkeeper, "Well, we have to see about getting some blacks in here," there would be black employees.

Another big problem many black communities face in becoming economically independent is to obtain capital. Part of our program was to get businesses to deposit their money in black banks, which are more likely to lend money to black businesspeople than are all-white banks.

In Chicago, Operation Breadbasket was ably led by Reverend Jesse Jackson, who later became SCLC national director for Operation Breadbasket, the economic development arm of SCLC, before going on to found his own organization, Operation PUSH. He is the president of the National Rainbow Coalition and has twice run for President of the United States.

The drive started with the milk companies and then spread all over Chicago, into practically all areas of living. Operation Breadbasket really did a tremendous job, not only in terms of getting more and better jobs for black people, but also, I think, in terms of the spiritual development of our people. It created a whole new way of life for many black men and women.

I attended one of Reverend Jesse Jackson's meetings in Chicago in October 1967, and I heard him give his regular message. It was terribly meaningful to me. There was a feeling of oneness and unity that seemed to me almost like the spirit of the early Christians. I have had a rich life, with many moving experiences, but I came away with the feeling that this was one of the greatest spiritual experiences I ever had.

I came home and said to Martin, "I think that Jesse Jackson and Operation Breadbasket have something that is needed in every community across the nation."

16

"You must be prepared to continue"

Though Martin had for a long time been concerned with the vital question of world peace, it was early in 1967 that he took the most explicit and outspoken steps in opposing the war in Vietnam. Prior to that he was in conflict about spending his very limited time and effort in the cause of international peace and dissipating his energies from the Movement for black freedom.

By 1966 it had become apparent to Martin not only that the Vietnam War was wrong, but that it was engulfing huge sums of money that could otherwise be spent fighting poverty. In January 1967, after long and serious deliberation, he decided to speak out. At a conference in Los Angeles he said, "The promises of the Great Society have been shot down on the battlefields of Vietnam. The pursuit of this widened war has narrowed domestic welfare programs, making the poor, white and Negro, bear the heaviest burdens. . . . It is estimated that we spend $322,000 for each enemy we kill, while we spend in the so-called war on poverty in America only about $53 for each person classified as poor. . . . We must combine the fervor of the Civil Rights Movement with the peace movement."

Martin made his first speech devoted entirely to Vietnam on April 4, 1967, at the Riverside Church in New York. I was very glad when Martin was able to take a strong position on the question of peace, because I felt that he had something important to contribute. I remember saying to him so many times, especially after he received the Nobel Peace Prize, "I think there is a role you must play in achieving world peace, and I will be so glad when the time comes when you can assume that role."

I realized that this was what I felt when Martin got the Nobel Prize. Then, when he made the statement on Vietnam, I had the strong feeling that this was the beginning of a larger work for him which would develop into something greater than we could conceive at the time. All along in our struggle one phase had led to another. As the years unfolded, it was like watching a scroll unfolding—you see more and more as you unroll it. There was a pattern and a process at work for the development of mankind; and though I had said it so often before, I felt again at the time of the 1967 statement on peace that Martin was an instrument of a Divine plan and purpose.

I think Martin believed this, but Martin had been, until 1967, carefully weighing the effect a peace statement might have on the Civil Rights Movement. He knew that it would take a long process of education to make people understand the relationship between peace and freedom. I felt that if anyone could do this, Martin could, because the people had faith in him. Although perhaps they sometimes did not fully comprehend what he was saying, they would decide, "If Dr. King says it, it must be so."

I believed that to combine the spiritual essence of the peace movement and the Civil Rights Movement would bring a lot of good people in this country together. The peace movement was composed primarily of whites who would be brought into closer cooperation with us. It would become one movement for good. You cannot separate peace and freedom; they are inextricably related.

At first Daddy King did not approve of Martin's stand. After some thought, he said, "I could not speak out against M.L. on the peace statement, though at the time I thought he was wrong. But when he finished his great speech, I knew—the whole audience knew—the man was right. He was a genius. I am not talking about my son when I say that, I'm talking about a world citizen. He moved beyond us early. He did not belong to us, he belonged to all the world."

The April 4, 1967, speech was made to an audience of clergy

and laymen. Martin was among the principal speakers, along with John C. Bennett, Dr. Henry Steele Commager, and Rabbi Abraham Heschel. Martin's address was called "Beyond Vietnam" and was, I think, one of the finest and most prophetic speeches he ever made. It was far-reaching in both content and import. In it he described the United States as the "greatest purveyor of violence today." He said, "If America's soul becomes totally poisoned, part of the autopsy must read Vietnam." He pointed out that African Americans were "dying in disproportionate numbers in Vietnam," a "reflection of the Negro's position in America." In summing up Martin said, "A nation that continues year after year to spend more money on military defense than on programs of social uplift is approaching spiritual death."

The reaction of the press to this speech was predictable—and quite controversial. But I think the fact that Martin came out and made such a strong statement had a tremendous impact on the thinking of many people in the country who might have been vacillating.

What we had not expected to be quite so strong was the reaction among Martin's colleagues in the Civil Rights Movement. At a board meeting of the NAACP on April 11, Roy Wilkins criticized Martin severely. Whitney Young, Jackie Robinson, and even Ralph Bunche also expressed publicly their disagreement with his position on Vietnam. Most of them felt that the Civil Rights Cause would be hurt by his pronouncements. Many people in the North and South felt that the two issues were going to be confused.

I replied to some of my friends, "Those persons who do not agree with my husband now do not understand the meaning of his whole life. You cannot believe in peace at home and not believe in international peace. He could not be a true follower of the non-violent philosophy and condone war. You think of him as a politician, but he feels that as a minister he has a prophetic role and must speak out against the evils of society. He sees war as an evil, and therefore he must condemn war."

I also pointed out that Pope Paul had recently visited this country and spoken against war, and my husband was really saying the same things. "When the Pope spoke, everyone applauded; but when a black man named Martin Luther King speaks, they criticize him. After all, Martin Luther King is a clergyman too, and taking the world as a whole, his influence may even be greater than that of the Pope."

In spite of all the criticism, Martin took part in the Spring Mobilization for Peace in New York on Saturday, April 15. I looked forward to being with him, because this was to be the first time we had been together in a peace demonstration. I tried to keep my calendar clear, but a couple of weekends beforehand Martin said to me, "I told the people who are staging the rally for peace in San Francisco that you would speak there. They need you out there." I must admit my disappointment in not being able to share this experience with Martin.

Of course, I went to San Francisco. There were sixty thousand people in the stadium, so it was extremely worthwhile. I would like to have been with Martin and to have seen the quarter million people he told me about, from all walks of life, who walked solemnly down the streets of New York that day.

After Martin led the demonstration for peace in New York, there was even more severe criticism. My husband answered it best in a talk he had with a young civil rights worker who had publicly denounced him. Martin called this man on the telephone, and I listened to their conversation.

Martin said, "I want you to know that this is a moral commitment with me, and I have had a great deal of anxiety over the fact that I haven't been able to take a position publicly earlier. When the day came when I could take a stand publicly on the war question, it was one of the happiest moments of my life.

"For a long time I encouraged my wife to be active in the peace movement. Finally I could no longer stand silently by. I have spoken my convictions that this is the most evil and unjust war in the history of our country."

Martin went on to review the history of the Vietnam War. When he finished, the young man said, "I see you do know what you're talking about. I admit that I just didn't understand it."

After this conversation, Martin turned to me and said, "I know I'm right. I know this is an unjust and evil war. I have made my decision to oppose it, and whatever people say, I am going to stick to my convictions."

As we reflect now on the course of events, Martin's peace activity marked incontestably a major turning point in the thinking of the nation. The tide began to turn to peace as the majority of the country saw the war as not only erroneous, impractical policy, but also unsound in morality. I think history will mark his boldness in speaking out so early and eloquently—despite singularly virulent opposition—as one of his major contributions. In defining these debasing national deficiencies and in offering constructive solutions, he was supporting the best in the American tradition.

There were more terrible riots in the summer of 1967. Martin often said, "Winters of delay bring about our summers of riots." He was terribly distressed, more so than I had ever seen him. He felt that people were looking to him for a creative solution, and he had not been able to propose one. He said, "People expect me to have answers, and I don't have any answers."

Many blacks were saying that the nonviolent Movement had failed, but I remember saying to Martin during those days, "There are millions of people who have faith in you and feel that you are our best hope."

Then I said to him, "I believe in you, if that means anything." And he replied, "Yes, it means a great deal."

As the summer went on, he continued to think hard about a real solution. He wrestled with these problems as he traveled all over the country speaking. Everywhere the press would ask him about the riots, and over and over again Martin would answer, "I condemn the violence of the riots; but I understand the conditions that cause them. I think we must be just as concerned about correcting those conditions as we are about punishing the guilty." His agony was all the more intense because he felt that our nation was not willing to face up to the basic causes of riots, which were in essence a moral issue. He would say, "I seriously question the will and moral power of this nation to save itself." He knew that only the nation could save itself from destruction.

Toward autumn he said to me, "We must have a program centered around jobs and economic opportunities. We have to think in terms of some creative nonviolent action in these areas." He was still searching for a way.

One person who helped him find that way was Marian Wright Edelman, who had been working among the poor of Mississippi. She had spent a good deal of time in Washington and knew of many programs that were available to poor people, but she had discovered that often the poor themselves knew nothing about them. Some way was needed to get these poverty programs initiated, particularly in states like Mississippi and Alabama. Marian had talked with a number of Congressmen and government officials, and she told Martin that they felt the climate was ready for some major thrust in the nonviolent Movement toward improvement of economic conditions. They thought that even the President might welcome some such move which would provide the federal government with a stimulus for action. Martin, in his usual fashion, began calling his trusted colleagues. He posed questions; he studied answers. His mind was crystallizing a plan.

My husband felt greatly encouraged by the knowledge that people in Washington were thinking along these lines. He came home that night radiating his old enthusiasm, and he said, "This is really it." He started talking about the possibility of a campaign in which poor people would go to Washington as their own representatives to plead their own case to all the relevant departments of government—Labor, Interior, Agriculture, Commerce. As he talked, Martin got more and more ideas, and I could see his excitement for the plan. He said, "We should get people from all the poverty areas, from the South and from the North, people who don't have jobs or resources. We must get them marching toward Washington. I think it would really dramatize the issue. It must not be just black people, it must be all poor people. We must include American Indians, Puerto Ricans, Mexicans, and even poor whites. . . ."

He realized that such a program would be a great change for the Movement, which had always focused on the rights of African Americans. Such a powerful coalition could really shake the established order and bring about needed structural changes to provide a better life for the poor. Martin felt the most difficult task might be to get the poor whites to see that they had a common interest with us. However, he was confident that it could be done.

That was the night the Poor People's Campaign was born. The plan was approved by the SCLC board, and the staff began to move. It was decided to concentrate on ten cities and five rural areas and to get two hundred people from each place. That would make the first contingent three thousand people. Of course, eventually the figure got much larger than that. Martin saw the Poor People's Campaign as a deterrent for the riots—giving people hope instead of despair and making them aware of programs already in existence. He also saw it as the answer to a pressing need for further programs. Our objectives, in Martin's words, were "economic security, decent sanitary housing, and quality education for every American."

As plans shaped up for the campaign, there was an enormous amount of preparatory work to be done. The sheer logistics of providing an encampment and food, medical supplies, water, and toilets for that many people was tremendous. In addition, coordinating the demands of the group was an enormous job that required patience and tact.

Martin believed in a guaranteed annual wage for all people. He believed that private industry must share the responsibility for training unskilled workers for better jobs. Government must help by subsidies. Martin would say that, after all, America had helped her immigrants to become adjusted. We gave them land. We gave them training. We helped businessmen—in the airlines, for example—to get started by giving them subsidies. So we were not proposing any extraordinary programs for black men, who, after all, had helped to build this country as unpaid slaves. We were asking only that we be given our fair share of the opportunity for life, liberty, and the pursuit of happiness.

Martin went on what we called "people-to-people tours" to recruit the poor for the great march. The response was terrific. People came out to hear him in large numbers, and they were eager and interested in the whole idea. He sometimes took the children with him and they came home all excited.

The enthusiasm of the people inspired Martin, as it always did. He had the novel idea of having a mule train go from Mississippi to Washington to dramatize the demonstration. Of course, being a city boy, he had never driven a mule train in his life, but the symbolism seemed so beautiful to him. As the plan grew and grew, Martin became more and more excited. He said to me, "This is a mammoth job. Before we have mobilized one city at a time. Now we are mobilizing a nation."

Early in March of 1968 Martin had the idea of bringing the leaders of other minority groups together in Atlanta—Puerto Ricans, Mexicans, Indians from the reservations, and poor whites from Appalachia. I was recuperating from surgery which I had in late January, but I went to the meeting because I thought of it as a historic occasion. I wanted to actually see for myself the different peoples sitting down in a room together discussing their common problems as they had never done before in this country. It was indeed a momentous occurrence.

At the meeting, the representatives talked about how they could participate in the campaign and whether they would be able to project their particular demands into the common program. It was a quite legitimate concern, because, as they said, "Our problems are different from yours."

The discussions were very friendly and we learned a lot from hearing each group describe its special needs. At the end of the meeting our program was endorsed, and the participants went home to recruit others to join us. We had all been united by one common problem—poverty.

There were, of course, other commitments that SCLC had to fulfill during these months. In the fall of 1967 there was a drive in Cleveland, Ohio, to register black voters. Though there were no legal impediments, disproportionately few African Americans were registered. A black candidate, Carl Stokes, was running for mayor, and Martin felt that his election would be a great inspiration to black people everywhere. Our drive succeeded in registering fifty thousand African Americans, and electing Carl Stokes to become the first black mayor of a major American city.

Throughout 1967, and during the planning of the Poor People's

Campaign early in 1968, we had, beyond everything, a sense of fate closing in. We did not let the feeling bow us down—we had lived with it too long for that. Years before, Martin had said to me, "You know, I probably won't live a long life, but if I die, I don't want you to grieve for me. You go on and live a normal life."

But death was not something he was morbid about; he just talked about it as he would any other experience. As the civil rights struggle went on, he saw the danger clearly. His knowledge of history made him realize that most men who had taken a strong moral position had to pay the price for their convictions. He even used the word "crucified" metaphorically, saying sometimes in his speeches, "I may be crucified for my beliefs, and if I am, you can say, 'He died to make men free.'"

Although Martin thought a lot about death, it did not seem to depress him. When people urged him to be careful, he said, "You know, I cannot worry about my safety; I cannot live in fear. I have to function. If there is any one fear I have conquered, it is the fear of death." He talked about it in his sermons and quoted again the phrase "If a man has not found something worth giving his life for, he is not fit to live."

Though no unusual dangers seemed to threaten when he said that, I think that, in a sense, my husband was preparing himself for his fate, without consciously saying to himself, "Now, it's going to happen this year." Yet, it seemed almost as if there were great forces driving him to complete his work. The last few months before his death were lived at a frantic pace. I think the feeling of tremendous urgency he had toward the Poor People's Campaign and the preparation that he tried to give his staff, so they could carry on without him, are indications of this. He worked at it as if it was to be his last and final assignment. At SCLC staff and board meetings he would say, with increasing frequency, "If anything happens to me, you must be prepared to continue."

Yet my husband was not gloomy about his own fate. As he said himself, "I'm just being realistic." Martin accepted the danger as a matter of course and it had little effect on his spirits. He was worried about the direction of the Movement and about the rise of violence, but, as a person, he was exuberant and full of spirit.

17

"I've been to the mountaintop"

The strategic planning for the Poor People's Campaign in 1968 would have been a full-time job for any man. In addition, Martin had a heavy schedule of speeches in connection with SCLC's tremendously expanded program; and, as I have mentioned, I had an operation in the latter part of January.

On February 23 Martin made an important speech in New York at the centennial ceremony honoring the memory of Dr. W. E. B. Du Bois, a great man whom Martin had long admired. Dr. Du Bois, breaking the pattern of "patience" set by George Washington Carver and Booker T. Washington, had been one of the first militant black leaders and was the particular hero of the black nationalists. Of course, Martin, too, preached that we "could not wait," nor "be patient" with injustice, and I think his speech in February was important in demonstrating to the nationalists, with whom Martin hoped to find reconciliation, that Du Bois was as much our hero as theirs.

In his speech Martin said that Du Bois had dedicated his brilliant talents to dismantling the myth of black inferiority, and quoted from Du Bois' great books, including *Black Reconstruction in America*. Martin said that Du Bois, "more than anyone else, demolished the lies about Negroes in their most important and creative period of history." After describing Du Bois' other great achievements, Martin said, "Dr. Du Bois has left us, but he has not died. The spirit of freedom is not buried in the grave of the valiant. He will be with us when we go to Washington to demand our right to life, liberty, and the pursuit of happiness."

As part of the preparation for the Poor People's Campaign, the program of getting local people ready to make the big trip, Martin continued the people-to-people tours. He and other SCLC staff members would go on tours of the various southern regions, make speeches, hold meetings, and recruit local leadership, always explaining to the people what they would have to do, how they would get to Washington, and so forth.

About March 23, 1968, Martin was going off on a people-to-people tour through rural Georgia. He had been away from home so much that I felt it would be wonderful if Marty and Dexter could go along with him. I wanted them, whenever it was possible, to see for themselves what their father was doing and to experience the inspiration of the Cause and of the people who followed Martin. I felt that being with him on some of these trips would help the boys to accept his absences and to share in his commitment.

It was Friday night when Martin and I discussed whether the boys would go with him on his trip. Martin had planned to leave first thing Saturday morning, and, since we got up rather late, what scurrying it took to get their clothes ready, to give everybody breakfast, and to get them off in time to make their plane!

In the hurry, I forgot to call the boys' athletic coach to explain that they would have to miss their Saturday-morning soccer game. Marty and Dexter were disciplined by their coach the following week for "cutting," but in the light of what happened to our family so soon after this trip, I will always be grateful to God that they went with Martin.

However, while they were gone, I worried quite a bit. Martin had told me that they would come home early that same evening, but the evening passed with nerve-racking slowness and no sign of them. I worried particularly because I knew they were flying in a very small chartered plane. Eleven o'clock rolled by, and then midnight, and I must confess that I became quite frantic about what had happened to "my boys." Bill Rutherford, our new executive director, telephoned me about another matter and he assured me that Martin and the boys were all right, but were running four hours behind schedule.

When they finally got in, in the small hours of the morning, Marty and Dexter were excited and utterly exhausted. They described how the crowds had responded to their daddy's speeches, how many people they'd seen, and how much territory they had covered.

Dexter, who was falling off his feet with sleepiness, rubbed his eyes, and said, "You know, Mommy, I don't see how my daddy can do so much and talk to so many people and not even get tired at all!"

It *was* amazing, for though Martin was tired, I'm sure, after he left the boys at the house he went off to his office to work on some writing he had to get done before the next day. Of course, he was so anxious that the work in which he was then engaged be successful that he spared himself nothing.

I think now that it was by the intervention of Divine providence that the boys were given this last trip with their father, so that they might carry with them for the rest of their lives the vivid picture of Martin giving of himself to the people.

Amid the enormous activity in connection with the Poor People's Campaign, there appeared a small but troublesome cloud on the horizon. In Memphis, Tennessee, the Sanitation Workers Union, most of whose members were black, had gone on strike because of the unjust treatment they were receiving from the newly elected Mayor, Henry Loeb. On February 23, while Martin was making his speech on Dr. Du Bois in New York, a small, peaceful march by the union had been brutally broken up by police using clubs and Mace, with squad cars as a sort of cavalry.

This action outraged not only black people in Memphis but many whites as well. What had been a small strike by an obscure local union became a citywide protest movement in which SCLC's local affiliate, headed by Jim Lawson, took a leading part. Predominantly white AFL-CIO unions joined in. Jim telephoned Martin for help. Martin went to Memphis to address a huge mass meeting, and while he was there, Lawson asked him to lead a protest march in Memphis on March 28. Against the advice of some of the SCLC staff, who feared such a diversion of effort might affect the planning for the Poor People's Campaign, Martin agreed to do so. Martin, though he also felt that he should not dissipate his efforts at that moment, could not turn down the Memphis request. He felt that his participation would be helpful and that it was important to give public support to this obviously righteous cause of black workers.

The strain of Martin's responsibilities was growing more intense. At the suggestion of his doctor, he decided to go away for a few days' rest. Then, on March 12, just before he was to leave, he called me on the telephone from his office and asked, "Did you get your flowers?"

I told him that none had come, and Martin explained that when he was downtown shopping for some much-needed clothing for himself, he had gone next door to the florist and purchased some flowers for me. The proprietor had promised to deliver them right away. I was touched by this gesture of love. By the time he had come home to pick up his bag to leave for the airport, the flowers had arrived.

They were beautiful red carnations, but when I touched them I realized they were artificial. In all the years we had been together, Martin had never sent me artificial flowers. It seemed so unlike him. I kissed him and thanked him. I said, "They are beautiful and they're artificial."

"Yes," Martin said. "I wanted to give you something that you could always keep."

They were the last flowers I ever got from Martin. Somehow, in some strange way, he seemed to have known how long they would have to last.

On March 28, I had been in Washington to participate in a joint press conference with Dorothy Hutchinson, then international president of the Women's International League for Peace and Freedom, in which she stated her proposal for "An Honorable Peace in Vietnam." In my own statement, I discussed the relationship of our domestic policy and the urban crisis to our Vietnam involvement.

I was just getting ready to board a plane from Washington to Atlanta when I decided to call our Washington office to express my regrets for not having been able to drop by, and to establish some personal contact since Martin had asked me to mobilize support from women's organizations for the Poor People's Campaign. As soon as I called, the director of our Washington office for the Poor People's Campaign informed me that while my husband was leading the demonstration in Memphis, violence had erupted. He added that Walter Fauntroy could give me the details of the incident. The news was terribly disturbing and I wondered whether my husband had been hurt. I immediately phoned Walter, who said that he had just talked with Martin and Ralph and they were all right, though some people had been injured. "Martin is extremely depressed," he said. I felt a great sense of relief, knowing that he was unharmed, yet all the way home I thought about Martin and how much he must be suffering.

Martin had returned from New York that day to lead the march in Memphis. Planes were late, and the march had already started when he got there, so he was rushed by automobile to the head of the line. He soon realized that the march was not well disciplined—there was never even a proper line formed. "Black Power" placards were being held by some marchers, and there were other things about the demonstration that Martin did not know—for example, some of the younger black nationalists had threatened to break up the march if they were not given recognition. This had been a problem throughout the Memphis strike, but no one had told my husband about it.

There was such a large crowd that Martin, though he now saw the "Black Power" signs, felt he had no choice but to get in front of the line and start to march. He had gone no more than a few blocks when he heard crashing glass and the sounds of rocks and bottles being thrown from the back of the line. It has been generally agreed that the trouble had been started not by the marchers but by gangs of young men who, using the parade as a cover, hurled rocks through windows and dodged in and out of the ranks to lose their identity among them. Some of the rioters were teenagers who had taken off from school to join the march.

It turned into a horrible situation. Mayor Loeb had brought the tension about in the first place by refusing even to discuss grievances. Now his police were ready, and they brutally moved in on the marchers. Loeb also sent for the National Guard. Many people were beaten up, and one young man was shot in the back and killed. When he got home, Martin told me that he felt that after the violence started the police were completely unrestrained.

When the trouble started, Ralph Abernathy, Bernard Lee, and Jim Lawson begged Martin to go back to his motel. They were so afraid that he might become the target for violence that Martin finally consented. He was terribly distressed. This was the first time violence had ever broken out in a march he was leading. Although he knew that he was not responsible, he felt he would be blamed.

When I got home to Atlanta, Martin called me. He was badly upset, and he said, "At the mass meeting I addressed ten days ago there was such a beautiful spirit of unity that I just knew everything would go smoothly. In the North I would have known what to expect, but I never knew there was a nationalist element in Memphis. *I* will be held responsible."

"You're not responsible for it," I said. "All the other demonstrations you have organized and led have not turned out this way."

"I was leading it," he answered, "so I will be blamed. It's just a misfortune."

Again I said, "You must not hold yourself responsible, because you are not."

But Martin felt terrible about what had happened.

Bernard Lee and Ralph Abernathy told me later that Martin held a press conference that night, and he was so deeply disturbed that it did not go well. However, the next morning, another press conference was called, in which Martin was to outline his future plans. At this meeting he was full of fire. He said to the reporters, "Gentlemen, this isn't going to be a regular press conference; it's going to be a press briefing." And he started talking with complete assurance, the words just flowing out of him as they did when he was inspired. Bernard Lee told me that the statement was like a sermon, a message concerning Martin's principles of nonviolence. He was trying to help the press understand what had gone wrong in Memphis. He spoke of the frustrations suffered by the black people there and how they could not be blamed. He restated his own total commitment to nonviolence. He poured out his soul!

Apparently it was so moving that Bernard said, "I have heard Martin speak many times, and I have been in a lot of press conferences, but I had never heard him in a press conference in which he was as eloquent, profound, and moving as that one. Martin must be called to do what he is doing. He could not have changed as he did in one night if God had not put his hands on him."

Ralph Abernathy told me the same thing. He said, "I saw a quality in Martin I hadn't seen before—a kind of lion quality."

One of the newsmen came up to Martin and asked, "Dr. King, what has happened to you since last night? Have you talked with someone?"

And Martin said, "No. I haven't talked with anyone. I have only talked with God."

The next day was Friday and Martin came home from Memphis. As always, the first thing he did when he came through the door was to call, "Where's Coretta?"

I came rushing from my bedroom and we kissed. Then we ate dinner together, and Martin talked about what had happened in Memphis. He was still sorrowful and disturbed. Afterward, when I thought back on that evening, I was very glad that we had shared it quietly together—I hope that I was able to give him some comfort.

The next day Martin called all the administrative staff of SCLC together, as well as Jim Lawson from Memphis and board members from other places, to try to decide whether or not we should continue to be involved in Memphis. You see, though it was not part of the Poor People's Campaign, it was consistent, because here were people, garbage workers, who were the worst paid and had the lowest status of any group, demanding better wages and better working conditions. My husband felt he should be identified with them. He said, "This is not a race war, it is now a class war."

This was a very important meeting for my husband. It was not held at headquarters, but in his study at Ebenezer. Martin was experiencing great anxiety, not only about Memphis, but also about the Poor People's March on Washington. There was much criticism in the press about so great a number of people converging on the city. It was felt that the demonstration would surely bring violence to the capital of the United States. During those days Martin kept saying that this was the last chance for nonviolence to work in America. He thought it could work. He felt very strongly about it and was ready to put all the resources of SCLC behind the preliminary skirmish in Memphis. He knew that what had happened there during the March 28 demonstration would heighten the fears of many people and make it more difficult for the Washington campaign to succeed. Martin's great task was to impress upon everyone how important it was to demonstrate peacefully in Memphis. Martin felt that the only way this would come about would be to concentrate our forces in Memphis to prepare the community for a nonviolent march. While this would temporarily delay the Poor People's Campaign, Martin felt that if nonviolence succeeded in Memphis—and he believed it could—it would redound to the advantage of the larger plan.

Martin was more blunt and emphatic than he had ever been before. He evaluated the weaknesses in the field organization, the quality of spirit, and the tendencies to be distracted from the principal goals of the hour. As one participant remarked, "When Martin combined his penetrating criticism with his eloquence, it was a withering fire."

All of the people present were themselves articulate and experienced. A vigorous discussion ensued and few were sparing in their self-criticism. In the light of what happened later, those who were involved in that genuinely soul-searching meeting have said it was a little like the Last Supper.

Members of the staff still talk a lot about that meeting. They remember it so well and the emotional impact it had on them. Martin felt so much agony and experienced so much conflict because the staff was not cooperative and supportive of his going back to Memphis. There was no enthusiasm; they hoped he would give up on the project. He kept talking to them and trying to prevail upon them. He went around the room and told each person what they needed to do; he criticized them one by one. It was like the way the Last Supper is described, when Christ told Judas that he would betray Him and then spoke to Peter and the others. Martin said that he wanted anyone in the organization who turned to violence to be fired, and then pointed out who was getting out of line. The meeting got very emotional, and he got upset and left. He knew that if he did that they would probably come around. That is just what they did.

During that interval, I telephoned to find out when my husband was coming home for supper. Ralph Abernathy said to me, "Martin left here a while ago. He seemed depressed and upset with the staff, and he left. But he is on his way back, and while he was gone, the Holy Spirit came by. We are all together now. We are going to Washington by way of Memphis."

Finally, when Martin came back they all decided to go through with the Movement in Memphis.

This was a very trying period for my husband because he felt very strongly that nonviolence was on trial, and that he had to go back to Memphis to prove that nonviolence was viable and that there could be a peaceful march. In the process, of course, he was killed. But that was part of the unfolding force. He had to meet his destiny.

When finally Martin came home, he told me that it had been decided to go ahead with the march in Memphis. We would be sending our top people to organize and prepare the community. Staff meetings were to be held in Memphis beginning Wednesday, April 3, and the march was to take place on Monday, April 8.

On March 31, we listened to President Johnson's famous speech in which he declined to run for another term as President and called for negotiations with North Vietnam. Like the rest of the country, we were greatly surprised, but we hoped that his action would bring us closer to peace among nations. The next day, Monday, April 1, Martin was busy planning for Memphis and

Washington. On Tuesday he met with the SCLC staff and then spent some time with the children. He was to go to Memphis Wednesday morning on a seven o'clock flight.

Ralph Abernathy came by the house to pick up Martin. I got up very early, as I always did whenever Martin was making an early start. I offered Ralph some breakfast, but he said he was not hungry. Neither Ralph nor Martin ate anything. They even refused coffee and juice. I followed Martin to the door, kissed him goodbye, and wished him well. The children were still asleep, and they did not see him off. It was an ordinary goodbye, like thousands of other times before. Martin said he would call me that evening.

Martin had been criticized in Memphis for staying at the Holiday Inn, which was considered too "fancy." The staff felt that it was the safest place for him, since it was away from where the demonstration would be held. However, sensitive to criticism, Martin reserved rooms in the black-owned-and-operated Lorraine Motel on Mulberry Street, which was near the Clayborn Temple on Mason Street, where the marches usually started.

Martin telephoned me that evening as he had promised. Things were going very well, he said. Bayard Rustin was arranging to bring a lot of people into Memphis from other cities, but Mayor Loeb had obtained a federal injunction against "nonresidents" marching or demonstrating in Memphis. Martin said he was going to lead the march on Monday, in spite of the injunction.

Then he asked me if I had listened to the news, because he was concerned about the peace talks the President had called for and he wondered if there had been any new developments. I told him I had not had a chance to watch the six-o'clock news. And he answered, "That's all right. I'll watch the eleven o'clock news. I have to go and speak at the mass meeting, but I'll be back in time to watch the news. Don't worry about it."

Then Martin said, "I'll call you tomorrow night. . . ."

Millions and millions of people for days and days, as the tape was run and rerun, watched Martin speak at the meeting that night. Yet, he almost had not gone because a violent rainstorm came up and Ralph Abernathy had felt that not many people would come. Martin needed rest, and Ralph volunteered to go and speak for him.

However, when Ralph got to Clayborn Temple, he found that about two thousand people had turned out, in spite of the weather. They applauded him politely, but he knew they were disappointed. Ralph left the platform and telephoned Martin, urging him to come to address the waiting crowd. Martin put on his raincoat and went directly to the meeting. Ralph said, "I knew this was not my crowd. They wanted to hear Martin."

Ralph, for some reason, took a much longer time introducing him than was usual, touching on all the highlights of Martin's life. It was an inspiring speech, and when Martin stepped to the platform the audience gave him a rousing ovation. As always, no matter how Martin had felt beforehand, the enthusiasm of the people inspired him. That night, completely spontaneously, he gave one of his greatest speeches. First, he told the citizens of Memphis that he was heart and soul with them, that their cause was just, and that he and his organization would fight for them. He said that even if the federal injunction was not lifted, he would lead the march on Monday. He had the audience roaring with excitement and he responded in kind.

Then the mantle of prophecy seemed to descend upon Martin. He told the people that his plane from Atlanta had been delayed that morning because "Dr. Martin Luther King is aboard," and there was a search for a possible bomb. He told of how, when he got to Memphis, there were threats and rumors of an attack on him. Then, Martin added,

> I don't know what will happen now. We've got some difficult days ahead. But it really doesn't matter to me now. Because I've been to the mountaintop. I won't mind.
>
> Like anybody else, I would like to live a long life. Longevity has its place. But I'm not concerned about that now. I just want to do God's will. And He's allowed me to go up to the mountain. And I've looked over, and I've seen the Promised Land.

I may not get there with you, but I want you to know
tonight that we as a people will get to the Promised Land.
So I'm happy tonight. I'm not worried about anything.
I'm not fearing any man. Mine eyes have seen the glory of
the coming of the Lord. . . .

So intense was the audience's emotional response to Martin's
words, so high was his own exaltation responding to their excitement, the action and reaction of one to the other, that he was
overcome; he broke off there. I believe he intended to finish the
quotation—"His truth is marching on." But he could not.

The next day, Thursday, April 4, 1968, Martin seemed almost
happy, despite his worry about the march. A.D. told me that it was
the same way it had been when they were young. That afternoon
they kidded each other and wrestled together boisterously like
boys. At one point Martin decided they should telephone their
mother. That was a little strange, because he almost never called
her when he was on a trip. They had a long, lively conversation
with Mamma King, in which A.D. and Martin fooled her for a
while, disguising their voices, each pretending to be the other. She
was so happy because she seldom talked to both her sons at the
same time.

Martin also talked with A.D. about the sermon my husband was
going to preach at Ebenezer on Sunday. It was to be called "Why
America May Go to Hell." Martin discussed it quite fully, going
over the points he intended to stress. (On that next Sunday, it was
A.D. who preached the sermon at Ebenezer, as he thought his
brother would have preached it.)

That afternoon passed at the Lorraine Motel and soon it was time
to get ready to go out to dinner. After Martin was dressed, he went
out on the little balcony facing the street toward a decaying room-
ing house two hundred feet away. Ben Branch, who was to play at
the meeting later that night, was standing below the balcony. Martin called down to him, "Be sure to sing, 'Precious Lord, Take My
Hand' for me tonight, Ben. Sing it real pretty."

Laughing, Branch said he would.

Solomon Jones, who was to drive the car that evening, called up. "It's getting chilly, Dr. King. Better take an overcoat."

Martin said, "O.K., I will."

It was almost time to go. Ralph Abernathy rushed into his room to put on some shaving lotion.

At that moment came the shot. They told me it sounded like a firecracker. . . .

That afternoon, Thursday, April 4, I went shopping with Yolanda. A few weeks before, I had decided not to buy the children Easter clothes. I have always felt that Easter should be regarded as a sacred holy day—not a spring festival as it is celebrated, a time to buy new clothes and show them off. But the children really seemed to have so much put upon them, what with their daddy's schedule, which took him away so much of the time, and all the rest, that I hated to add to their burdens by forcing them to be the only ones in Sunday school without new clothes. Martin agreed with me, and I had bought the boys new suits the Friday before. On Thursday I took Yoki downtown and bought some dresses for her. I had not been home very long when the telephone rang. It was Jesse Jackson. He said, "Coretta, Doc just got shot. I would advise you to take the next thing smoking."

It hit me hard—not surprise, but shock—that the call I seemed subconsciously to have been waiting for all our lives had come. I asked for details, and Jesse, trying to spare me, said, "He was shot in the shoulder."

I sensed that it was quite serious, and I wanted to ask how seriously hurt he was, but I was afraid. I said, "I'll check the next flight."

"They've taken him to St. Joseph's Hospital," said Jesse. "Why don't you come to the hotel, and then we'll get you to the hospital?"

Somehow I felt it might have been fatal, and I called Dora McDonald and asked her to come over. Then Andy Young called from Memphis and told me Martin's condition was very serious. "He's not dead," Andy said.

It was about seven twenty then, and I told him I'd be on the eight twenty-five flight. Andy said, "All right. We'll be looking for you. He was shot in the neck. Bring someone with you."

"Dora is on her way over here," I answered.

"Bring Dora," Andy said.

"Maybe Juanita Abernathy can come—I'll call her," I added.

I turned on the television. They were talking about Martin, reporting what I already knew. By that time the children had come into the room, and although I tried to turn the TV down, they had already heard enough to know that something had happened to their father.

They asked, "What is it?"

Yoki said, "Don't tell me! Don't tell me!" and ran crying from the room.

But she soon came back. I said to her, "I'm getting ready to go to Memphis, because your daddy has been shot." All the children were in the room, and Yolanda started to help me pack. It was the first time she had ever offered to do so.

Then the telephone rang again. The voice said, "Mrs. King, this is Mayor Allen. I called to ask if there is any help I can give you."

I said, "Well, I'm leaving for Memphis on the eight twenty-five flight."

Mayor Allen said, "I'm coming over myself, and I'll try to get there before you leave. I'll send an officer over to go with you."

While I was getting ready, friends from all over town began coming in. There was a call from Mother King, who told me Christine was on the way to my house. Then Mayor Allen came, with his wife. Dora McDonald had come and then gone home to get her things and meet me at the airport.

It was now eight o'clock. As I started to leave, Dexter asked me, "Mommy, when will you be back?"

I said, "Dexter, I'll call you from Memphis and let you know when I'll be back."

"Mommy, when will Daddy be back?"

"Dexter, I'll call you from Memphis and let you know."

Then, of course, I kissed all the children goodbye.

Christine and her husband, Isaac, came with me to the airport, with the Mayor and Mrs. Allen, and Reverend Fred Bennette and his wife, Bernita. As we walked up the long corridor full of hurrying people, it all seemed unreal, nightmarish. Mayor Allen said to me, "It is such a senseless thing. When will people ever learn?"

Then I heard my name echoing over the public address system.

"Someone is paging me," I said.

And I had a strange, cold feeling. For I knew that it was the word from Memphis and that the word was bad. By this time, we had reached the gate to board the plane. I asked the Mayor to have someone check the page for me.

A few minutes later I saw Dora McDonald walking toward me very fast, and I noticed the expression on her face. As she came running up, she said, "Come on! We need a room where we can sit down."

Then I knew Martin was dead.

We went into the outer entrance of the ladies' lounge.

Mayor Allen went to try to get definite confirmation, but Dora didn't say anything. We just clung to each other.

Mayor Allen came back looking grave and white. Very formally he said, "Mrs. King, I have been asked to tell you that Dr. King is dead."

Of course I already knew. But it had not yet been *said*. I had been trying to prepare myself to hear that final word, to think and accept it—I was trying to make myself believe that Martin was dead.

We all stood there stunned and weeping. Mayor Allen took my hand and said, "Mrs. King, what do you want to do? Do you want to go on to Memphis, or do you want to go back home?"

I said, "I should go back home and see about the children. And then decide about going to Memphis."

Juanita Abernathy, who had brought her children to the airport, returned to my house and Mayor Allen and I, and Christine and Isaac, rode home together. We were all silent. It was comforting to have Isaac and Christine with me as well as the Mayor of our city, who was first of all a good friend. As I reflected, groping for meaning in this experience, I realized that this was the Lenten season, the week leading up to Passion week. It was somewhat strange, yet reassuring, that his death would come so close to the anniversary of the death of his Lord and Master. I thought of how often Martin had drawn analogies in life to Good Friday and Easter. Good Friday, the day of sorrow, the apparent triumph of evil over good. Then Easter Morn and the Resurrection, the coming of Joy, the triumph of life over death!

Martin had often talked of the meaning of Easter in human life. He would say that the moments of despair and doubt were the Good Fridays of life. But, Martin always added, even in the darkest moments something happens, and you hear the drums of Easter. As the clouds of despair begin to disperse, you realize that there is hope, and life, and light, and truth. There is goodness in the universe. That is what Martin saw as the meaning of Easter.

My husband had always talked of his own readiness to give his life for a cause he believed in. He felt that giving himself completely would serve as a redemptive force in its inspiration to other people. This would mean that he would be resurrected in the lives of other people who dedicated themselves to a great cause. Martin had felt a mystical identity with the spirit and meaning of Christ's Passion. And even in those first awful moments, it went through my mind that it was somehow appropriate that Martin Luther King's supreme sacrifice should come at the Easter season.

Then I began to think of what I was going to tell my children. I was afraid that by this time they must have heard—without me beside them. But when I got home, Dexter and Bernice had been put to bed, and Bernice was asleep. Yolanda was sitting calmly in the foyer talking on the telephone. Marty was still up, but Yolanda followed me to my bedroom; and she said to me, "Mommy, I'm not going to cry! I'm just not going to cry, because my daddy's not really dead. He may be physically dead, but his spirit will never die, and I'm going to see him again in heaven."

All this time she was insisting that she was not going to cry, tears were running down her soft cheeks. She said, "Mommy, you're such a strong and brave lady. I don't know what I would do if I were in your shoes."

Then she said, "Mommy, should I hate the man who killed my daddy?"

I said, "No, darling, your daddy wouldn't want you to do that."

She stopped crying before she finished talking. I put my arms around her and said, "But you have been so wonderful and so brave yourself. I'm proud of you; and your daddy would have been so proud of you too."

Marty and Dexter were waiting for me in their room. Marty seemed a little confused; he wanted to talk, but he didn't know what to say. Dexter, who was only seven, said, "Mommy, when is Daddy coming home?"

My heart was breaking, but keeping calm, I said, "Dexter, do you know your daddy was shot?"

He said, "Yes."

I went on. "He was hurt very badly. You go to sleep, and I'll tell you about it in the morning."

He said, "All right," and he seemed to go calmly to sleep.

But that was only the beginning of a nightmare night.

Though people were wonderful to me, nothing could really help during those hours. President Johnson called and said, "I want you to know how deeply Mrs. Johnson and I feel for you and your family." And he said, "I'm getting ready to go on television to make a statement." In the telecast the President announced that he would call an extraordinary joint session of Congress to hear him outline a program of action—"of constructive not destructive action—in this hour of national need."

Robert Kennedy, who was now a United States senator, called to express his distress and sympathy. "I'll help in any way I can," he said.

I told him, "I'm planning to go to Memphis in the morning to bring back Martin's body," and he said, "Let me fly you there, I'll get a plane down there. I'll be glad to do that."

Then, knowing the large number of telephone calls that would be coming into the house during those days, Senator Kennedy had three more telephones installed in my house that same night.

Harry Belafonte called next, and said, "Coretta, I want to come down tomorrow to be with you and the children. I just want to be there at your side and do any little menial thing to serve you in any way I can. I want to share this sorrow with you, and I want you to know you can call on me for anything you need."

Harry did come down on Friday, and was there when I got back from Memphis. He was a tremendous help throughout this period, because of his wisdom, insight, and sensitivity about people.

Of course, I talked with Daddy and Mother King. Daddy King was terribly shaken. "I always felt I would go first," he said, over and over, and my heart broke for him as well as for myself. But Daddy King was strong when he needed to be.

Perhaps the most touching incident was the arrival of Bill Cosby and Robert Culp—at the time the famous integrated spy team of television's "I Spy." They did not even ask to see me, but spent most of the afternoon at the house playing with my boys, because they felt that this was the best contribution they could make. In addition, there were thousands who came whom I did not know, nor had they ever met my husband, but they loved him dearly. He had given his life trying to make a better world for them. Their presence was deeply meaningful to me.

In addition to the excellent coverage by the three major networks of the activities and events pertaining to my husband's death and funeral, each of them carried the funeral service for about six hours. Many schools, local government offices, and business enterprises closed in Martin's memory. President Johnson proclaimed Sunday, April 7, a national day of mourning. Important sports events, entertainment, and other programs were canceled or postponed, as were many TV and radio programs. Now forty-eight states honor Martin with an official holiday. Perhaps soon all fifty will.

There was a tremendous outpouring of concern throughout the entire nation. Everybody was being helpful. There was genuine love and brotherhood throughout the world during this period. We received telegrams, cards, and letters by the tens of thousands, scores of floral pieces from people all over the world, gifts, and valuable contributions.

I kept thinking, and sometimes saying aloud, "I wish Martin could see how much people really care about him." I felt that he had never known how much people thought of him. I remembered the times he had been depressed and needed a lift, and I thought that if he could only see how much people really cared, he would feel his sacrifices were worth it.

It is true that some of the emotional reactions to my husband's death had unfortunate repercussions. There were riots in sixty-three cities across the nation, the worst in Washington, D.C. It lasted for three days and devastated many blocks of the capital. Though I fully understood the desperate frustration with which the rioters reacted to Martin's death, it seemed an ironic tribute to the apostle of nonviolence.

However, it seemed clear that this violence was in no way encouraged by any faction of the Movement, but was an expression of the despair and hopelessness of so many of our people.

On Friday morning, I flew to Memphis with close friends and family in the plane Senator Kennedy had provided. I waited inside while Martin's body was brought onto the plane and then traveled home with him to Atlanta.

The children were brought to the Atlanta airport to meet us on our return. They boarded the plane by the front entrance while Martin's body was removed by the rear door. I remember Bernice, who was five, being carried by Andy Young. She started looking around and she asked, "Mommy, where's Daddy?"

I was silent, and she said again, "Mommy, where *is* Daddy?" By this time my heart was breaking.

Finally, I took her in my arms and sat down with her, and I said, "Bunny, Daddy is lying down in his casket in the back of the plane, and he is asleep. When you see him, he won't be able to speak to you." I could not explain any more to her, but I knew that we would go to Hanley's Funeral Home from the plane and that we would open the casket, and perhaps that would help her understand better what I had told her.

There were crowds of people at the airport and crowds at the funeral home waiting to get a glimpse of the casket. When we got inside, I told the funeral director to open the casket so that the children and I might see Martin. Bernice just stood there looking at her daddy. His face looked so young and smooth and unworried against the white-satin lining of the casket; there was hardly any visible damage. I said to Bernice, "Daddy has gone to live with God, and he won't be coming back."

She did not fully understand, but as the days unfolded, she gradually began to comprehend the meaning of death. She would sometimes ask to see her daddy, saying she missed him.

When we got home, we began planning the funeral. It was difficult to arrange the funeral to accommodate all the people who would want to come and yet keep it simple, as Martin would have wanted it. In fact, in his sermon at Ebenezer, on February 4, 1968, exactly two months prior to his death, Martin had talked about his own funeral. At that time he said, as he had said often to me, "If any of you are around when I have to meet my day, I don't want a long funeral."

I knew Martin did not want any fanfare or extravagant tributes. The main thing he was concerned about was that his funeral be in keeping with the kind of life he had led and the principles he had lived by. I don't think he would have been concerned that a large number of people attended.

Yet, we felt that this ceremony should be shared by all those people whom he loved so much and had served during his lifetime, and that those who came from far-off places to honor him should be able to view his body for the last time. This meant he must lie in state for a considerable time. Also, at some point, the people should have an opportunity to be a part of the funeral service as they so evidently desired. We were aiming for simplicity, dignity, and a really meaningful experience for everyone, that the multitude who loved him might see him in death as they had seen him in life.

We decided to let Martin lie in state in Sister's Chapel at Spelman College from Saturday afternoon until Monday afternoon, when he was carried to Ebenezer Baptist Church to stay until nine o'clock Tuesday morning, the day of the funeral.

Many thousands of people of all classes and all colors waited for hours at Sister's Chapel to pay homage to him. When I went with the children to Ebenezer on Monday night to view his body for the last time, there were lines of people that went all around the block from Auburn to Boulevard to Edgewood Avenue and back. I saw for myself how the people waited to pay their last respects to this man, who, as a drum major for Justice, Peace, Righteousness, and Brotherhood, had given his life for them and for the Cause.

On Saturday Harry Belafonte said he thought I should make some sort of public statement, and we invited the press to meet with us at Ebenezer. There I told them that Martin would have wanted SCLC to continue under the leadership of Ralph Abernathy, Andrew Young, and the others. I thanked all our friends at SCLC, at Ebenezer, and throughout the world who had rallied to help at this painful time.

Then I talked about Martin and said,

> My husband often told the children that if a man had nothing that was worth dying for, then he was not fit to live. He said also that it's not how long you live, but how well you live. He knew that at any moment his physical life could be cut short, and we faced this possibility squarely and honestly. My husband faced the possibility of death without bitterness or hatred. He knew that this was a sick society, totally infested with racism and violence that questioned his integrity, maligned his motives, and distorted his views, which would ultimately lead to his death. And he struggled with every ounce of his energy to save that society from itself.
>
> He never hated. He never despaired of well-doing. And he encouraged us to do likewise, and so he prepared us constantly for the tragedy.
>
> I am surprised and pleased at the success of his teaching, for our children say calmly, "Daddy is not dead; he may be physically dead, but his spirit will never die."
>
> Ours has been a religious home, and this too has made this burden easier to bear. Our concern now is that his

work does not die. He gave his life for the poor of the world—the garbage workers of Memphis and the peasants of Vietnam. Nothing hurt him more than that man could attempt no way to solve problems except through violence. He gave his life in search of a more excellent way, a more effective way, a creative rather than a destructive way.

We intend to go on in search of that way, and I hope that you who loved and admired him would join us in fulfilling his dream.

The day that Negro people and others in bondage are truly free, on the day want is abolished, on the day wars are no more, on that day I know my husband will rest in a long-deserved peace.

The march in Memphis was still scheduled to be held on Monday, as Martin had planned it and as he would have wished. That Saturday morning Harry Belafonte said to me, "I want to talk to you about something that has been on my mind. You don't have to agree, but think about it. I think you should go to Memphis and march on Monday if it isn't too much for you. It would mean a great deal to people throughout the nation, for you just to be there."

Immediately I replied, "I agree. I think Martin would have wanted me to go. I had not thought about it before, but now that you raise the question, I would really like to go. I may even take the children."

So on Monday I flew to Memphis with Harry Belafonte, Justine Smadback, and my three oldest children in a plane Harry provided. As director of the Jessie Smith Noyes Foundation when it gave me a scholarship to the New England Conservatory of Music, Justine had helped me to meet my destiny; we had come full circle. There was no difficulty in Memphis. In the shock and sorrow of Martin's death the federal injunction against the march was either forgotten or rescinded; there was hardly a person in America who would have dared or even wanted to enforce it. We were rushed from the airport to the head of the line, and we marched about a mile to City Hall, Ralph Abernathy and the children walking beside me. There were twenty-five thousand, perhaps fifty thousand people marching, some of whom had come to Memphis from all parts of the country for this demonstration. There were dense crowds of people along the route who did not cheer or wave, but stood silent in Martin's memory. Even my children seemed to sense the sympathy and compassion those people felt for us.

Of course, the children sat on the platform with me at City Hall. There were several speeches. The theme of them was Martin Luther King, Jr., and the many things he had accomplished, his greatness and his simplicity. I know that Yolanda and Marty and even little Dexter were comforted to hear these good things said about their daddy.

When it came my turn to speak, Harry Belafonte introduced me. I talked about Martin's qualities as a leader and as a husband and father. I talked about his work, his great hope for social and economic justice for all. I explained Martin's concept of redemptive suffering and that he had been prepared to give his life to the Cause in which he believed.

However, in closing, I asked a question: "How many men must die before we can really have a free and true and peaceful society? How long will it take? If we can catch the spirit and the true meaning of this experience, I believe that this nation can be transformed into a society of love, of justice, peace, and brotherhood where all men can really be brothers."*

When I finished, I received an accolade from my daughter. Yolanda said, "Mommy, you were real good."

That experience in Memphis, and the inspiration I derived from it, helped me to get through those first days and also the long days ahead. I was so uplifted by the spirit of the people. The inspiration I gained from them I hope I gave back to them by being there.

You see, I feel strongly that Martin's work must go on. In the same way that I had given him all the support I could during his lifetime, I was even more determined to do so now that he was no longer with us. Because his task was not finished, I felt that I must

* The full text of this speech appears on page 311 of the Epilogue.

rededicate myself to the completion of his work. Also, I felt not only that I must do this, but that if enough individuals joined in the work, Martin's dream would be realized, and his death would have served the redemptive purpose which he talked about so often.

Not that I can do what Martin did; but I hope to make my contribution in my own way. In some small way, perhaps I can serve, as he did, the aspirations of oppressed people of all races, throughout the world.

Martin's funeral was held at Ebenezer Baptist Church on Tuesday, April 9, 1968. The church would hold only seven hundred and fifty of the one hundred and fifty thousand who had come to pay their respects to him, and we were deeply sorry that they could not all be accommodated. But this was his church, his father's, and his grandfather's. There he was baptized, and had grown up, and been imbued with the deep religious faith which had guided his life and informed his spirit; there he and his family had preached for three generations. Ebenezer was one of Martin's great loves. It was only fitting that it should be the scene of his funeral.

Ralph Abernathy, Martin's closest friend and companion, officiated at the service. The people who came were truly representative of the total society. There were diplomats; high government officials; congressmen; governors; legislators; mayors; aldermen; judges; professionals from the religious, educational, and business communities; civil rights leaders; and the people. They were black, white, brown, red, and yellow. They were rich and poor, old and young, believers and nonbelievers; conservatives, moderates, liberals, and militants. It was a beautiful example of the brotherhood which he worked for in life and achieved in death.

It was a short service, but very beautiful. There were readings from the Old and New Testaments, a prayer, a short tribute, excerpts from some of Martin's own sermons, and music. We had chosen some of Martin's favorite hymns—"When I Survey the Wondrous Cross," "In Christ There Is No East Nor West." These were followed by a special favorite of Martin's, "Softly and Tenderly," and, then, appropriately to his whole life, "Where He Leads

Me I Will Follow." The choir of Ebenezer sang more beautifully and movingly than I have ever heard them. Mrs. Mary Gurley, Martin's favorite meditation singer, sang beautifully one of his favorite hymns, "I Trust in God." Mrs. Jimmie Thomas sang "If I Can Help Somebody."

The tribute was given by Dr. L. Harold DeWolf, Martin's major professor from Boston University, who had been a real inspiration to Martin. Dr. DeWolf said that he too had been greatly inspired by his pupil.

Then in conclusion, we played a tape of Martin's own words, taken from the sermon he had preached at Ebenezer on February 4, 1968, in which he talked about his own funeral. We played parts of the tape of that sermon so Martin's own beloved voice could be heard pronouncing the words. "I'd like somebody to mention that day that . . . Martin Luther King, Jr., tried to give his life serving others. I'd like for somebody to say that day that . . . Martin Luther King, Jr., tried to love somebody. . . ."* It was a very moving experience for me and for our children.

How painfully beautiful the service at Ebenezer was and, at the same time, how fulfilling. I felt that Martin would have been pleased and proud.

When we came out of the church into the sunlight there were tens of thousands of people standing in all the streets who had been listening to the service over the loudspeakers. Martin's casket was brought out and placed on a flatbed farm wagon drawn by a pair of mules. We chose the mule train to transport Martin's body through the streets of Atlanta because it was symbolic of the Poor People's Campaign and of the conditions among the poor of this nation with whom he wanted to be identified; and it characterized the struggle that he had waged for them throughout his life. I was pleased that so many people whose rights he championed were there to see that his identification with them persisted even in death.

Then we began our march from Ebenezer Church to Morehouse College, halfway across the city; and all the people marched with us. We marched at his funeral because Martin had spent so

---

* Excerpts from the text of this sermon are on page 314 of the Epilogue.

much of his life marching for justice and freedom, and marching for human dignity. This was his last great march. We had thought there would be twenty-five to fifty thousand people who would come to pay their last respects to him. We were awed and deeply grateful that one hundred and fifty thousand people had come, so that even in death, Martin was leading one of the greatest marches ever held.

It was also fitting that the final memorial service should be held at Morehouse College, where Martin had grown from youth to manhood, and had been shown the way to his ministry. And it was right that Dr. Benjamin Mays, his mentor, his friend, should deliver the eulogy. Dr. Mays had come to see me that night Martin was shot down in Memphis. I said to him, "You know, Dr. Mays, Martin always said he wanted you to preach his eulogy." And he replied, "I always wanted him to preach mine."

It was a long, difficult march to Morehouse. So many people, the slow clop, clop of the mules, the huge crowds standing respectfully silent or kneeling to pray, then following on with us. We finally reached the green campus and stopped in front of Harkness Hall, with its classic portico serving as a platform. The casket was taken from the mule train. Again, Ralph Abernathy officiated at the service.

The service at Morehouse had been carefully planned so as to give it an ecumenical quality. After all, the man whose memory we were honoring not only transcended race and class lines, but religious divisions as well.

Before the final service began, the Morehouse College Glee Club, of which Martin had been a member, sang "O God Our Help in Ages Past"; and Martin's college friend Bob Williams, in his beautiful tenor voice, sang "Witness," one of Martin's favorite spirituals. After the prayers and Scripture readings, Mahalia Jackson sang "Precious Lord, Take My Hand," which Martin had asked Ben Branch to sing, moments before he died. I think she sang more beautifully than I had ever heard her sing before.

Only Dr. Mays could have spoken the eulogy as he did. It was pronounced with such admiration and such love for the boy-man whose footsteps he had guided, whose work and life he had so much admired:

"We have assembled here from every section of this great nation and from other parts of the world to give thanks to God that He gave to America, at this moment in history, Martin Luther King, Jr. Truly God is no respecter of persons. How strange! God called the grandson of a slave on his father's side, and said to him: *Martin Luther, speak to America about war and peace; about social justice and racial discrimination; about its obligation to the poor; and about nonviolence as a way of perfecting social change in a world of brutality and war.*"

Now it was time for the interment. Though we had not yet decided where Martin's final resting place would be, we felt that, for a time at least, he should lie among his people in South View Cemetery.

As we started for the graveside, A.D., who had been at my side all that long day, whispered in a husky voice, "Coretta, I don't think I can go with you all the way. Would you mind if I didn't?"

I said, "Of course, I understand. I will ask my father and Harry Belafonte to escort me there, and sit beside me at the graveside."

I wanted my father, with his strength and forbearance, and I wanted Harry, because of what Harry had meant to Martin and to me all these years. Of course, the rest of the family were present, but I sat between those two. Ralph Abernathy spoke the short burial ceremony and paid a brief and emotional final tribute to Martin. Then the casket was put into the crypt.

In the deep pain of sorrow at that moment, I was comforted by the thought that everything had been so beautiful, so right, so much in the spirit befitting the man who had lived.

There was one more test of my strength that day. When we got home and the boys had been put to bed, Marty wanted to talk to me. I sat on his bed, and he asked me questions about his daddy. And he said, "Mommy, it just makes me mad that I don't have a daddy anymore."

I said, "Marty, I understand how you feel, but really your daddy will never die; and the thing we have to think about is how much, even by his death, how much he has helped other people and inspired them; how many people have already said that they are going to help bring about the fulfillment of your daddy's dream."

Then I told Marty that I heard Marlon Brando say on television that he was going to give a tenth of his earnings to the Cause; and he had urged other people to do the same thing.

Marty said, "Yes, that's right. My principal, Mrs. Douglas, seems to understand better now, too."

"Many, many people have begun to understand much more about what your daddy was trying to do in his lifetime," I said.

Marty repeated, "Mrs. Douglas *does* seem to understand better now. Of course, she doesn't understand everything, but she understands better."

I could see that Marty's hurt was somewhat eased as he talked. He felt better and seemed not to think so much about his own loss, but about what his daddy did, and will continue to do in his eternal lifetime, for mankind.

After we had talked, Marty was able to go to sleep.

Marty's daddy slept, too, in his crypt in South View Cemetery.

Upon it have been carved the triumphant words he quoted on that Great Day in Washington:

FREE AT LAST, FREE AT LAST
THANK GOD ALMIGHTY
I'M FREE AT LAST

Epilogue

Thousands of tributes have been paid to my husband since his death on April 4, 1968, but the one which best describes the meaning of my husband's life and death was written by two of his most devoted and trusted friends, Harry Belafonte and Stanley Levison:

> In a nation tenaciously racist, a black man sensitized its somnolent conscience; in a nation sick with violence, a black man preached nonviolence; in a nation corrosive with alienation, a black man preached love; in a world embroiled in three wars in twenty years, a black man preached peace.
>
> When an assassin's bullet ended Martin Luther King's life it failed in its purpose. More people heard his message in four days than in the twelve years of his preaching. His voice was stilled but his message rang clamorously around the globe.
>
> He was stoned, stabbed, reviled, and spat upon when he lived, but in death there was a shattering sense that a man of ultimate goodness had lived among us.
>
> Martin Luther King died as he lived, fighting to his last breath for justice. In only twelve years of public life he

evoked more respect for black people than a preceding century had produced.

We who knew him intimately cannot recall a single instance when he expressed a word of hatred for any man. Yet his indictment of segregation, discrimination, and poverty was a hurricane of fire that opened a new era of struggle for freedom.

Martin Luther King was not a dreamer although he had a dream. His vision of a society of justice was derived from a stirring reality. Under his leadership millions of black Americans emerged from spiritual imprisonment, from fear, from apathy, and took to the streets to proclaim their freedom. The thunder of millions of marching feet preceded the dream. Without these deeds, inspired by his awesome personal courage, the words would merely have woven fantasy. Martin Luther King, the peaceful warrior, revealed to his people their latent power; nonviolent mass protest, firmly disciplined, enabled them to move against their oppressors in effective and bloodless combat. With one stroke he organized his armies and disorganized his adversaries. In the luminescent glare of the open streets he gave a lesson to the nation revealing who was the oppressed and who was the oppressor.

He was incontestably one of history's preeminent black leaders. Yet he was, as well, a leader to millions of white people who learned from him that in degrading black men they diminished themselves, that in supporting black liberation they enriched themselves.

Few people know how humble this giant was. He had an inexhaustible faith in people, and multitudes felt it with their hearts and their minds, and went beyond respect almost to worship. And even fewer knew how troubled he was, and even tortured, because he doubted his own capacity to be unerring in the fateful divisions thrust upon him.

He drained his closest friends for advice; he searched

within himself for answers; he prayed intensely for guidance. He suspected himself of corruption continually, to ward it off. None of his detractors, and there were many, could be as ruthless in questioning his motives or his judgment as he was to himself.

Today when millions of his portraits hang in simple cabins, in ordinary homes, and in stately halls, it is hard to recall that he forbade his own organization to reproduce his picture. He did not want to be idolized; he wanted only to be heard.

He wrote his own obituary to define himself in the simple terms his heart comprehended. "Tell them I tried to feed the hungry. Tell them I tried to clothe the naked. Tell them I tried to help somebody."

And that is all he ever did. That is why, in the nobility of man, he is matchless; that is why, though stilled by death, he lives.

The following speech by Mrs. Martin Luther King, Jr., was given on April 8, 1968, at the Memphis City Hall.

To my dear friends in Memphis and throughout this nation:

I come here today because I was impelled to come. During my husband's lifetime I have always been at his side when I felt that he needed me, and needed me most. During the twelve years of our struggle for human rights and freedom for all people, I have been in complete accord with what he stood for.

I came because whenever it was impossible for my husband to be in a place where he wanted to be, and felt that he needed to be, he would occasionally send me to stand in for him. And so today, I felt that he would have wanted me to be here.

I need not say to you that he never thought in terms of his personal welfare, but always in terms of the Cause which he dedicated his life to, and that Cause we shared with him. I have always felt that anything I could do to free him to carry on his work, that I wanted to do this, and this would be the least that I could do.

Three of our four children are here today, and they came because they wanted to come. And I want you to know that in spite of the times that he had to be away from his family, his children knew that Daddy loved them, and the time that he spent with them was well spent. And I always said that it's not the quantity of time that is important but the quality of time.

I have been deeply gratified, and my spirit has been uplifted, because so many thousands of persons and followers of my husband, like you, have done so many wonderful things and said so many kind things to lift my spirit and that of our family. Your presence here today indicates your devotion, and I would say your dedication to those things which he believed in, and those things that he gave his life for.

My husband was a loving man, a man who was completely devoted to nonviolence, and I don't need to say that. And he, I think, somehow was able to instill much of this into his family. We want to carry on the best we can in the tradition in which we feel he would want us to carry on.

And this hour to me represents much more than just a time to talk about and to eulogize my husband, who I can say was a great man, a great father, and a great husband. We loved him dearly, the children loved him dearly. And we know that his spirit will never die.

And those of you who believe in what Martin Luther King, Jr., stood for, I would challenge you today to see that his spirit never dies and that we will go forward from this experience, which to me represents the Crucifixion, on toward the resurrection and the redemption of the spirit.

How many times have I heard him say that with every Good Friday there comes Easter. When Good Friday comes, these are the moments in life when we feel that all is lost, and there is no hope. But then Easter comes as a time of resurrection, of rebirth, of hope and fulfillment.

We must carry on because this is the way he would have wanted it to have been. We are not going to get bogged down. I hope in this moment we are going to go forward; we are going to continue his work to make all people truly free and to make every person feel that he is a human being. His campaign for the poor must go on.

Twelve years ago in Montgomery, Alabama, we started out with the bus protest, trying to get a seat, the right to sit down on the bus in any seat that was available. We moved through that period on to the period of desegregating public accommodations and on through voting rights, so that we could have political power. And now we are at the point where we must have economic power.

He was concerned about the least of these, the garbage collectors, the sanitation workers here in Memphis. He was concerned that you have a decent income and protection that was due you. And this was why he came back to Memphis to give his aid.

We are concerned about not only the Negro poor, but the poor all over America and all over the world. Every man deserves a right to a job or an income so that he can pursue liberty, life, and happiness. Our great nation, as he often said, has the resources, but his question was: Do we have the will? Somehow I hope in this resurrection experience the will will be created within the hearts, and minds, and the souls, and the spirits of those who have the power to make these changes come about.

If this can be done, then I know that his death will be the redemptive force that he so often talked about in terms of one giving his life to a great cause and the things that he believed in.

He often said, unearned suffering is redemptive, and

if you give your life to a cause in which you believe, and which is right and just—and it is—and if your life comes to an end as a result of this, then your life could not have been lived in a more redemptive way. And I think that this is what my husband has done.

But then I ask the question: How many men must die before we can really have a free and true and peaceful society? How long will it take? If we can catch the spirit and the true meaning of this experience, I believe that this nation can be transformed into a society of love, of justice, peace, and brotherhood where all men can really be brothers.

Excerpt from the sermon of Martin Luther King, Jr., preached at Ebenezer Baptist Church on February 4, 1968, and played at his funeral.

Every now and then I guess we all think realistically about that day when we will be victimized with what is life's final common denominator—that something we call death. We all think about it. And every now and then I think about my own death, and I think about my own funeral. And I don't think of it in a morbid sense. Every now and then I ask myself, "What is it that I would want said?" And I leave the word to you this morning.

If any of you are around when I have to meet my day, I don't want a long funeral. And if you get somebody to deliver the eulogy, tell them not to talk too long. Every now and then I wonder what I want them to say. Tell them not to mention that I have a Nobel Peace Prize, that isn't important. Tell them not to mention that I have three or four hundred other awards, that's not important. Tell them not to mention where I went to school.

I'd like somebody to mention that day that . . . Martin Luther King, Jr., tried to give his life serving others. I'd like for sombody to say that day that . . . Martin Luther King, Jr., tried to love somebody. I want you to say that day that . . . I tried to be right on the war question. I want you to be able to say that day that . . . I did try to feed the hungry. And I want you to be able to say that day that . . . I did try, in my life, to clothe those who were naked. I want you to say, on that day that . . . I did try, in my life, to visit those who were in prison. I want you to say that . . . I tried to love and serve humanity.

Yes, if you want to say that I was a drum major, say that I was a drum major for justice; say that I was a drum major for peace; I was a drum major for righteousness. And all of the other shallow things will not matter. I won't have any money to leave behind. I won't have the fine and luxurious things of life to leave behind. But I just want to leave a committed life behind.

And that's all I want to say . . . if I can help somebody as I pass along, if I can cheer somebody with a word or song, if I can show somebody he's traveling wrong, then my living will not be in vain. If I can do my duty as a Christian ought, if I can bring salvation to a world once wrought, if I can spread the message as the master taught, then my living will not be in vain.

Chronology

(CS = Coretta Scott; CSK = Coretta Scott King;
MLK = Martin Luther King, Jr.; JFK = John Fitzgerald
Kennedy; LBJ = Lyndon Baines Johnson)

1863	Emancipation Proclamation
1865	Civil War ends
1868, 1870	Passage of Fourteenth, Fifteenth Amendments provides vote, legal equality to blacks
1873	Jeff Scott (CSK's grandfather) born
1880s–90s	"Grandfather clauses" deprive blacks of voting rights
1896	*Plessy* v. *Ferguson* ("separate but equal") decision of U.S. Supreme Court
1900	Obadiah Scott (CSK's father) born
1920	Obadiah Scott marries Bernice McMurry
Jan. 15, 1929	MLK born
About 1941–42	Jeff Scott dies
Thanksgiving 1942	Scott house burns down
1943	Edythe Scott (CSK's sister) goes to Antioch College
1944	MLK goes to Morehouse College

Dec. 5, 1946	President Truman appoints President's Committee on Civil Rights
1947	MLK ordained; becomes assistant pastor, Ebenezer Baptist Church
1947	CS enters Antioch College
1948	MLK graduates from Morehouse College
1951	CS leaves Antioch College
	MLK graduates from Crozer Theological Seminary
1952	CS meets MLK
June 18, 1953	CS and MLK married
1954	CSK graduates from New England Conservatory of Music
May 17, 1954	Supreme Court's *Brown* v. *Board of Education* decision
July 1954	Kings' first trip to Montgomery
Spring 1955	MLK gets his Ph.D.
1955	Supreme Court's "all deliberate speed" decision
Nov. 17, 1955	Yolanda King born
Dec. 1, 1955	Rosa Parks incident
Dec. 5, 1955	Montgomery bus boycott begins
Mar. 22, 1956	MLK convicted on boycott charges
May 1956	Federal court rules bus segregation is unconstitutional
Nov. 13, 1956	Supreme Court upholds federal court ruling on bus segregation
Dec. 20, 1956	Montgomery Mayor Gayle agrees to desegregate buses
Feb. 14, 1957	SCLC formed
May 17, 1957	Prayer Pilgrimage of Freedom, Washington, D.C.
Oct. 23, 1957	MLK III born
Sept. 3, 1958	MLK arrested on flimsy charge of disobeying an officer
Sept. 5, 1958	MLK convicted
Sept. 17, 1958	MLK's *Stride Toward Freedom* published
Dec. 19, 1958	MLK stabbed in Harlem

Mar. 9, 1959	Kings arrive in India
Nov. 1959	MLK resigns as pastor of Dexter Avenue Church in Montgomery
Jan. 1960	MLK becomes co-pastor at Ebenezer Baptist Church in Atlanta
Early 1960	MLK indicted on tax charges
Feb. 1960	Sit-ins at lunch counters begin, Greensboro, N.C.
April 1960	SNCC formed
May 1960	MLK tax trial; he is declared innocent by all-white jury
Fall 1960	MLK arrested in sit-in; MLK sentenced to six months on traffic violation; JFK calls CSK; MLK released
Jan. 30, 1961	Dexter King born
Mar. 1961	Freedom Rides begin
Nov. 25, 1961	Albany Movement begins with sit-in at bus terminal dining room
Jan. 1962	Boycott of segregated Birmingham stores begins
Fall 1962	James Meredith desegregates University of Mississippi
Nov. 1962	George Wallace elected Governor of Alabama—slogan "Segregation Forever"
Jan. 1963	MLK, Ralph Abernathy, and Fred Shuttlesworth meet with JFK and Robert Kennedy, who say Kennedy Administration plans no civil rights legislation in 1963
Mar. 28, 1963	Bernice King born
April 3, 1963	Birmingham Movement begins; lunch counter sit-ins
April 12, 1963	MLK arrested in Birmingham
April 1963	MLK writes "Letter from a Birmingham Jail"
April 20, 1963	MLK released
May 2–3, 1963	Marches in Birmingham
May 10, 1963	Desegregation agreement in Birmingham
June 12, 1963	Mississippi NAACP leader Medgar Evers killed

Aug. 28, 1963	March on Washington; "I Have a Dream" speech
Sept. 15, 1963	Four children die in bombing of Sixteenth Street Baptist Church, Birmingham
Nov. 22, 1963	JFK assassinated
June 21, 1964	Disappearance of civil rights workers James Chaney, Michael Schwerner, and Andrew Goodman
Aug. 4, 1964	Bodies of Chaney, Schwerner, and Goodman found
Oct. 1964	MLK wins Nobel Peace Prize
Nov. 14, 1964	CSK's first Freedom Concert, New York City
Dec. 10, 1964	MLK is awarded Nobel Prize in Oslo
Dec. 18, 1964	MLK received at White House
Jan. 1965	Demonstrations for voting rights in Selma
Feb. 3, 1965	CSK meets Malcolm X; 18 days later Malcolm is killed
Feb. 18, 1965	Jimmy Lee Jackson shot in Marion, Alabama
Feb. 26, 1965	Jimmy Lee Jackson dies
Mar. 7, 1965	First Selma-to-Montgomery march (MLK does not march); violent clash on Edmund Pettus Bridge
Mar. 9, 1965	MLK leads another Selma-to-Montgomery march—urges marchers to turn back James Reeb attacked in Selma
Mar. 11, 1965	James Reeb dies
Mar. 15, 1965	LBJ's "We Shall Overcome" speech
Mar. 21, 1965	Another Selma-to-Montgomery march begins, led by MLK, after injunction against marching is lifted
Summer 1965	MLK goes to Chicago
Aug. 6, 1965	Voting Rights Bill signed into law
Aug. 1965	Riots in Watts neighborhood of Los Angeles
Jan. 1966	SCLC lays groundwork for Chicago Movement
Early 1966	MLK moves into a slum apartment in Chicago
June 6, 1966	James Meredith shot
June 1966	Mississippi March
July 10, 1966	"Freedom Sunday" rally, Chicago

July 11, 1966	MLK meets Chicago Mayor Daley, who rejects demands
July 11–12, 1966	Riots in Chicago
Jan. 1967	MLK first denounces Vietnam War
April 4, 1967	First full speech by MLK on Vietnam War
1967–68	Planning of Poor People's Campaign
Feb. 4, 1968	MLK's speech at Ebenezer discussing his funeral
Feb. 23, 1968	MLK's speech praising W. E. B. Du Bois
	Demonstration of Sanitation Workers Union in Memphis broken up violently by police
Mar. 28, 1968	MLK leads a demonstration in Memphis that turns violent
Mar. 31, 1968	LBJ announces that he won't run for President
April 3, 1968	MLK's "Mountaintop" speech in Memphis
April 4, 1968	MLK killed in Memphis
April 8, 1968	March in Memphis; CSK speaks
April 9, 1968	MLK's funeral
July 21, 1969	A.D. King (MLK's brother) dies
June 30, 1974	Alberta Williams King (MLK's mother) is killed in Atlanta
Nov. 11, 1984	Martin Luther King, Sr. (MLK's father) dies

Index

McMurry, Martin (CSK's
grandfather), 20, 28, 29, 36
McMurry, Mrs. Martin (CSK's
grandmother), 21, 37
McMurry, Ruth (CSK's cousin),
26
McMurry, Willie (CSK's cousin),
26
McNair, Christopher, 226
McNeil, Joseph, 172
Malcolm X, 238–39, 240–41
Manhattan Center, 133–35
Manley, Norman Washington, 143
Mann, Horace, 42
March on Washington for Jobs
and Freedom (1963), 218–
25
Marshall, Burke, 191, 214
Marx, Karl, 56
Materialism, 162–65
Maxwell, O. Clay, 153
Maynard, Aubré D., 156
Mays, Benjamin E., 16, 49, 50,
81, 83, 124, 146–47, 169,
306–7
Memphis, Tenn., sanitation
workers' strike in, 283–93,
302–3
Men of Montgomery, 137
Meredith, James, 258–60
Methodist Church, 29, 50, 237
Ministerial Alliance of Albany,
187
Mississippi Freedom Democratic
Party, 230
Mississippi March (1966), 258–
60
Mitchell, Judge, 178, 179, 181
Mobile Movement, 139
Montgomery, march from Selma
to (1965), 241–50

Montgomery bus boycott, 101–
37, 142, 172, 249
arrests in, 114–16, 123–26
benefit concert for, 133–35
desegregation after, 132–33,
135–36
initiation of, 103–6
lessons of, 138, 139
MLK's speeches in, 107–9
organization of, 110–12
Parks incident and, 102–3
threats and violence in, 113–
14, 116–20, 122–23, 128,
133, 136–37, 140
white supporters of, 127–28
Montgomery Improvement
Association (MIA), 106–7,
111, 112, 128, 131, 133,
149, 151, 168, 169, 184, 187
Morehouse College, 55, 63, 75,
76, 78, 81–84, 114, 122,
146–47, 305–7
Morgan, Juliette, 127
"Mother to Son" (Hughes), 247–
48
Motivos de Son (Roldán), 86
Mount Tabor A.M.E. Zion
Church, 19, 27–30
Muhammad, Elijah, 238, 240

Nashville Student Movement,
186
National Association for the
Advancement of Colored
People (NAACP), 3, 42, 80,
101, 146, 187, 274
National Council of Negro
Women, 3
National Rainbow Coalition, 270
National Urban League, 46, 48
Negro Voters League, 187

Segregation (*cont.*)
  of schools, 32–33, 41, 48, 80–81, 158
  see also Desegregation; Discrimination
Seigenthaler, John, 184
Sellers, Clyde, 118, 119, 120, 130, 152, 188
Selma Movement, 235–50
  first casualty of, 236–37
  Johnson's congressional address and, 245–46
  march to Montgomery and, 241–50
"Separate but equal" facilities, 22, 101
Sharecroppers, 72–73
Shuttlesworth, Fred Lee, 139, 140, 201–2, 203, 215–16, 221
Simone, Nina, 247
Sit-ins, 172–77, 183, 205
Sixteenth Street Baptist Church (Birmingham), 213, 225–26
Slavery, 6, 23, 79
Smadback, Justine, 302
Smiley, C. T., 119
Smiley, Glenn, 127, 135, 136
Smith, Lillian, 177
Smitherman, Joe T., 241
Soul music, 29
Southern Bedspring Mattress Company, 82
Southern Christian Leadership Conference (SCLC), 3, 15, 78, 114, 127, 133, 139, 140–42, 149, 169, 181, 183, 192, 219, 235, 236, 241, 242, 254, 258, 301
  activities of, expanded into

North and West, 252–53, 257–58, 260–71
  Birmingham Movement and, 201, 202–17
  founding of, 140–41
  fund-raising concerts for, 231–32, 243
  Memphis strike and, 283–84, 287–89, 290
  nonviolence ideal and, 141–42, 172
  Poor People's Campaign of, 278–85, 287–90, 305
  staff of, 186–87
  students organized by, 172–73
Southern Conference on Transportation and Nonviolent Integration, 140–41
Spelman College, 75
Spingarn Medal, 146
Spring Mobilization for Peace (1967), 275
Spring Street School (Atlanta), 234
Steele, C. K., 139, 140
Stokes, Carl, 279
"Story of the Struggle from 1955 to 1965, The," 230–31
Stride Toward Freedom (MLK), 126, 149, 153
Student Movement, 253
  Freedom Rides and, 183–86
  sit-ins and, 172–77, 183, 205
Student Nonviolent Coordinating Committee (SNCC), 3, 172–73, 183, 187, 236
Supreme Court, U.S., 22, 100–101, 109, 141, 158